MICH-AGAIN'S DAY

A panorama of major and trivial, human-interest and historical, and informative and entertaining events that have taken place on each of Michigan's past days.

by Gary W. Barfknecht

Friede Publications

MICH-AGAIN'S DAY

Copyright, 1984

by Gary W. Barfknecht

*Friede Publications
510 North Lapeer Street
Davison, Michigan 48423
Printed in the United States of America*

ISBN 0-9608588-2-2

To Mom and Dad

ACKNOWLEDGEMENTS

Editing and Composition — Dorothy Hohn

Cover Design — Jeanine Ackerman Smith

Title — Tom Powers

Two urban mountaineers scale Michigan's highest peak, the 74-story Plaza Hotel in the Detroit Renaissance Center (see July 4). - *Detroit Free Press* photo -

JANUARY

1 1982   FOOTBALL FIRSTS
    Coach Bo Schembechler's University of Michigan football team
    trounced UCLA 33-14 in the Blue Bonnet Bowl at the Houston
Astrodome, one of the nation's first enclosed stadiums. The game was the
first the Michigan squad had ever played in Texas and the first they had ever
played indoors.

1978   DURABLE MAYOR STEPS DOWN
    After serving for thirty-five years and surviving recall votes, libel suits,
grand-jury investigations, a federal indictment, and a crippling stroke,
Dearborn Mayor Orville Hubbard, Michigan's longest-serving mayor, completed his sixteenth and final term in office.

1972   A DAY OF WINE AND ROSES
    Governor William G. Milliken and California Governor Ronald
Reagan bet a bottle of wine on the outcome of the University of Michigan-
Stanford Rose Bowl game. When Stanford kicked a last-second field goal to
win 13-12, Milliken promptly packed a bottle of Michigan's finest in Lake
Superior snow and shipped it to the future president.

1972   NEW AGE OF MAJORITY
    The age of adulthood in Michigan was lowered, without exception,
from twenty-one to eighteen. Six years later, the legislature returned the
drinking age to twenty-one. (See December 23.)

1970   FIRST BLACK FORD DEALERS
    By officially assuming ownership of Detroit's oldest Ford franchise,
U.S. Representative John Conyers and his brother Nathan became
Michigan's first black Ford dealers and second black "Big Three" franchise
holders. (See also November 12.)

1

1966   ACCIDENTALLY FIRST

At 3:15 a.m. two automobiles crashed together on Flint streets. The accident resulted in the first claim against a new state fund set up by the legislature to pay victims of accidents involving uninsured motorists. The fund operated through 1973 when all Michigan drivers were required to carry "no fault" insurance. (See October 1.)

1961   EXPENSIVE NAME CHANGE

The Detroit Tigers officially renamed their home field "Tiger Stadium." The changeover from "Briggs Stadium" cost the team more than $20,000 for new signs and stationery.

1942   MICHIGAN CAP FLIES

The Michigan wing of the Civil Air Patrol, a volunteer, civilian auxiliary of the U.S. Air Force, was formally activated.

1926   ON THE ROAD AGAIN

The Michigan State Highway Department took over the entire cost of construction and maintenance of all Michigan highways, and the state levied a two-cent-per-gallon gasoline tax to fund the department's projects. The department, prior to this date, had supervised and funded road-building, but the actual planning and construction of roads was left up to local officials who built farm-to-market, hit-and-miss roads that ignored cross-country or cross-state traffic patterns. (See also July 1.)

1907   FOR THE BIRDS

A bounty on English sparrows, considered a nuisance by the area's farmers, went into effect in Genesee County. City, village, or township clerks, who began paying two cents for each dead bird, were inundated by people who, in anticipation of the law, had killed hundreds of sparrows months before and salted (embalmed) them.

1879   CAPITOL CEREMONIES

The present domed state Capitol building at Lansing was formally dedicated and occupied.

2 1973   YOU'RE SO VAIN

Governor William G. Milliken signed into law a bill authorizing the sale of "vanity" license plates. The law allowed motorists, for a $25 fee, to personalize their license plates by choosing, within limitations, their own combinations of six letters and numbers. (See also October 11.)

1970   FIRST BLACK COLLEGE PRESIDENT

C. R. Wharton Jr. took charge as the fourteenth president of Michigan State University and became the first black in the country to preside over a predominantly white major college.

1969   JUDGING PROFESSIONALLY

District judges, all of whom were required to be attorneys, replaced all municipal judges and justices of the peace throughout Michigan, and, for the first time in a hundred years, all justice in Michigan was in the hands of professionals.

1920   BETTER RAID THAN RED

Local and state authorities, as part of a nationwide, communist-hunting "Red Raid" organized by J. Edgar Hoover, arrested more than a thousand Detroit, Grand Rapids, and Flint residents, nearly all of whom were innocent of any crime except that of being a "foreigner" or of being in the wrong place at the wrong time. Justice Department officials finally admitted that they had arrested innocent citizens, asked reporters not to mention that fact in their stories, then praised Michigan law-enforcement agencies for their cooperation in ending the "red menace" in their state.

1902   FIRST SMELL OF ROSES

At Pasadena, Coach Fielding H. Yost's first Michigan football squad, nicknamed the "point-a-minute" team, demolished Stanford 49-0 in the first Rose Bowl game ever played.

1837   FIRST LEGISLATURE CONVENES

The first regular session of the legislature of the State of Michigan began at Detroit.

1889   The village of Fife Lake (Grand Traverse County) incorporated.

3 1977   BREAKING UP IS HARD TO DO

Boyne City and East Jordan residents, after eight-and-a-half years of competition to locate a new consolidated school building in their respective communities, called it a draw and voted overwhelmingly to terminate the 1968 merger agreement that had created the Twin Valley School District. In doing so, Twin Valley became the first consolidated school district in Michigan history to split up.

1933   DEATH START

A 22-year-old Battle Creek man, who forgot to take his car out of gear, was killed when he crank-started the vehicle and it lurched forward, pinning him to his house.

1848   GUBERNATORIAL FIRST

Epaphroditus Ransom, Democrat, was inaugurated as Michigan's seventh governor and the first to be sworn in at the new capital at Lansing (see December 25). During the former judge's single two-year term, the Kalamazoo Asylum for the Insane was established and the first telegraph line from New York to Detroit was completed.

4

1930   EARLY DREAM

Governor Fred W. Green revealed to the press that the state was seriously considering the construction of bridges to connect the Upper and Lower Peninsulas. Green also reported that, since "a single-unit bridge straight across the Straits (of Mackinac) from St. Ignace to Mackinaw City would present too many engineering problems," a series of bridges starting at Cheboygan would reach St. Ignace by "island-hopping."

1910   BATTLEWAGON PUT IN SERVICE

The *U.S.S. Michigan*, one of the first "battlewagons" built by the U.S. Navy, was commissioned. Used as a troopship during World War I, she carried more-than-a-thousand troops home from Europe before being decommissioned in 1922.

1843   FIRST GOVERNOR DIES

Stevens T. Mason, the State of Michigan's first governor 1835-40, died of pneumonia at New York at the age of thirty-one. Mason, only twenty-four when inaugurated, was a popular, energetic and progressive man. As governor he requested a state geological survey, proposed establishment of the University of Michigan at Ann Arbor, recommended that the Soo Canal be built, and encouraged the building of a state prison at Jackson.

But by the end of his second term, a severe depression had swept the nation, and Mason became the scapegoat for all of Michigan's problems. Depressed and discouraged, he moved to New York City in 1841 where he practiced law until his death. (See also October 27.)

VILLAGES INCORPORATED THIS DAY
1866   Schoolcraft (Kalamazoo County)
1867   Algonac (St. Clair County) which incorporated as a city December 4, 1965.
1877   Litchfield (Hillsdale County) which incorporated as a city November 5, 1968.

5 1971   BING'S HELPING HAND

Dave Bing became the first Detroit Piston basketball player to pass the two-thousand mark for career assists as the Pistons beat the Atlanta Hawks 98-90 at Atlanta. Bing finished the season with a team record 2,213 points and ended his Piston career in 1975 with 4,330 assists, also a team record.

1914   ALL IN A DAY'S PAY

At a time when the average American worker's pay was only a few pennies an hour and ten- to twelve-hour workdays were common, Henry Ford startled the nation by announcing he would pay his auto workers $5.00 for an eight-hour day. Ford said he decided to do so because it seemed unfair that the only people in America who could not afford to buy a car were the men who made them.

1870   LADIES FIRST

University of Michigan Regents voted to allow women to attend their college for the first time in its history. (See also February 2.)

1863   FORMER GOVERNOR DIES

Moses Wisner, Michigan governor 1859-60, died at Lexington, Kentucky. A year and a half after leaving the governor's office, Wisner raised a regiment of infantry from Oakland County, received his commission as colonel, and left for Kentucky to fight in the Civil War. There Wisner was seized with typhoid and died never having been in battle. (See also June 3.)

1942   The city of Hazel Park (Oakland County) incorporated.
VILLAGES INCORPORATED THIS DAY
1861   Galesburg (Kalamazoo County) which incorporated as a city July 2, 1931.
1899   Climax (Kalamazoo County).

6   1914   MAKE ROOM FOR DADDY

Entertainer Danny Thomas was born at Deerfield as Amos Muzyad Jacobs (Jahood). The fifth of nine children of Lebanese immigrants, Thomas began his career in 1934 as a singer at a Detroit radio station then worked his way into nightclubs and later television where he starred in "Make Room for Daddy," and "The Danny Thomas Show."

1853   GOVERNOR BORN

Woodbridge N. Ferris, Michigan governor 1913-16, was born at Spencer, New York. As governor, Ferris advocated prohibition and sent the state militia to the Upper Peninsula during a copper miner's strike. In 1922 the Democrat was elected to the U.S. Senate but is best remembered for founding the Ferris Technological Institute, now called Ferris State College.

VILLAGES INCORPORATED THIS DAY
1859   Lyons (Ionia County).
1876   Oxford (Oakland County).
1891   Copemish (Manistee County).
1892   Thompsonville (Benzie County).

7   1984   BOWLING RECORD SET

Dave Kowalski, 28, bowled a state record 878 three-game series at a tiny church-owned bowling center in Bay City. Kowalski rolled games of 299, 300, and 279 for the third-highest series in sanctioned-bowling history.

1971   NUCLEAR NEAR HIT

An unarmed Air Force B-52 bomber crashed into Lake Michigan ten miles from Charlevoix, killing nine crew members. Had the plane crashed eleven seconds later, it would have hit the Big Rock Point nuclear power plant.

1929   FIRST FLORIDA FLIGHT

Michigan pilots William Brock and Edward Schlee completed the first-ever nonstop Detroit-to-Miami airplane flight, making the trip in nine hours and twenty minutes.

1858   Muskegon County was established.
1887   The village of Athens (Calhoun County) incorporated.

8   1948   LEARN WHILE LISTENING

WDTR-FM (Detroit) went on the air as the state's first educational FM radio station.

1831 DAILY BUT NOT SPEEDY DELIVERY

For the first time, mail began arriving daily at Detroit from the East, but it took fourteen days and nights to receive a letter from New York City.

1963   The city of Luna Pier (Monroe County) incorporated.
VILLAGES INCORPORATED THIS DAY
1863   Fenton (Genesee County) which incorporated as a city April 1, 1963.
1887   Lake City (Missaukee County) which incorporated as a city April 11, 1932.

9 1973 MARQUETTE NOT FINE

The federal government fined the Marquette Airport, along with only three others throughout the rest of the country, for failing to comply with a mandated Federal Aviation Administration anti-hijack program. Faced with continuing $1000-per-day fines, Marquette airport officials, who had claimed the strict regulations were too expensive to implement, reluctantly hired armed guards and installed required metal detectors.

1925 EARLY FORCED-BUSING MEASURES

The Michigan Public Utilities Commission ordered the owners of Michigan passenger buses to follow several new safety rules including: passengers may not occupy the same seat as the driver unless all other seats are filled; passenger-carrying vehicles may not be heated with stoves; and buses must have emergency-exit doors.

VILLAGES INCORPORATED THIS DAY
1894   Elberta (Benzie County).
1896   Beaverton (Gladwin County) which incorporated as a city March 13, 1903.
1903   Mulliken (Eaton County).

10 1964 GETTING THE LION'S SHARE

William Clay Ford, Henry Ford's grandson, took over as the sole owner of the Detroit Lions after purchasing the franchise from other stockholders for $6 million.

1872 FARMERS ORGANIZE

Michigan's first Grange, the Burnside Grange, organized at Lapeer County. By 1875, six-hundred local Granges had formed throughout Michigan and, though first formed for educational and social purposes, they became a forceful lobbying group, leading the fight, for example, to lower railroad rates.

1836 DON'T THROW STONES

A window-glass factory, the first in Michigan, opened at Monroe. Before the shop's opening, installation of glass in Michigan buildings had been a luxury and a broken window a disaster.

MICH-AGAIN'S JANUARY

VILLAGES INCORPORATED THIS DAY
1888   Caledonia (Kent County).
1889   Leonard (Oakland County).

11 1945   SILENCING A SENATOR

The day before he was scheduled to testify before a special one-man grand jury investigating legislative bribery and political corruption, state Senator Warren G. Hooper was murdered in his car while traveling from Lansing to his Albion home. The murder of the key witness all but ended the grand-jury investigation and Hooper's killer was never found.

1940   AUTO MAKER REACHES MILESTONE
General Motors produced its twenty-five millionth car.

1805   MICHIGAN CREATED

As a preliminary step to statehood for the area, the United States Congress formed, from parts of the Indiana and Northwest Territories, the Territory of Michigan with Detroit as its seat. The Territory, until 1818, included only the Lower Peninsula and the easternmost tip of the Upper Peninsula. In 1818 the Territory expanded to include all of (present-day) Michigan, all of (present-day) Wisconsin, and the eastern tip of Minnesota.

12 1980   TRANSSEXUAL SEEKS OFFICE

A 27-year-old Jackson woman, who admitted undergoing a sex operation in 1978, declared her candidacy for the Republican nomination to congress in Michigan's 6th Congressional District. Michelle (formerly Oscar) Strom did not gain the nomination.

1904   SPEED ON ICE
Henry Ford, in a publicity stunt designed to attract national attention, drove one of his automobiles a world-record 91.37 miles per hour on cinders strewn atop frozen Lake St. Clair.

1903   TIGERS LOSE WIN
Shortly after being named manager of the Detroit Tigers, former Tiger pitcher Win Mercer committed suicide in a San Francisco hotel.

1878   FOR THE LADIES
The first women's section of the *Detroit Free Press*, called "The Household," rolled off the presses.

1819   Oakland County was established.

8

VILLAGES INCORPORATED THIS DAY
1867 St. Charles (Saginaw County).
1904 Colon (St. Joseph County).
1906 Dimondale (Eaton County).
1960 Mattawan (Van Buren County).

13 1977 FIRST RESOURCEFUL WOMAN

Mrs. Joan L. Wolfe (Belmont) became the first woman chairman of the Michigan National Resources Commission. In accepting her appointment, Mrs. Wolfe also became the first woman in state history to chair a major state commission and the first woman in the country to head a resources commission.

1921 MICHIGAN BECOMES CITIFIED

The United States Census Bureau reported that, for the first time in the nation's history, more than half of the country lived in urban areas (defined as any town or city with more than 2,500 people) and that Michigan's urban growth (47.2% in 1910 to 61.1% in 1920) had been the largest of any state.

14 1977 PROUD TREE

President Gerald R. Ford planted a six-foot easter white pine from the Proud Lake Recreation Area (Oakland County) on the White House grounds.

1914 REVOLUTIONARY ASSEMBLY

Henry Ford revolutionized the manufacturing world by inaugurating his new "assembly-line" technique. By assembling a car while it was in continuous motion, Ford workers cut production time for one automobile from twelve-and-a-half hours to ninety-three minutes.

1879 GRAVE UNDERTAKINGS

Twenty-six undertakers met at Jackson and formed the Undertakers Association of Michigan, the first such organization in the nation.

1870 FORMER GOVERNOR DIES

John S. Barry, Michigan governor 1842-45 and 1850, died at Constantine. Barry, Michigan's only nineteenth-century, three-term state executive, had returned to Constantine to continue his mercantile business upon leaving office. (See also January 29.)

1857 MSU GETS FIRST LEADER

Joseph R. Williams (Constantine), a prominent politician, maufacturer, and Harvard graduate, was appointed as the first president of

9

Michigan State University, then called the Michigan Agricultural College.

1904   The village of Frankenmuth (Saginaw County) incorporated. On March 9, 1959, Frankenmuth became a city.

15   1968   HONORABLE MENTION

In the midst of an attack by a North Vietnamese battalion, army Sergeant Dwight Johnson (Detroit) jumped from his immobilized tank near Dak To, Vietnam, and, using machine guns, pistols, and even the stock of a weapon, killed twelve enemy soldiers while rescuing a fellow officer. As a result of his heroics, Johnson, in 1969, became the first Michigan Congressional Medal of Honor winner from the Vietnam War.

1950   SNOWED IN

A snowstorm began at Calumet that eventually lasted five days and dropped a state-record 46.1 inches of snow on the upper-peninsula community.

1919   LADIES LAY DOWN THE LAW

When all-male juries twice were unable to determine the guilt or innocence of a Flint man charged with being intoxicated, the judge, defense attorney and prosecutor all agreed to pick Michigan's first all-woman jury. The six women quickly agreed on a guilty verdict, and the man was ordered to pay a $50 fine or spend sixty days in jail.

1818   Macomb County was established.
1868   The village of Saugatuck (Allegan County) incorporated. On July 2, 1984, Saugatuck incorporated as a city.

16   1891   SKI ENTHUSIASTS ORGANIZE

Ten regional ski clubs met at Ishpeming, formed the nation's first major ski association, and held their first tournament. Thirteen years later, the National Ski Association formed at Ishpeming. (See February 21.)

1888   MICHIGAN MAN BECOMES MAIL BOSS

Don M. Dickinson, longtime Michigan resident and University of Michigan graduate, became postmaster general in the Cabinet of President Grover Cleveland. Dickinson served for two years then returned to Michigan, making his home at Trenton.

17   1977   FORD LOSES — MAN WINS

An Onsted man won $1,893,742, Michigan's largest lottery prize to that time. The 23-year-old carpenter, as a result of a special bicentennial lottery promotion, received $1 for every Michigan vote cast for losing presidential candidate Gerald Ford in 1976.

1939   MICHIGANIAN BECOMES TOP LAW OFFICIAL

Frank Murphy, former judge, Detroit mayor, and Michigan's first Catholic governor, became attorney general in the Cabinet of President Franklin D. Roosevelt.

1924   LIVING IN THE PAST

The head of the University of Michigan Department of Archaeology, the director of University Museums, and an officer of a philanthropic foundation met at Lansing and formed the Michigan State Archaeological Society.

1907   The village of Onsted (Lenawee County) incorporated.
1955   The city of Madison Heights (Oakland County) incorporated.

18 1947   TIGERS SELL NUMBER FIVE

The Detroit Tigers sold Hank Greenberg to Pittsburgh for $35,000, but the aging star played for the Pirates for only one season before retiring. Greenberg, who interrupted his Tiger career during his prime by enlisting for a four-year hitch in the army, still compiled a .313-lifetime-batting average, scored 1,051 runs, and slugged 331 home runs.

1943   NOT A SLICE OF BREAD AVAILABLE

To save manpower and steel-cutting equipment, commercial bakeries in Michigan and the rest of the nation were directed to stop the sale of sliced bread for the duration of World War II, and only whole loaves lined Michigan's grocery-store and bakery shelves.

1802   BIRTH OF A METROPOLIS

With the approval of the Northwest Territorial government, the town of Detroit incorporated. The new town's second annual budget totaled only $137.25, but the five-member board of trustees still finished the fiscal year with a $35.36 surplus.

1932   The village of Beulah (Benzie County) incorporated.

19 1955   FILM AT 11

At Washington, D.C., President Dwight D. Eisenhower admitted cameramen to his regular meeting with the press, and Michigan residents, along with the rest of the country, watched the first presidential news conference ever covered by television.

1841   FIELD CORRESPONDENTS

The first issue of Michigan's first farm journal, the *Western Farmer*, was published at Detroit. The eight-page, semimonthly folio was published for two years, then folded because of financial problems.

20 1975   CAPTIVATED STUDENTS

Jackson Community College presented twenty Associate degrees to inmates of Southern Michigan Prison (Jackson) in the nation's first college commencement exercises ever held within the walls of a prison.

1934   WANT A WALNETTO?

Comedian Arte Johnson, best remembered for his award-winning performances in the television show "Laugh In," was born at Benton Harbor.

1880   THE CANADIAN CONNECTION

The world's first international telephone line opened between Detroit and Windsor.

1837   LOCOMOTION

The Erie & Kalamazoo Railroad put the first locomotive ever to run on Michigan tracks into service on their 33-mile, Adrian-to-Toledo route. Prior to the locomotive's arrival, horses had pulled the railroad cars along the tracks. (See also October 1.)

1837   FIRST AMERICANS CEDE LAST LAND

The Saginaw Bay Chippewas signed a treaty and turned over to the United States the last Indian-owned land in the Lower Peninsula.

1815   GOVERNOR BORN

Josiah W. Begole, Michigan governor 1883-84, was born at Groveland, New York. The farmer and state legislator was elected on a "Fusion ticket" of Democrats and Greenbacks. (See also June 5.)

21 1961   FORD OFFICER IS MADE DEFENSE SECRETARY

Only a month after he had been named Ford Motor Company president, Robert S. McNamara, the first person outside the Ford family to hold that position, resigned to become secretary of defense in the Cabinet of President John F. Kennedy. While serving under Kennedy and Lyndon B. Johnson, McNamara became a leading architect of American strategy in Vietnam. McNamara resigned in 1967 to head the World Bank.

1953 FLINT AUTO DEALER HEADS U.S. POST OFFICE

Arthur E. Summerfield (Pinconning) became postmaster general in the Cabinet of President Dwight D. Eisenhower. The University of Michigan graduate, longtime Flint automobile dealer and former Republican National chairman, served as the nation's postmaster until 1961.

1934 CAMPERS GET GRILLED

Because fallen timber and other free wood had run out, the Michigan Department of Conservation began replacing the state parks' wood stoves with charcoal grills.

1918 The village of Caspian (Iron County) incorporated. On November 12, 1949, Caspian incorporated as a city.

22 1974 SPINNING THEIR WHEELS

The World Football League, formed to rival the National Football League, held its first college draft, and the Detroit entry, which had no name, no coach, and no general manager, picked an obscure quarterback. The club later named themselves the "Detroit Wheels," started their first season, but disbanded before the league did the same. (See October 11.)

1971 FIRST SKYJACKING

The first hijacking in Michigan airspace took place when a man holding a hatchet and claiming to have a bomb in a briefcase forced a Boeing 727 to land at Detroit Metro Airport and refuel before flying to Cuba. The jet, which carried fifty-three passengers and six crew members, landed safely at Havana, dropped off the hijacker, then returned with all passengers to Miami.

1969 MICHIGAN GOVERNOR HEADS HUD

Governor George Romney resigned in mid-term to become secretary of housing and urban development in the administration of President Richard M. Nixon.

1932 ACTRESS BORN

Actress Piper Laurie was born at Detroit as Rosetta Jacobs. Laurie began her movie career as a sex symbol who appeared in several films with Tony Curtis but switched to more serious roles for which she received two Oscar nominations. Laurie's films included: *The Days of Wine and Roses* (TV, 1958), *The Hustler* (1961), and *Carrie* (1976).

1881 THE MICHIGAN CONNECTION

The State Telephone System, the state's first phone company, went into operation and connected, for the first time, some two-hundred Michigan cities and villages.

1860   GOVERNOR BORN

Chase S. Osborn, Michigan governor 1911-12, was born at Huntington County, Indiana. During Osborne's self-proclaimed single term, the former journalist achieved passage of a workman's-compensation law, accumulated a large surplus in the state treasury, and supported women's suffrage.

1813   REMEMBER THE RIVER RAISIN

During the War of 1812, more than 1200 British soldiers, with strong support from Indians, completely surprised seven-hundred American troops camped at Frenchtown (present-day Monroe) on the River Raisin. During the bloodiest battle ever fought in Michigan, the British captured more than five-hundred Americans, eighty of whom were injured too seriously to be moved. Then, in an act of deliberate savagery, British officers left the wounded Americans with drunk and angry Indians who killed and scalped them. "Remember the River Raisin" became the American battle cry for the remainder of the war.

23   1979   A CONVENTIONAL CHOICE

A site committee of the National Republican Convention officially selected Detroit as the site of their 1980 national convention. (See also July 14.)

1961   A FORD IN THEIR FUTURE

In a move calculated to thwart disgruntled stockholders who planned to oust Detroit Lions President Edwin J. Anderson, William Clay Ford took over as the club's president. Three years later, Ford became sole owner of the National Football League's Detroit franchise.

1944   GOAL GLUT

The Detroit Red Wings set a National Hockey League record by scoring fifteen consecutive goals while beating the New York Rangers 15-0 at Olympia stadium.

1923   COMEDIAN BORN

Comedian Dick Martin was born at Detroit. The former auto worker wrote radio comedy before forming a nightclub act with car-salesman Dan Rowan. The pair rocketed to fame with NBC's 1967-through-1973 television production of "Rowan and Martin's Laugh-In."

1915   JUSTICE IS BORN

Potter Stewart, supreme court justice of the United States from 1958 to 1981, was born at Jackson.

1968   The village of Rosebush (Isabella County) incorporated.

24 1983   SMOKE 'EM IF YOU GOT 'EM

Jim Purol (Livonia), while appearing on a Detroit-area television show, stuffed 140 cigarettes into his mouth and smoked them for one minute, breaking his own Guinness Book world record by five smokes.

1982   SUPER SUNDAY

The National Football League held their Super Bowl XVI championship game at the Pontiac Silverdome. More than 81,000 fans and a national television audience of about 105 million watched the San Francisco 49ers beat the Cincinnati Bengals 26-21 in the first Super Bowl to be played at a northern city.

1977   UNIQUE TRANSPLANT

Michigan State University physicians successfully performed a rare thymus-gland transplant, the first in Michigan, on a 1½-year-old Marshall boy to strengthen his immunity against infection and disease.

1907   FORMER GOVERNOR DIES

On the eve of his retirement from the U.S. Senate, Russell A. Alger, Michigan's nineteenth governor, died at Detroit. After completing his first term as governor in 1886, Alger decided not to run for a second term and, instead, unsuccessfully sought the Republican nomination for president. Alger then served as President William McKinley's secretary of war, 1896-1899 (see March 5), and, upon the death of Senator James McMillan in 1902, the Michigan legislature elected Alger to serve out the unexpired term. (See also February 27.)

1889   The village of Crystal Falls (Iron County) incorporated. On March 23, 1899, Crystal Falls became a city.

25 1979   ROBOT KILLS REPLACEMENT

When a Dearborn Heights auto worker climbed into a bin to retrieve parts that a robot, which was programmed for the job, wasn't getting fast enough, the robot smashed the man's head, killing him instantly. (Photo following page.)

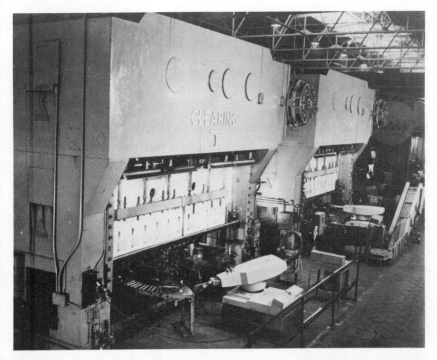

The fast-moving "hand" of an industrial robot killed a Detroit-area auto worker (see January 25).

1976   NCAA SENTENCES MSU

The National Collegiate Athletic Association (NCAA) placed the Michigan State University football program on probation for three years and also banned the team from appearing on any televised games or participating in post-season play during that period. The sanctions resulted from an investigation into seventy alleged recruiting violations involving the MSU football coaching staff.

1945   LOOK, MA, NO CAVITIES

Grand Rapids became the first community in the country to fluoridate its municipal water supply to reduce tooth decay.

1913   The village Eastlake (Manistee County) incorporated.

26 1978 SNOWBOUND

Michigan's worst twentieth-century blizzard struck when two feet of snow fell and was whipped by sixty- to seventy-mile-per-hour winds into ten-foot drifts. The storm killed twenty people and left some 400,000 stranded along Michigan highways.

1976   FORMER GOVERNOR SENTENCED

Former Governor John B. Swainson received a sixty-day prison sentence on three counts of perjury. The charge and subsequent sentence was based on testimony that he had given to a federal grand jury arising from charges that he, as a Michigan Supreme Court justice, had accepted a bribe in return for getting a retrial for a convicted thief.

1969   AN ARRESTING REVIEW

Ann Arbor police officers arrested six actors and four actresses who had stripped naked during a play at the University of Michigan. The members of the New York company had performed in *Dionysus 69*, a three-hour play which included two fifteen-minute nude scenes.

1953   IKE PICKS GM PRESIDENT

President Dwight D. Eisenhower appointed Charles E. Wilson, General Motors vice-president (1929-39), executive vice-president (1939-40), and president (1941-53), as the nation's secretary of defense.

1925   ACTRESS BORN

Joan Leslie was born at Detroit as Joan Agnes Theresa Sadie Brodel. Leslie, who starred in films at age sixteen, was cast predominantly as the wholesome "girl next door." After appearing in films such as *Camille* (1936), *Sergeant York* (1941), *Yankee Doodle Dandy* (1942), and *Hellgate* (1952), Leslie left films to devote time to her family and later became a successful dress designer.

1875   THIS WON'T HURT

George F. Green (Kalamazoo) patented the nation's first electric dental drill, but his version of the tool never caught on because it was too heavy and the batteries were too expensive for general use.

1847   THE CROSSWHITE INCIDENT

Four Kentuckians and a deputy sheriff arrived at a farm near Marshall in search of the Adam Crosswhite family, black slaves who had escaped from Kentucky and settled in the area years earlier. But Marshall residents, both black and white, rescued the Crosswhites, sent them to safety in Canada, then threatened to tar and feather the Kentucky slave hunters. Their actions helped lead to the passage of a strict Fugitive Slave Law by congress (see February 13).

1837   MICHIGAN JOINS UNITED STATES

Michigan was officially admitted to the United States of America as the 26th state.

27 **1967   MICHIGAN ASTRONAUT DIES**

Astronaut Roger Chaffee (Grand Rapids), along with Gus Grissom and Edward White III, died in a flash-fire aboard an Apollo I module while simulating what would have been his first venture into space.

1893   CAPITOL BURNS

Michigan's first capitol building, which had been used by the Detroit Board of Education since 1848, burned in a Detroit fire.

1885   GOVERNOR BORN

Frank D. Fitzgerald, Michigan's thirty-fourth governor, was born at Grand Ledge. The longtime Republican official and officeholder served one term as governor, 1935-36, lost reelection to Frank Murphy, then achieved a Michigan gubernatorial first by coming back to beat Murphy in 1938 to win a second term. (See also March 16.)

28 **1984   SPEED ON SNOW**

Tom Earhart (Kalamazoo) set a world snowmobile speed record when radar guns clocked his quarter-mile run at a Minocqua, Wisconsin, strip at 155.5 miles per hour.

1973   FINAL CASUALTY

Lt. Col. William Nolde (Mt. Pleasant) died in a communist artillery barrage in Binh Long Province. Eleven hours later, a cease-fire ended the role of American soldiers in Vietnam and made Nolde the last American soldier to die in that conflict.

1973   FASTEST GOAL

Henry Boucha of the Detroit Red Wings set a National Hockey League record for the fastest-opening goal when he scored six seconds after the puck had been dropped to start a game against the Montreal Canadiens. Detroit won the game 4-2 at Montreal.

1979   PLAYING THE PERCENTAGES

The Detroit Pistons hit fifty-six of eighty-one shots from the floor, shooting a National Basketball Association record 69.1% in a 128-118 victory over San Diego at the Pontiac Silverdome.

1958   FIRST BLACK TIGER

The Tigers, in a trade with the San Francisco Giants, obtained infielder Ozzie Virgil who became the first black ever to play for Detroit. Virgil stayed with the team until the middle of the 1960 season when he went to

Kansas City.

1826 MAPPING THEIR STRATEGY

Michigan's first road map was published at Washington, D.C. Engineers and surveyors who were developing a road from Detroit to Chicago sent their plans and an accompanying plat to congress which published them.

29 1983 REMARKABLE RECOVERY

In an NBA game against Chicago, Detroit Piston Kelly Tripucka, who had missed a game the night before while recovering from the flu, scored twenty-eight points in the first half. The 6'6'' forward came back in the second half to score twenty-eight more, breaking Dave Bing's single-game scoring record by two.

1945 MAGNUM P.I. BORN

Actor Tom Selleck was born at Detroit. Selleck, an unknown commercial and bit-part actor, hit it big with female television viewers in 1980 when he won the starring role in the show "Magnum P.I."

1802 GOVERNOR BORN

John S. Barry, Michigan's fourth governor, was born at Amherst, New Hampshire. The lawyer/businessman applied strict business principles to the operation of the state and improved Michigan's financial condition during his three terms in office. (See also January 14.)

30 1962 CIRCUS TRAGEDY

During a Shrine Circus performance at the Detroit State Fairgrounds Coliseum, the seven-member Flying Wallendas' "human pyramid" collapsed, and seven-thousand shocked children and adults watched two of the performers fall thirty-six feet to their deaths.

1933 HI YO SILVER AWAY

"The Lone Ranger" radio program made its first public broadcast over Detroit radio station WXYZ. By the end of the decade, more than four-hundred stations nationwide carried the popular program.

1914 THEATRE STAR BORN

Actor David Wayne was born at Traverse City as W. D. McKeekan. After a brilliant career in the theatre, Wayne went to Hollywood in the forties but returned to the theatre after filmmakers had cast him predominantly in supporting roles.

1894 WERE EARPLUGS INVENTED NEXT?

C. B. King (Detroit) patented the nation's first pneumatic hammer.

31 1980 FISH TALE

Tom Courtemanche (Pinconning) caught a world-record eighteen-pound, four-ounce burbot near Pickford.

1971 MICHIGAN'S CAPE CANAVERAL

Thirty scientists from NASA launched a 28-foot Nike-Apache research rocket from a University of Michigan launching pad ten miles from Copper Harbor. The rocket and one launched two days earlier from the same clearing along the shore of Lake Superior were the largest, at that time, launched from a Michigan rocket pad.

1945 RARE EXECUTION

World War II private Eddie Slovik (Detroit) died before a firing squad in the snowy forests of France and became the only soldier shot for desertion since the Civil War.

VILLAGES INCORPORATED THIS DAY
1885 Fowler (Clinton County) and West Branch (Ogemaw County). On March 9, 1905, West Branch incorporated as a city.
1887 Mayville (Tuscola County) and Dryden (Lapeer County).

FEBRUARY

1 1977   PRESS FIRED

A raging fire destroyed the Detroit Tiger Stadium press box, which had been slated for replacement under stadium renovation plans.

1968   ALL IN THE FAMILY

The Michigan Historical Commission presented their 2,500th "Centennial Farm" marker to a Bridgeport Township couple. In 1948, the commission began the program to certify Michigan farms that have been owned by the same family for at least a hundred years and, through 1983, placed 5,068 markers.

1967   FINAL CONNECTION

A seven-mile section of I-94 opened through St. Clair Shores and Roseville. The new section completed the 275-mile, New Buffalo-to-Port Huron highway and made Michigan the first state in the nation to have a border-to-border interstate freeway.

2 1936   FIRST HALL OF FAMER

The newly formed Baseball Hall of Fame at Cooperstown, New York, selected their first player — Ty Cobb. Though Cobb, who played twenty-two years for the Detroit Tigers, retired in 1929, he still holds more-than-twenty-five major-league records including: highest lifetime average (.367), most hits (4,191), and most steals of home (35).

1926　ACTRESS BORN
Elaine Stritch, character actress of stage, screen and television, was born at Detroit.

1870　FIRST UNIVERSITY OF MICHIGAN CO-ED
Madeline Stockwell (Kalamazoo) officially registered as the first woman to attend the University of Michigan. Stockwell received a Bachelor of Arts degree in June 1872.

1704　MICHIGAN'S FIRST WHITE CHILD
Two-and-a-half years after Antoine de la Mothe Cadillac founded Detroit, his daughter, the first white child known to be born in Michigan, was baptized at the settlement. The records of any French children who may have been born prior to Cadillac's were destroyed in a fire that burned St. Anne's church.

3　1956　SPEED ZONE AHEAD
New statewide speed limits of sixty-five-miles-per-hour-by-day and fifty-five-miles-per-hour-at-night went into effect. Prior to the law, motorists had been limited only by their own judgment as to how fast they could safely drive on Michigan highways, so the highway department, at a cost of $26,000, installed some 2,500 signs to notify drivers of the new limits.

1944　DOUBLE HAT TRICK
Syde Howe became the first and only Detroit Red Wing ever to score six goals in one game. Howe's effort came in a game at Olympia in which the Wings beat the New York Rangers 12-2.

1862　EDISON RAILROADS READERS
Thomas A. Edison became the first publisher in the nation to distribute a newspaper on a train when he sold copies of the first issue of his one-page *Weekly Herald* on a run between Port Huron and Detroit.

1859　The legislature changed the name of the town of Boston (Ionia County) to Saranac. Ten years later, on March 4, 1869, Saranac incorporated as a village.

VILLAGES INCORPORATED THIS DAY
1887　Carsonville (Sanilac County) and Brown City (Sanilac-Lapeer counties) which incorporated as a city March 19, 1907.

4　1979　HOOP STARS AT PONTIAC
The National Basketball Association played their twenty-ninth annual All Star game at the Pontiac Silverdome before a crowd of 31,745. Only one Detroit Piston, Bob Lanier, was voted to the East team

which lost 134-129.

1964   BARBER BRINGS HOME GOLD
Terry McDermott, a barber from Essexville, cracked the Soviet Union's longtime speed-skating monopoly by winning an Olympic gold medal in the 500-meter event at Innsbruck, Austria.

1948   ROCK STAR BORN
Vincent Damon Furnier was born at Detroit. In 1971 Furnier donned makeup and transformed himself into Alice Cooper who *Time* magazine once descibed as the "King, Queen . . . and Godzilla of schlock rock." During his five-year career, Cooper routinely featured simulated hangings, electrocutions and decapitations at his performances.

1922   FORD RESCUES LINCOLN
The Ford Motor Company bought a bankrupt luxury-car manufacturer, the Lincoln Motor Company, at a receiver's sale for $8,000,000.

1902   LUCKY LINDY BORN
Charles A. Lindbergh was born at Detroit. As an unknown airmail pilot, Lindbergh purchased a plane he named the "Spirit of St. Louis" and captured the attention, admiration, and love of the world when, in May 1933, he became the first person to fly nonstop from New York City to Paris.

1859   The village of Lowell (Kent County), which exactly two years earlier had changed its name from Danville, incorporated. On December 31, 1959, Lowell incorporated as a city.

5 1976   DETROITER CAPTURES SILVER
Sheila Young (Detroit) won a silver medal in the 1976 Olympic 1500-meter women's speed-skating event at Darvos, Switzerland.

1974   KING HONORED
Nine years before President Ronald Reagan signed a bill declaring a national holiday for Martin Luther King Jr., Governor William G. Milliken signed into law a bill designating the second Sunday in January as a legal Michigan holiday to honor the slain civil-rights leader.

1663   FIRST RECORDED EARTHQUAKE
An earthquake shook the area of North America known as New France which, at the time, included Michigan. The reports of the quake, as recorded by Catholic missionaries in *Jesuit Relations*, are the earliest written account of a Michigan earthquake.

1847   The legislature changed the name of the town of Truago (Wayne County) to Trenton. Trenton incorporated as a village February 10, 1855, and as a city January 21, 1957.

6 1976   YOUNG WINS GOLD

Sheila Young (Detroit) won a gold medal, her second Olympic medal, by winning the 500-meter speed-skating event in a world-record 40.91 seconds at Darvos, Switzerland.

1924   FIRST ROAD SIGNS INSTALLED

The state highway department placed the first of 10,000 metal signs along Michigan highways that notified drivers, for the first time, of railroad crossings, route markers, mileposts, and danger points.

1950   Livonia Township (Wayne County) incorporated as the city of Livonia.

7 1979   FIRST TO BE CANNED

A Southfield party-store operator and his employee/sister were the first in the state to be arrested for selling nonreturnable throwaway cans and bottles after Michigan's new bottle-return law took effect. (See November 2.) A judge later dismissed the charges, however, ruling that the law provided for enforcement by the Liquor Control Commission, not the courts.

1976   FIRST U.S. TRIPLE MEDAL WINNER

Sheila Young (Detroit) became the first American to ever win three medals in one winter Olympics when she captured her third, a bronze, in the 1000-meter speed-skating event at Darvos, Switzerland. (See also February 5 and 6.)

1870   FREEDOM ROUTES CLOSE

Detroiters held a celebration to mark the official closing of the state's "underground railroad," a secret system of nationwide routes that had been used to transport more than 50,000 slaves to freedom before the Civil War. The two main routes in Michigan, one of the nation's foremost anti-slavery centers, led to Detroit where slaves could be escorted across the river to Canada.

1887   Gogebic County was created.
VILLAGES INCORPORATED THIS DAY
1887   East Jordan (Charlevoix County) which incorporated as a city February 14, 1911; Durand (Shiawassee County) which incorporated as a city July 18, 1932; and Carson City (Montcalm County) which incorporated as a city October 27, 1958.

8 1971   FORMER GOVERNOR DIES

Harry F. Kelly, Michigan's thirty-ninth governor, died. In 1953, six years after he had left the capital, Kelly became the first Michigan governor in over a century to be elected to the state Supreme Court where he served until shortly before his death. (See also April 19.)

Detroit's Sheila Young, one of the nation's greatest female athletes, practices before her record-setting Olympic performance (see February 7). - *Detroit Free Press* photo -

1966   LION SUSPENDED

For the first time in their thirty-one year history, the Detroit Lions suspended a player. Coach Harry Gilmer suspended veteran end Gail Cogdill indefinitely for making detrimental remarks about the team and coaches during personal public appearances. In August Cogdill returned with the rest of the team to the Lions' pre-season training camp.

1962   A FAST DECISION

After being pressed for months to enter the Republican race for Michigan governor, George W. Romney, a devout Mormon, made national news by announcing he would not reach a decision until he had concluded a 24-hour fast and session of personal prayer. Two days later, he threw his hat into the ring and won the election in November.

1818   CIVIL WAR GOVERNOR BORN

Austin Blair, Michigan governor 1861-65, was born at Caroline, New York. Four months after the lawyer and antislavery Republican took office, the nation plunged into Civil War and Blair raised money from private sources to form the First Michigan Infantry Regiment, the first Western regiment to report for duty at Washington, D.C. (See also August 6.)

1870   The village of Escanaba (Delta County) incorporated. On March 27, 1883, Escanaba incorporated as a city.

9   1951   DRAFT EVADER GETS WISH

A fire raged uncontrolled through the top floor of the seven-story Michigan State Office Building (Lansing) destroying countless state records including Michigan's original land surveys and the records of all prison inmates. A nineteen-year-old confessed that he had deliberately set the fire but claimed he had intended to put it out so that he could be arrested for attempted arson and escape the draft. He was sentenced to jail for two to ten years.

1934   BABY IT'S COLD OUTSIDE

The coldest temperature in Michigan history, $-51°$ F., was recorded at Vanderbilt.

1847   DUTCH CITY FOUNDED

A group of Dutch immigrants, led by the Rev. Albertus C. Van Raalte, reached the head of Black Lake in Ottawa County and founded Holland, Michigan.

1859   The legislature changed the name of the village of Fremont (Alpena County) to Alpena. On March 29, 1871, Alpena incorporated as a city.

VILLAGES INCORPORATED THIS DAY

1855   Albion (Calhoun County) which incorporated as a city March 26, 1885.
1859   Bay City (Bay County) which, two years before, had been called Lower Saginaw. On March 21, 1865, Bay City incorporated as a city.

10   1942   THE ARSENAL OF DEMOCRACY

Michigan factories turned out the last civilian cars as the automobile capital of the world quickly and efficiently switched to the production of World War II materials and became known to the rest of the world as the "Arsenal of Democracy."

1930 ACTOR BORN

Robert Wagner was born at Detroit. The son of a wealthy Detroit metals manufacturer, Wagner was a young rebel who, after being expelled from several fashionable prep schools, landed a job at Warner Bros. as an extra. Wagner landed bit parts in 1950s' films, then starring roles in movies such as *It Takes a Thief*, before moving into television.

1922 SYMPHONY ENTERS LIVING ROOMS

The Detroit Symphony Orchestra, conducted by Ossip Gabrilowitch, gave the nation's first complete symphony concert ever presented by radio. The Detroit News radio station (later called WWJ) broadcast the performance.

1855 NO FREEZE ON LIQUOR

An enterprising entrepreneur erected a small shanty in the middle of the frozen Detroit River and sold liquor from it.

VILLAGES INCORPORATED THIS DAY
1855   Lexington (Sanilac County), Jonesville (Hillsdale County), and Dundee (Monroe County).
1859   Marquette (Marquette County) which became a city February 27, 1871.

11 1937 HISTORIC RECOGNITION

In a one-page, nineteen-paragraph document, General Motors guaranteed, for the first time, that it would recognize the United Auto Workers (UAW) as its employees' bargaining agent. The agreement came after an historic 44-day strike that began in Flint and ultimately affected 150,000 workers and closed more-than-sixty plants in fourteen states. (See also December 30.)

1930 TOP-FLIGHT AIRPORT

The Pontiac Municipal Airport became the first in the nation to receive the U.S. Department of Commerce's highest rating, A1-A.

1859   The village of Paw Paw (Van Buren County) incorporated.

12

1955   MSU COMMEMORATED

The U.S. Post Office issued a three-cent green and white stamp at East Lansing that commemorated the founding of Michigan State University, the first land grant college in the nation. (See May 13.)

1931   NEWSPAPER GETS OFF THE GROUND

The first autogiro in the nation to be used commercially was delivered to the *Detroit News* which used the small half-helicopter half-airplane to gather news and take aerial photographs. (*Detroit News* Photo.)

1781   THE CITY OF FOUR FLAGS

A small force of Spanish, French, and Indians seized Fort St. Joseph (Niles), looted the stockade, then abandoned it. During the 24-hour occupation, the raiders raised a Spanish flag and gave Niles the distinction of being the only area in Michigan ever to have the banners of four nations — England, France, Spain, and the United States — fly over it.

MICH-AGAIN'S FEBRUARY

VILLAGES INCORPORATED THIS DAY
1835   Niles (Berrien County) which became a city February 12, 1859.
1853   Hudson (Lenawee County) which became a city February 17, 1893.
1855   Dexter (Washtenaw County).

13 1925   WWJ JOINS FIRST NETWORK

Detroit radio station WWJ, New York station WEAF, and a small group of other stations around the country organized the first radio network. The network later grew into a broadcasting giant, the National Broadcasting Company (NBC).

1855   MICHIGAN PROTECTS FLEEING SLAVES

The state legislature prohibited the use of county jails for the detention of escaped slaves and directed county prosecuting attorneys to defend the runaways if necessary. The law was a direct countermeasure to the federal Fugitive Slave Act which directed that runaway slaves be arrested and held in any state where they were found.

1847   WAR MONEY

The state legislature appropriated $10,000 to outfit the first Michigan Regiment to serve in the war with Mexico congress had declared on May 13, 1846. At the war's end, July 1848, the Michigan soldiers returned home but would, thirteen years later, form the backbone of the state's initial Civil War involvement.

1855   The city of Flint (Genesee County) incorporated.
1869   The legislature changed the name of the town of Centreville (Tuscola County) to Caro. On February 21, 1871, Caro incorporated as a village.
VILLAGES INCORPORATED THIS DAY
1855   Hastings (Barry County) which became a city March 11, 1871, and Three Rivers (St. Joseph County) which became a city May 24, 1895.
1905   Alanson (Emmet County).

14 1970   SNOWMOBILERS PAY TOLL

Thirteen members of an upper-peninsula snowmobile club called the Pathfinders crossed the Mackinac Bridge during a 400-mile cross-country expedition from Marquette to Cadillac. One lane of the bridge was closed during the snowmobile crossing, the first in the bridge's history.

1933   UNWELCOME HOLIDAY

After nearly two-hundred Michigan banks had failed, Governor William Comstock, in order to prevent further panic withdrawals, ordered a bank "holiday" which closed the state's few remaining banks for nine days.

29

15

1935   IMPOTENT BEER

The head of the Michigan Liquor Control Commission's brewery division announced that Michigan beers contained only 3.5% alcohol compared to pre-Prohibition strengths of 5.6%. The official, who had tested the state's beers in response to consumer complaints about lack of "kick," said that brewers had deliberately lowered the alcohol content because, "bartenders and brewers don't want to sell a beer which intoxicates on three or four bottles. They cannot make money with such potency."

1926   AIRMAIL COMMEMORATED

The nation's first contract airmail flight took place from Dearborn to Cleveland. Fifty years later, on March 19, 1976, the U.S. Post Office issued a thirteen-cent blue and multicolored stamp at Chicago, Illinois, to commemorate the flight.

VILLAGES INCORPORATED THIS DAY
1859   Orion (Oakland County) which changed its name to Lake Orion on March 11, 1929.
1879   Edmore (Montcalm County) and Marcellus (Cass County).
CITIES INCORPORATED THIS DAY
1859   Owosso (Shiawassee County) and Lansing (Ingham-Clinton-Eaton counties).

16

1974   BIG FISH TALE

Joe Maka (Grand Haven) speared the largest fish ever caught in Michigan waters, a 193-pound, 87-inch lake sturgeon, at Mullett Lake (Cheboygan County).

1940   I'VE GOT YOU, BABE

Entertainer Sonny Bono was born at Detroit as Salvatore Bono. Bono met his wife Cher when they both sang backup for a group called the Ronettes. Sonny and Cher became overnight stars when they released a single, "I've Got You, Babe," then later developed a Las Vegas act that led to an enormously successful comedy, musical and variety television show. During the late 1970s, both the show and their marriage ended.

1925   LAST LINCOLN DELEGATE DIES

Addison G. Proctor (St. Joseph), the last surviving member of the 1860 Republican convention that nominated Abraham Lincoln for president, died at the age of eighty-six.

30

1914   PRISONER JAILED ALMOST FOR LIFE
Castra Nova, 21, was sentenced to a life term for the first-degree murder of a Detroit police officer. Nearly fifty-six years later, Governor William G. Milliken commuted Nova's sentence and he was released after spending more time behind bars than any other prisoner in Michigan history.

1819   CONGRESS GRANTS MICHIGAN SUFFRAGE
Citizens of the Territory of Michigan voted in their first United States congressional election and sent William Woodbridge to the house of representatives as Michigan's first congressman.

1899   The village of Onaway (Presque Isle County) incorporated. On March 26, 1903, Onaway became a city.

17 1932   JUST PEACHY
The Michigan Agricultural College horticultural department announced the successful development of a new peach variety called the Hale Haven. The tough-skinned, early ripening peach, developed at South Haven orchards, quickly became a favorite of commercial growers.

1918   GERMANS NOT WELCOME
Following up on a policy spawned by anti-German sentiment that swept the nation after the declaration of World War I, the U.S. Department of Justice sent instructions to "war bureaus" throughout Michigan to arrest all German aliens who had failed to register. As a result, many of Michigan's 80,000 German-born and 20,000 Austrian-born residents who had not registered with the government faced internment or deportation.

1863   BLACK SOLDIERS ORGANIZE
The First Michigan Colored Infantry was mustered into the service of the United States with 895 names on its rolls. White officers commanded the regiment which became the 102nd United States Colored Infantry Regiment, the only Michigan unit in the Civil War to lose its state name.

1857   Bay County was established.
1857   The city of Saginaw (Saginaw County) incorporated.
VILLAGES INCORPORATED THIS DAY
1865   Ionia (Ionia County) which became a city March 22, 1873.
1885   Harrison (Clare County) which incorporated as a city May 7, 1891.
1887   Baldwin (Lake County).
1893   Addison (Lenawee County).

18

1984   TOP-SCORING AMERICAN

Reed Larson, defenseman for the Detroit Red Wings, assisted on three of Detroit's goals in a 6-0 win over the Chicago Black Hawks at the Joe Louis Arena. The three points brought Larson's career total to 432 (144 goals and 288 assists) and made the Minnesota native the highest-scoring U.S.-born player in National Hockey League history.

1977   UP IN THE AIR

Karl Thomas, a 28-year-old adventurer from Troy, landed his hot-air balloon on a remote island beach fifteen miles northeast of Jacksonville, Florida, and ended a record eighteen-day solo voyage across the United States.

1839   BOATERS ORGANIZE

The Detroit Boat Club, the first of its kind in the country, was founded.

1963   Portage Township (Kalamazoo County) incorporated as the city of Portage.
VILLAGES INCORPORATED THIS DAY
1879   Farwell (Clare County).
1887   East Tawas (Iosco County) which incorporated as a city March 20, 1895.

19 1970   PITCHER SUSPENDED

Baseball Commissioner Bowie Kuhn suspended Detroit Tiger pitcher Denny McLain indefinitely for his involvement with bookmakers. McLain, the first major-league ball player suspended since 1924, was permitted to join the Tigers the following July but, on August 28, Tiger management suspended the Cy Young-award winner for dousing a sportswriter with water. Two weeks later, Commissioner Kuhn again suspended McLain, this time for carrying a gun, and on October 9 the Tigers traded their former star to the Washington Senators.

1940   MOTOWN GIANT BORN

William "Smokey" Robinson was born at Detroit. Robinson has succeeded enormously in a dual career as a member of the group, Smokey Robinson and the Miracles, and as the creative kingpin of Motown Records.

1830   HOW DRY THEY WERE

The Detroit Society for the Suppression of Intemperance, Michigan's first temperance society, organized at Detroit. In March 1833 the organization expanded into the Michigan Temperance Society.

1875   Baraga County was created.
1909   The village of Ahmeek (Keweenaw County) incorporated.
1951   The city of Harper Woods (Wayne County) incorporated.

20 1977   HELP ARRIVES

One-hundred-ten state troopers from posts throughout Michigan reported to Detroit as members of a permanent city-freeway patrol team. The state police who, at the request of the understaffed Detroit Police Department, had temporarily cruised Detroit's 62.5-mile freeway system since August had so successfully curbed crime and lawlessness that Governor Milliken made the patrol permanent.

MICH-AGAIN'S FEBRUARY

1929   FIRST TAXPAYER-PAID FLIGHT
Governor Fred W. Green and fifteen other state officials flew from Lansing to a Kalamazoo conference on the state's first aviation junket.

1919   MICHIGAN WOMEN DEBATE THEIR ROLES
The keynote speaker at a meeting of the Michigan State Federation of Women's Clubs at Battle Creek chided Michigan women for holding so many "scattering-chicken-feed, pink-tea programs" and urged those in attendance to involve themselves in meaningful and worthwhile projects. But in rebuttal, another speaker expressed concern that women were becoming too involved and sarcastically remarked that she was surprised that women "hadn't asked to be included at the (World War I) peace conferences."

VILLAGES INCORPORATED THIS DAY
1889   Lake Odessa (Ionia County), Marion (Osceola County), and Fennville (Allegan County) which incorporated as a city June 30, 1960.

21 1978   THE CAT'S MEOW
Seventy-five noisy fifth-graders jammed into Governor William G. Milliken's office to watch him sign into law their bill protecting house cats from hunters. The St. Clair elementary-school students had initiated the legislation by bombarding their state senator with letters protesting a 1929 law that made it legal to shoot cats.

1972   A GEM OF A LAW
Governor William G. Milliken signed into law a bill that designated chlorastrolite, a green opaque stone found only in the northernmost reaches of Michigan, as the official state gem.

1904   SKIERS ORGANIZE
A group of skiing enthusiasts led by Carl Tellefson organized the National Ski Association at Ishpeming.

1907   The city of Whittemore (Iosco County) incorporated.
VILLAGES INCORPORATED THIS DAY
1883   LeRoy (Osceola County), McBride (Montcalm County), and Essexville (Bay County) which incorporated as a city December 4, 1933.
1887   Reese (Tuscola County), Oakley (Saginaw County), and Coleman (Midland County) which incorporated as a city March 29, 1905.

22 1973   FEELS LIKE A MILLION
Hermus Millsaps (Taylor) became the state's first million-dollar-lottery winner. The man's former wife, whom he divorced in 1969, filed a lawsuit the next day asking for a share of the prize, but a judge denied her request.

34

1973   COURT ENDS 135-YEAR-OLD ARGUMENT

The United States Supreme Court ruled that a mineral-rich area in Lake Erie, called the "Toledo Strip," belonged to Ohio and ended a 135-year-old dispute over the 200-square-mile, pie-shaped segment of water. Michigan had brought the suit to court claiming that the U.S. had never established an official water boundary between the two states.

1837   FIRST FLAG UNFURLED

Stevens T. Mason, Michigan's first state governor, presented Michigan's first official state flag to the Brady Guard at Detroit.

1814   GOVERNOR BORN

Henry P. Baldwin, Michigan governor 1869-72, was born at Rhode Island. The former state senator served two terms as governor during which money was appropriated for the construction of the present capitol building.

23

1976   MICHIGAN FLAG FEATURED

The United States Post Office issued a thirteen-cent stamp at Washington, D.C., that featured the Michigan state flag.

1922   RECORD SNOW

Michigan's greatest recorded daily snowfall, twenty-nine inches, fell on Ishpeming.

1911   GOVERNOR BORN

G. Mennen Williams, Michigan governor 1949-60, was born at Detroit. Nicknamed "Soapy" because of his maternal grandfather who founded the Mennen Company, manufacturers of soaps and toiletries, Williams was one of the few American governors to be elected to six or more consecutive terms. One of Williams' accomplishments while in office was to link Michigan's two peninsulas by the Mackinac Bridge. Williams was elected in 1970 to the Michigan Supreme Court and reelected in 1978.

1882   The village of St. Ignace (Mackinac County), Michigan's second-oldest continuous settlement, incorporated. On March 14, 1833, St. Ignace incorporated as a city.

24

1928   FIRST POT LAW

The Detroit City Council passed an ordinance forbidding the use and sale of a new drug that was finding its way into the city from Mexico. The council took the action because the new substance, marijuana, was not covered by state and federal laws.

1844 COLLEGE FOUNDED

The Rev. John J. "Father" Shepherd and thirty-nine Congregationalist followers, believing that God had directed them to find a spot to build a coeducational Christian college, arrived by ox cart at an oak grove on a wilderness hilltop near (present-day) Olivet. Fifteen years later the school received its charter as Olivet Institute and later changed its name to Olivet College.

25 1976 NO LICENSE TO PROFIT

Michigan's attorney general ruled that the State Corrections Department could not make a profit on the manufacturing of license plates.

1888 ISHPEMING STAGES FIRST JUMP

Crowds of spectators gathered at Ishpeming to watch professional ski jumpers compete for cash prizes as Michigan's first ski club sponsored its first public ski-jumping meet. The winner jumped thirty-five feet.

1863   The state legislature changed the name of the town of Fred (Montcalm County) to Stanton. Stanton incorporated as a village February 24, 1869, and as a city March 10, 1881.

VILLAGES INCORPORATED THIS DAY

1885   Gladwin (Gladwin County) which became a city March 4, 1893.
1887   Bessemer (Gogebic County) which incorporated as a city April 10, 1889.
1893   Deckerville (Sanilac County).

26 1971 MARATHON SKATE

At the Fuller Ice Skating Rink (Ann Arbor), Kirt Barnes skated one-hundred miles in five hours, thirty-four minutes, 1.45 seconds and became the first ice skater in the world to cover that distance in less than six hours.

1921 PERFORMER BORN

Betty Hutton, blonde, blue-eyed actress, comedienne and singer, was born at Battle Creek as Betty June Thornburg. Hutton appeared in many films including: *Duffy's Tavern* (1945), *The Perils of Pauline* (1947), and *Annie Get Your Gun* (1950).

1914 I HEAR A SYMPHONY

At the Detroit Opera House, the Detroit Symphony gave its first concert.

1906 WHAT A CIRCUS

At Detroit's Moslem Shrine Temple, three-thousand spectators

Above: Competitors at Michigan's first ski tournament (see February 25) jumped only slightly more-than-thirty feet. Below: Eighty-two years later jumpers at the Western Hemisphere's first ski "flying" meet (see February 27) soared more-than-five-hundred feet. - National Ski Hall of Fame photos -

watched the nation's first Shrine Circus. The one-ring show grew to become a major fund-raiser for Shrine temples throughout the country.

1903   The village of Peck (Sanilac County) incorporated.

27

1970   SKIERS GO AIRBORNE

Ironwood hosted the Western Hemisphere's first tournament for ski "flyers" who jump more than five-hundred feet through the air, nearly two-hundred feet more than the best ski "jumpers."

1955   WINGS STREAK BEGINS

The Detroit Red Wings beat Chicago 3-2 at Chicago to begin a National Hockey League-record fifteen-game winning streak. The Wings won their next eight regular season games and six play-off games before losing to Montreal on April 7.

1904   FOR THE BIRDS

The Michigan Audubon Society met, at Detroit, for the first time.

1836   GOVERNOR BORN

Russell A. Alger, Michigan governor 1885-86, was born at Lafayette Township, Ohio. During his administration, the former lawyer/lumberman sent state troops into the Saginaw Valley during a lumber strike and also created the state parole board.

1863   Benzie County was established.
VILLAGES INCORPORATED THIS DAY
1879   Brooklyn (Jackson County); Petoskey (Emmet County) which became a city March 8, 1895; and White Cloud (Newaygo County) which became a city May 22, 1950.
1956   Goodrich (Genesee County).

28

1977   TOURNEY TELEVISED

Prep basketball star Earvin Johnson scored twenty-seven points and helped hold fellow all-stater Jay Vincent to four points while leading Lansing Everett to a 63-41 win over Lansing Eastern in a district high-school basketball tournament opener. The game was the first in Michigan High School Athletic Association history to be televised live.

1975   HAIR-RAISING OPINION

Michigan's attorney general ruled that hair transplants by the use of skin grafts to the scalp constitute surgery and may only be performed by licensed physicians.

1893   The village of Coloma (Berrien County) incorporated. On December 22, 1941, Coloma incorporated as a city.

29

1948   SPEEDERS BEWARE

Police in several major Michigan cities began experimenting with a new piece of equipment called radar to see if the portable, speed-detecting devices could be useful in traffic-law enforcement.

1940   DOGS LOCKED UP

Barry County became the sixth county, following Saginaw, Genesee, Calhoun, Eaton and VanBuren, to impose a ninety-day dog quarantine in an attempt to control a widespread rabies outbreak.

1837   The village of Coldwater (Branch County) incorporated. On February 28, 1861, Coldwater incorporated as a city.

MARCH

1 1972   EXPENSIVE WHITTLING
The Cranbrook Academy (Bloomfield Hills) sold a 75-inch wooden carving by Henry Moore for $260,000, a world record for price paid for a work by a living sculptor.

1965   THE VOICE OF YESTERYEAR DIES
Brace Beemer, who's hearty "Hi yo, Silver, away" thrilled *Lone Ranger* radio audiences for a generation, died of a heart attack at Oxford, Michigan. Beemer, broadcasting from the studios of Detroit radio station WXYZ, where the *Lone Ranger* originated (see January 30), had personified the masked hero from 1932 through the 1940s.

1962   THANK YOU FOR SHOPPING AT K MART
The S.S. Kresge Company opened the nation's first K mart at Garden City. Over the next twenty years the firm opened more than two thousand of the discount stores nationwide.

1954   REPRESENTATIVE SHOT
Rep. Alvin M. Bentley (Owosso) was among five U.S. congressmen wounded by a group of Puerto Ricans who fired shots from the House gallery.

1949   THE BOMBER RETIRES
Detroit's Joe Louis announced his retirement from the ring after a record eleven years, eight months and one week as world heavyweight boxing champion. A year-and-a-half later, Louis attempted to regain his title but lost to Ezzard Charles in a fifteen-round decision at New York City.
(See also May 23, June 22, June 25 and September 27.)

1848   THE EASTERN CONNECTION
The O'Reilly Telegraph Company (Detroit) completed the first New

40

York (Buffalo)-to-Detroit telegraph line and transmitted a dispatch that day.

1887   Luce County was created.
1889   The city of Gladstone (Delta County) incorporated.

2 1974 LAW SAVES LIVES, ENERGY AND FUNDS

To comply with a federal-government policy designed to reduce gas consumption and traffic fatalities, Governor William G. Milliken signed into law a bill lowering Michigan's speed limit from sixty-five to fifty-five miles per hour. Had Michigan not met the federally suggested limits, the state would have lost $170 million in federal highway funds.

1824 APPEALING SPEECH

Father Gabriel Richard, in his only recorded speech as territorial representative of Michigan, asked the U.S. Congress to appropriate $1,500 to build a 285-mile road from Detroit to Chicago. His appeal was so eloquent that congress doubled the amount. (See also May 24.)

1799 CUSTOMARY COLLECTIONS BEGIN

Detroit became an official port-of-entry with jurisdiction over lakes Erie, St. Clair, and Huron west of the Miami River to Mackinac. The first collector earned a $250 annual salary plus three percent of any customs fees he took in.

1831   Allegan, Arenac, Clinton, Gladwin, Gratiot, Ionia, Isabella, Kent, Livingston, Midland, Montcalm, Oceanna, and Ottawa counties were established.

VILLAGES INCORPORATED THIS DAY
1867   Hubbardston (Clinton-Ionia counties).
1871   Linden (Genesee County) and Vassar (Tuscola County) which became a city September 18, 1944.
1881   North Branch (Lapeer County).

3 1875 MICHIGAN GETS NATIONAL PARK

Congress established Mackinac Island National Park, the nation's second, following the creation of Yellowstone by only three years. Twenty years later, the federal government turned the fort and park over to Michigan, and the island became our first state park.

1801 POSTMARKED "MICHIGAN"

The first post road (mail route) in Michigan was established, and mail, carried by men on horseback and on foot, began arriving quarterly at Detroit from Washington, D.C.

VILLAGES INCORPORATED THIS DAY
1881   North Adams (Hillsdale County).
1885   Elsie (Clinton County).
1947   New Lothrop (Shiawassee County).

4

1964   LABOR LEADER FOUND GUILTY

A federal grand jury convicted International Brotherhood of Teamsters President James Hoffa of attempted jury-tampering. Four-and-a-half months later, another jury convicted Hoffa on charges of fraudulently using his union's pension fund, and in 1967 the labor leader, who grew up on Detroit's west side, entered prison. In 1975, four years after President Richard M. Nixon had commuted his sentence, Hoffa mysteriously disappeared. (See July 30).

1947   LIVE FROM DETROIT

Though less than one-hundred families in the area had receivers, the state's first television station, WWJ-TV (Detroit), began daily broadcasts consisting, at first, of test patterns and studio presentations.

1853   GOVERNOR RESIGNS

Two months after taking office for a second term, Governor Robert McClelland resigned to become secretary of the interior in the administration of President Franklin Pierce.

VILLAGES INCORPORATED THIS DAY

1871	Coopersville (Ottawa County) which became a city June 1, 1966.
1879	Columbiaville (Lapeer County) and Galien (Berrien County).
1881	Gaylord (Otsego County) which became a city March 13, 1922
1887	Sherwood (Brand County), Stockbridge (Ingham County), and Scottville (Mason County) which incorporated as a city February 26, 1907.
1893	McBain (Missaukee County) which became a city March 8, 1907.

5

1973   THE GREAT PIZZA FUNERAL

A Michigan frozen-food manufacturer, after being told by the federal Food and Drug Administration that he had used contaminated mushrooms, buried 44,000 pizzas on an Ossineke farm.

1921   MICHIGAN MAN COMMANDS NAVY

Edwin Denby, University of Michigan graduate, Detroit attorney, and Michigan and U.S. congressman, became secretary of the navy in the Cabinet of President Warren G. Harding.

1897   MICHIGAN GOVERNOR HEADS WAR DEPARTMENT

Former Michigan Governor Russell A. Alger became secretary of war in the Cabinet of President William McKinley. Alger became a scapegoat for the wretched conditions suffered by American troops during the Spanish-American War (see April 24) and on August 1, 1899, resigned in disgrace.

1829   FIRST JOURNALIST JAILED

The Michigan Territorial Supreme Court fined John P. Sheldon, editor of the *Detroit Gazette,* for printing editorials critical of their decisions and, when Sheldon refused to pay, jailed him for contempt of court. Angry Detroit citizens, however, collected and paid Sheldon's fine and held a festive reception upon his release.

VILLAGES INCORPORATED THIS DAY
1867   Plymouth (Wayne County) which incorporated as a city March 14, 1932.
1887   Port Hope (Huron County) and Grandville (Kent County) which incorporated as a city May 5, 1933.
1895   Frazer (Macomb County) which changed its name to Fraser March 12, 1928, and incorporated as a city June 4, 1956.

CITIES INCORPORATED THIS DAY
1867   Wyandotte (Wayne County).
1888   Iron Mountain (Dickinson County).

6

1923   H...E...R...E...'S ED

Ed McMahon, television-star Johnny Carson's longtime announcer, was born at Detroit.

1896   FAMOUS FIRST DRIVE

After two years of private testing on Belle Isle, Charles B. King, a 27-year-old college-trained engineer, became the first man in Michigan to publicly drive a horseless carriage powered by a gasoline engine. But, during the test drive on Detroit's main sreets, King's handmade vehicle broke down, and spectators jeered, "Get a horse."

1877   FIRST TELEPHONE MUZAK

Eight months after copper-mining companies had set up Michigan's first telephone lines at Ontonagon, Alexander Graham Bell's telephone made its Detroit debut. A Detroit men's organization set up the instrument at their club, then listened to a musical performance transmitted from Chicago.

1863   FIRST INTERRACIAL RIOT

Detroit suffered its first interracial riot when a mob of whites, angered by President Lincoln's Emancipation Proclamation and conscription orders, swept through the black section of town burning homes and brutally beating and kicking blacks. One white and at least one black were killed.

1857   MICHIGAN MAN HEADS STATE DEPARTMENT

Lewis Cass, former Michigan territorial governor, U.S. secretary of war, U.S. senator, and presidential candidate, became secretary of state in the administration of President James Buchanan. (See also May 29, June 17, and October 9.)

VILLAGES INCORPORATED THIS DAY
1871   Homer (Calhoun County) and Ishpeming (Marquette County) which incorporated as a city April 1, 1873.
1893   Stevensville (Berrien County) and Grant (Newaygo County) which became a city December 9, 1969.

7 1984   CONSERVING YOUTH

Governor James J. Blanchard signed into law a bill creating the Michigan Conservation Corps. The $2.6-million, six-month pilot program provided public-works jobs at department of natural resources residential camps for five-hundred unemployed young adults.

1983   PANTHER FIRST

The Michigan Panthers, members of a newly created United States Football League (USFL), played their first game and beat the Birmingham Stallions 9-7 at Birmingham. The Panthers went on to win the USFL's first championship. (See July 16.)

1932   RIOT AT THE ROUGE

Three-thousand desperate, unemployed auto workers marched toward Henry Ford's Dearborn Rouge Assembly Plant to demand relief for laid-off employees, union recognition, and better working conditions. As the crowd surged toward the plant's gates, police and Ford security guards leveled their guns and fired hundreds of shots, killing four marchers and wounding nearly a hundred more.

VILLAGES INCORPORATED THIS DAY
1834   St. Joseph (Berrien County) which incorporated as a city June 5, 1891.
1843   Jackson (Jackson County) which incorporated as a city February 14, 1857.
1863   Buchanan (Berrien County) which incorporated as a city March 11, 1929.
1867   Brighton (Livingston County) which incorporated as a city February 16, 1928, and Greenville (Montcalm County) which incorporated as a city March 10, 1871.
1889   Shepherd (Isabella County).
1907   Buckley (Wexford county).

8 1971   BACHELOR FATHER

Allan R. Kerr, a Detroit bachelor, adopted a second son. A year earlier, the social-science teacher had become the first bachelor in Michigan history to adopt a child.

1918   SOLDIERS TAGGED

At Fort Custer (Battle Creek) the U.S. Army issued two identification tags to each of the thirty-thousand Michigan and Wisconsin draftees who had trained at the new army camp. As the men prepared to leave for World War I overseas duty, the army instructed them to put one tag around their neck and the other around their wrist "to make identification certain in case of explosion where portions of the body might be blown to pieces."

VILLAGES INCORPORATED THIS DAY
1837   White Pigeon (St. Joseph County).
1865   Holly (Oakland County).
1869   Augusta (Kalamazoo County) and Burlington (Calhoun County).
1883   Springport (Jackson County).
1889   Mancelona (Antrim County).
1893   Standish (Arenac County) which incorporated as a city March 4, 1904.

9

1979   PORTER ASSISTS TEAMMATES

Kevin Porter set a Detroit Piston single-game assists record when he set up twenty-five baskets in a National Basketball Association 160-117 victory over Boston at the Pontiac Silverdome. Three weeks later, Porter duplicated his record in a 116-105 loss to Phoenix.

1977   WIFE ENDS ABUSE

Francine Hughes, a 33-year-old Dansville woman whose husband allegedly beat and choked her repeatedly, poured gasoline under the sleeping-man's bed and set the house afire, killing him. Seven-and-a-half months later, a jury found the mother of four not guilty of first-degree murder by reason of temporary insanity, a decision lauded by feminists as a landmark in married-women's right to self-defense.

1976   FULL OF HOT AIR

Governor William G. Milliken signed a bill making manned hot-air balloon flights from and over Michigan legal once again. The new act replaced a 1931 law that had outlawed the sale or use of such balloons in Michigan.

1908   FLOOD SALE

Shoppers fled from five Albion stores as glass windows shattered and flew from their frames. Moments later, as the flooded Kalamazoo River washed away the dirt beneath the stores, they all toppled into the muddy waters.

VILLAGES INCORPORATED THIS DAY

1838	Romeo (Macomb County) and Utica (Macomb County) which incorporated as a city December 16, 1936.
1865	Mason (Ingham County) which incorporated as a city March 20, 1875.
1867	Dansville (Ingham County).
1883	Bancroft (Shiawassee County).

10

1953   FORMER GOVERNOR DIES

Alexander Groesbeck, Michigan's twenty-ninth governor, died at Detroit. In 1927, after losing in a bid for a fourth consecutive two-year term as governor, Groesbeck returned to his Detroit law practice and tried twice more, unsuccessfully, to gain the Republican party's nomination for governor. (See also November 7.)

1918   WOMEN ADVISED TO AVOID DETROIT

Social workers broadcast a "stay-away-from-Detroit" message to young women in cities throughout Michigan and the east coast. The social investigators reported that many women who had flocked to Detroit after the outbreak of World War I to earn big wages in factories had found jobs in short supply and had become charity cases or prostitutes.

1906   PHONEY WEATHER

The Michigan State Telephone Company introduced the state's first "weather-report" phone service.

VILLAGES INCORPORATED THIS DAY
1881   Maple Rapids (Clinton County) and Marlette (Sanilac County).
1885   Milan (Washtenaw-Monroe counties) which incorporated as a city March 13, 1967.
1887   Kalkaska (Kalkaska County) and Gagetown (Tuscola County).
1902   Ortonville (Oakland County).
1903   Wolverine (Cheboygan County).

11   1967   STATE FIRM BUILDS STATE HELICOPTER

The R.J. Enstrom Company (Menominee) delivered Michigan's first state-owned helicopter to the conservation department which used it to spot forest fires, count deer, check timber, and nab game-law violators.

1902   LANSING ELIMINATES DRUG PEDDLERS

The common council of Lansing enacted an ordinance prohibiting the distribution of medicine and drug samples throughout the city by leaving them on doorsteps.

1861   Keweenaw County was created.
1905   The city of Alma (Gratiot County) incorporated.
VILLAGES INCORPORATED THIS DAY
1871   Vermontville (Eaton County).
1881   Lakeview (Montcalm County).

12   1984   RECORD CONTRACT

The Detroit Pistons signed NBA all-star guard Isiah Thomas to an eleven-year contract worth an estimated $12 million, the highest compensation and longest contract ever extended by the club.

1975   THOUSAND-HOUR CALL BEGINS

Students at Western Michigan University (Kalamazoo) began the longest phone call ever recorded by the *Guinness Book of World Records*. The students, in an effort to raise money for a burn center, sat at a phone in one-hour shifts for 41-2/3 days.

1974   BAD TIMING

Michigan became the first state to exempt itself from year-round, nationwide daylight savings time imposed by the federal government to save fuel during an energy shortage. Michigan took the action when a study showed that the time change had increased traffic hazards for children who had to walk to school in the morning darkness and had saved little energy.

1972   NUMBER 9 RETIRED

In pre-game ceremonies at Olympia Stadium, the Detroit Red Wings honored Gordie Howe and officially retired his jersey. Howe, who had retired in 1971, quickly became dissatisfied with his office job with the Wings, and in 1973 he and his sons Marty and Mark joined the Houston Aeros of the newly formed World Hockey Association (WHA). The Howe family played with the Aeros for four years then went to the WHA New England Whalers. New England joined the NHL in 1979, the final year of Howe's amazing 32-year career. (See also October 16, November 10, and November 27.)

1965   ON THE RIGHT TRACK

At Detroit's Cobo Hall, Missouri won the first-ever National Collegiate Athletic Association (NCAA) indoor track-and-field championships.

VILLAGES INCORPORATED THIS DAY
1873   Capac (St. Clair County).
1885   Sanilac Center (Sanilac County) which changed its name to Sandusky and incorporated as a city June 15, 1905.
1907   Melvin (Sanilac).

13

1952   PHARMACEUTICAL FIRST

At Holland, Michigan, the Parke Davis and Company opened the nation's first facility to exclusively produce a synthetic antibiotic. Parke Davis built the hundred-yard-long, forty-foot-high building to commercially manufacture chloromycetin.

1938   FASTEST HAT TRICK

Detroit Red Wing Carl Liscombe set a club record for fastest three goals when he scored his hat trick in 1:52 of the first period in a 5-1 win over Chicago at Olympia Stadium.

1917   OTHERS STILL SAY IT

In a hearing before a Michigan house committee on taxation, state Attorney General Alexander Groesbeck said, "The history of the important utilities in Michigan is a history of exploitation, overcapitalization, and mismanagement."

1846   The legislature changed the name of the town of Newburg (Lapeer County) to Almont. On February 12, 1855, Almont incorporated as a village.
1867   The legislature changed the name of the town of Mears (Muskegon County) to Whitehall. Six days later, Whitehall incorporated as a village and, on December 14, 1942, incorporated as a city.
VILLAGES INCORPORATED THIS DAY
1837   Centreville (St. Joseph County), Constantine (St. Joseph County), and Mount Clemens (Macomb County) which incorporated as a city March 20, 1879.
1867   The town of Dower (Genesee County) changed its name and incorporated as the village of Mt. Morris. On November 26, 1929, Mt. Morris incorporated as a city.
1867   Northville (Oakland-Wayne County) which incorporated as a city May 23, 1955.
1879   Sebewaing (Huron County).
1885   Hanover (Jackson County).
1906   South Range (Houghton County).

14
1967   HAPPY TO BE DRAFTED
Michigan State University football stars Bubba Smith, George Webster, Gene Washington and Clint Jones were four of the first eight men selected in the NFL-AFL professional-football draft.

1920   WHISKEY FISHING
A truck loaded with illegal whiskey attempted to cross the frozen Livingstone Channel in the Detroit River from Canada but fell through the ice and sank. When federal agents investigated, they discovered an underwater "graveyard" of many missing cargoes of Canadian liquor, and when word of the discovery leaked to the public, the agents had to issue an order forbidding people from "fishing" for the liquor.

1907   SOME NICOTINE FIT
A Spring Lake man broke every window in one of the town's office buildings causing $100 worth of damages. Doctors, who judged the man insane and committed him to an institution, attributed his behavior to "excessive use of cigarettes."

1865   The village of Bronson Harbor (Berrien County) changed its name to Benton Harbor. On June 5, 1891, Benton Harbor incorporated as a city.

VILLAGES INCORPORATED THIS DAY

1837   Tecumseh (Lenawee) which incorporated as a city June 29, 1953.
1863   Howell (Livingston County) which incorporated as a city December 14, 1914.
1873   Howard City (Montcalm County).
1882   Minden (Sanilac County) and Sand Beach (Huron County) which changed its name to Harbor Beach on March 23, 1899, and incorporated as a city July 6, 1965.
1893   Kingston (Tuscola County) and Luther (Lake County).

15
1978   BILLY BEER ARRIVES
Billy Beer, the short-lived brewing brainchild of President Jimmy Carter's beer-guzzling brother, made its first appearance on Michigan's retail shelves.

1975   FIRST PREP HOCKEY CHAMPS
Lansing Catholic Central (Tier I) and St. Clair Shores Lakeview (Tier II) won the first high-school ice-hockey championships sponsored by the Michigan High School Athletic Association.

1972   ARCHERS GET BEAR
Fred Bear (Grayling), big-game hunter, manufacturer of archery equipment and promoter of archery, became the first person to be inducted into the Archery Hall of Fame located at Grayling, Michigan.

1887   FIRST GAME WARDEN HIRED
The State of Michigan hired William Alden Smith (Grand Rapids) as the state's and the nation's first salaried game and fish warden.

1867   TAXING FOR THE MIND
The state legislature, by approving a levy of 1/20th of a mill on each dollar of taxable property in the state, made the University of Michigan the nation's first university to be supported by a direct property tax.

1861   PREPARING FOR CIVIL WAR
The state legislature gave the governor broad powers to furnish men to serve in a federal army to put down any rebellion by southern states against the federal government. (See also May 16.)

VILLAGES INCORPORATED THIS DAY
1865   Otsego (Allegan County) which incorporated as a city March 11, 1918.
1883   Pinckney (Livingston County) and Mecosta (Mecosta County).
1905   Owendale (Huron County).

16 1977   BLACK WARDEN APPOINTED
Charles E. Anderson was appointed as the head of Southern Michigan Prison (Jackson) and became the first black warden in Michigan prison history. Anderson, an Albion College graduate and twenty-year, up-through-the-ranks veteran of the Michigan corrections system, was promoted from the head of Southern Michigan Prison's Reception and Guidance Center.

1947   WING SETS RECORD
The Detroit Red Wings' Billy Taylor set a National Hockey League record when he assisted on seven goals, the most ever by one player in a NHL game, as the Wings beat Chicago 10-6 at Chicago.

1939   GOVERNOR DIES IN OFFICE
Governor Frank D. Fitzgerald, after serving only two-and-a-half months of his second term as Michigan governor, died at age fifty-four, making him the only Michigan governor to die while in office. (See also January 27.)

1849   The legislature changed the name of the town of Groveland (Jackson County) to Parma which incorporated as a village December 31, 1864.
VILLAGES INCORPORATED THIS DAY
1847   Hillsdale (Hillsdale County) which incorporated as a city March 8, 1869.
1861   Decatur (Van Buren County) and Muskegon (Muskegon County) which incorporated as a city April 3, 1869.
1867   Pentwater (Oceana County), Manchester (Washtenaw County), and Newaygo (Newaygo County) which incorporated as a city September 11, 1967.
1887   Port Austin (Huron County).
1899   Sunfield (Eaton County) and DeTour (Chippewa County).
CITIES INCORPORATED THIS DAY
1867   Grand Haven (Ottawa County).
1869   Manistee (Manistee County).
1883   Menominee (Menominee County).

17

1929   SOCIAL INTERCOURSE BANNED

The president of the University of Detroit, claiming that he was "tired of seeing girls act like campus widows," threatened to expel any coed caught talking to boys. "It would not be so bad," he added, "if they were content to talk with one boy at a time, but they insist on chatting with seven or eight."

1905   STRONG WORDS

Dr. Julia A. White of the Battle Creek Sanitarium, in a speech before a Battle Creek church audience on the subject "Dress Healthful and Beautiful," predicted that "with proper attention to dress, diet and exercise, American girls will, by another decade, prove themselves equal to boys in strength and physical development."

1847   LAST DETROIT LAWMAKING

The state legislature met for the final time at Detroit before moving permanently to Lansing.

1885   Alger County was created.
VILLAGES INCORPORATED THIS DAY
1885   Manistique (Schoolcraft County) which incorporated as a city February 7, 1901.
1903   Applegate (Sanilac County).

18

1968   PARDON ME

Governor George Romney approved a pardon that wiped out all traces of the prison record of an Ypsilanti man who had served two years in prison for conspiring to violate gambling laws. The pardon was the first under new "clean-the-slate" guidelines for former prisoners who have demonstrated six years of exemplary conduct after returning to their communities.

1905   FORMER GOVERNOR DIES

Cyrus G. Luce, Michigan's twentieth governor, died at Coldwater. Luce, a farmer, believed that agriculture furnished the basis for national prosperity and devoted his governorship and life to the elevation and education of the farming community. Luce County was named after him. (See also July 2.)

1898   GOVERNOR BORN

Murray D. VanWagoner, Michigan governor 1941-42, was born at Kingston, Michigan. The former state highway commissioner was the first governor in the nation to call a special war session of the legislature after the bombing of Pearl Harbor.

1837   EDUCATION ON THE MOVE

The state legislature authorized the relocation of the University of Michigan from Detroit to Ann Arbor. The school opened in 1841 and granted its first degrees in 1845.

VILLAGES INCORPORATED THIS DAY

1865   Pine River (Gratiot County) changed its name and incorporated as the village of St. Louis. On March 12, 1891, St. Louis incorporated as a city.
1871   Concord (Jackson County), Vernon (Shiawassee County), Richland (Kalamazoo County), and Cedar Springs (Kent County) which incorporated as a city June 22, 1959.
1881   Bloomingdale (Van Buren County).
1891   East Grand Rapids (Kent County) which incorporated as a city December 14, 1926, and Royal Oak (Oakland County) which incorporated as a city June 2, 1921.

19   1925   FREE FISHING ENDS

The state senate passed a law that required, for the first time, anglers to purchase licenses to fish in Michigan.

1770   WHAT'S A BODY TO DO

An English newspaper reported that food was so scarce in Michigan that Detroit residents ". . . have been obliged to keep two human bodies, that they had found unburied upon the shore, in order to collect and kill the ravens and eagles that come to feed on them for their subsistence."

1845   Houghton County was created.
1863   Menominee County was established.

VILLAGES INCORPORATED THIS DAY

1867   Olivet (Eaton County) which incorporated as a city December 2, 1957.
1869   Petersburg (Monroe County) which incorporated as a city November 13, 1967.
1875   Red Jacket (Houghton County) which changed its name to Calumet June 3, 1929.
1885   Shelby (Oceana County) and Bad Axe (Huron County) which incorporated as a city March 15, 1905.

20   1881   YOU LIGHT UP MY LIFE

The Hotel Bancroft at Saginaw featured the first incandescent electric lamps used commercially in Michigan.

1836   MICHIGAN ISSUES FIRST IOU

The State of Michigan borrowed its first funds, $36,000, from Robert Hollingsworth (New York) who charged six-percent-a-year interest payable over twenty years.

1680   FANTASTIC VOYAGE

Robert Cavalier de la Salle set foot across the southern part of Michigan and became the first known white man to move across the interior of the Lower Peninsula. While awaiting the return of his supply-ship *Griffin*, LaSalle had set out from a fort at (present-day) St. Joseph to reach the mouth of the Mississippi River. While in Illinois, LaSalle received word that the *Griffin* had disappeared and he began his incredible thousand-mile journey across Michigan to Fort Frontenac at the eastern end of Lake Ontario. (See also August 23 and November 1.)

1867   The legislature changed the name of Varna (Genesee County) to Clio which incorporated as a village April 18, 1873, and as a city March 12, 1928.

VILLAGES INCORPORATED THIS DAY

1837   Pontiac became Oakland County's first and the state's fourteenth incorporated village. On March 15, 1861, Pontiac incorporated as a city.

1838   Allegan (Allegan County) which became a city June 12, 1907.

1879   Richmond (Macomb County) which incorporated as a city October 27, 1964.

1885   Ontonagon (Ontonagon County).

1893   Tustin (Osceola County).

1901   Millersburg (Presque Isle County).

1905   Waldron (Hillsdale County).

21 1927 FIRST YOUNG CANDIDATE

Robert J. Garner, the first eighteen-year-old to run for office after the state lowered its age of majority to eighteen (see January 1), lost in his bid for the Independence Township (Pontiac) clerk's job.

1946 PREMIER FOR PATIENTS

The Percy Jones Hospital (Battle Creek) installed the nation's first microcfilm projector. The hospital used the machine, which was made by University Microfilms (Ann Arbor) and Argus Cameras (Ann Arbor), to project enlarged images on the ceilings of rooms of their bedridden patients.

VILLAGES INCORPORATED THIS DAY

1865   Marine (St. Clair County), which changed its name to Marine City and incorporated as a city June 8, 1887.

1877   Millington (Tuscola County), Otisville (Genesee County), Bangor (Van Buren County) which incorporated as a city March 13, 1967, and Flushing (Genesee County) which incorporated as a city April 1, 1963.

1891   Eau Claire (Berrien County) and Gaston (Wexford County) whose name was changed by the legislature to Harrietta on March 4, 1893.

22 1977 THE BABY-SITTER

Police discovered the body of the fourth child within a year to be abducted and ritualistically murdered by a mysterious killer dubbed "the baby-sitter," who prowled Detroit's affluent northern suburbs. The slayings prompted the largest law-enforcement investigation in Michigan history but the killer was never found.

1954 SHOPPERS FLOCK TO SUBURBS

Northland, the country's first regional shopping mall, opened at Southfield and began an American shopping revolution. (Photo following page.)

1907 CLEARING HIS THROAT

A seventy-year-old Port Huron man, who had carried a bullet in his neck for forty years as the result of a hunting accident, coughed and spit the lead shot out his mouth.

1867   The village of Berrien Springs (Berrien County) incorporated.

1873   The city of Ludington (Mason County) incorporated.

America's first shopping mall (see March 22).

23

1984 UNIQUE BABY BORN

A Hazel Park woman gave birth to Michigan's first "test-tube" baby, a seven-pound thirteen-ounce boy, at Detroit's Hutzel Hospital. Almost exactly nine months before, doctors had removed four eggs from the woman, fertilized them in a small glass saucer with her husband's sperm, then transferred one fertile egg back into the mother's uterus where the baby developed normally.

1917 FIRST AIR ROUTES

The United States Aero Club named Grand Rapids and Detroit as two Michigan cities to be included in the nation's first four main transcontinental airways.

1835 COLLEGE FOUNDED

Three Methodist Episcopal churchmen, after traveling over icy forest trails, arrived at Detroit to secure a charter for a "literary school in the wilderness" from the legislative council of the Territory of Michigan. The council granted the charter and the men returned to Spring Arbor to build a "Spring Arbor Seminary." The Spring Arbor school never opened but instead, in November 1843, opened its doors as the Wesleyan Seminary at Albion. In 1861 the school became Albion College.

1893   The city of Belding (Ionia County) incorporated.

VILLAGES INCORPORATED THIS DAY

1867   New Baltimore (Macomb County) which incorporated as a city March 9, 1931.

1893   Gobleville (Van Buren County) which changed its name to Gobles and incorporated as a city March 11, 1957.

24
1980 BIG PAYOFF

The largest pay-out for the state's legal "numbers" lottery game occurred when number 222 paid $3,026,750 to 8,478 winners.

1970 U.P. HEARS SYMPHONY

The Detroit Symphony Orchestra presented a concert at Northern Michigan University (Marquette), the first upper-peninsula performance in the symphony's 56-year history.

1965 PROTESTOR DIES

On a road from Selma to Montgomery, Alabama, four members of the Ku Klux Klan killed Mrs. Viola Liuzzo (Detroit), a white civil-rights worker who had marched in a protest to demand equal voting rights for the state's blacks. Her children unsuccessfully sued the federal government when an FBI informer revealed he had been with the Klansmen who were convicted of violating Mrs. Liuzzo's civil rights.

1936 HOCKEY MARATHON

At Montreal, the Detroit Red Wings and Montreal Maroons began an NHL Stanley Cup play-off game that ended after sixty minutes of regulation play and 116 minutes, thirty seconds of overtime, the longest Stanley Cup game every played. Detroit won 1-0 and went on to win not only the semifinal series but also their first Stanley Cup. (See April 5.)

1917 FIRST BASKETBALL CHAMPIONS

Detroit Northwestern High School beat a team from Jackson 24-21 in the finals of the first basketball championship held in the state of Michigan. The thirty-six teams that arrived for the three-day tournament sponsored by the University of Michigan were housed at fraternities and rooming houses at the Ann Arbor campus.

1902 FAMOUS LOSER BORN

Thomas E. Dewey, governor of New York and two-time Republican presidential nominee, was born at Owosso.

VILLAGES INCORPORATED THIS DAY
1869 Spring Lake (Ottawa County), Lawrence (Van Buren County), Ovid (Clinton County), and Rochester (Oakland County) which incorporated as a city September 20, 1966.
1875 Blissfield (Lenawee County) and Gaines (Genesee County).
1893 Dearborn (Wayne County) which incorporated as a city February 15, 1927.
1958 Novi (Oakland County) which incorporated as a city May 20, 1968.

25
1982 CARRYING PARTISANSHIP INTO SPACE

During a telecast from the third Columbia space-shuttle voyage, the camera zoomed in on a wall above Michigan native and University of Michigan-graduate Jack Lousma's head and zeroed in on a maize-and-blue "M-Go-Blue" bumper sticker.

1942   FIRST LADY OF SOUL BORN

Singer Aretha Franklin, who during the 1960s practically defined soul music with hits such as "Respect," "Natural Woman," and "Chain of Fools," was born at Detroit.

1926   LICENSE PLATES LETTERED

In anticipation of Michigan registering, for the first time, one-million automobiles, the state department revised their license-plate numbering system. The department directed that, as in the past, they would number the plates beginning with 1 and, upon reaching 999999, would begin again with M 1.

1922   AUTOMOBILERS BECOME BROADCASTERS

Radio station WWI, owned and operated by the Ford Motor Company, went on the air at Detroit as the first of only two Michigan radio stations ever to be operated by auto companies. The other, WREO (Lansing), owned by the REO Motor Car Company, went on the air in 1924. WWI stopped broadcasting in 1926 and WREO in 1927.

1867   The city of Holland (Allegan-Ottawa County) incorporated.
VILLAGES INCORPORATED THIS DAY
1867   Farmington (Oakland County) which incorporated as a city February 19, 1926.
1871   Muir (Ionia County).

26

1982   STREAK ENDS

The Detroit Red Wings ended a club-record fourteen-game losing streak by beating the Toronto Maple Leafs 2-1 in a National Hockey League game played at Toronto.

1979   MSU WINS NCAA

Michigan State University became the state's first NCAA Division I basketball champion by beating Indiana State 75-64 at Salt Lake City.

1944   SUPERSTAR BORN

Recording superstar Diana Ross was born at Detroit. Motown Records signed Ross and two of her friends who called themselves the Primettes, rechristened the group the Supremes, and launched them on a spectacular career that made them the 1960s' best-selling group behind the Beatles. In 1969 Ross began a solo career and later expanded into acting *(Lady Sings the Blues)*.

1922   GOVERNOR BORN

William G. Milliken, Michigan's longest-serving governor, was born at

Traverse City. The former department-store owner and lieutenant governor took over when George Romney resigned (see January 22) in 1969. Milliken was reelected in 1970, 1974 and 1978.

1836 SUPREME COURT BEGINS

The state legislature created the first Michigan State Supreme Court composed of three judges who also presided over the state circuit courts. Four months later, with William S. Fletcher as chief justice, the court organized and conducted sessions at various Michigan cities until moving permanently to Lansing in 1873.

1804 FIRST LAND OFFICE

The federal government established the first United States land office, in what is now the state of Michigan, at Detroit and began settling disputes over deeds issued during French and English rule.

VILLAGES INCORPORATED THIS DAY
1869   Nashville (Barry County).
1877   Port Sanilac (Sanilac County) and Hartford (Van Buren County) which incorporated as a city December 2, 1963.
1903   Kinde (Huron County).
1907   Baroda (Berrien County).

27 1871 FIRST FEMALE ALUMNI

Amanda Sanford received a Doctor of Medicine degree and Sarah Killgore, a Bachelor of Laws degree, and became the first women to graduate from the University of Michigan. One year earlier, when the college first allowed women to enroll, both ladies had transferred from other schools to complete their education.

VILLAGES INCORPORATED THIS DAY
1867   Middleville (Barry County).
1869   Merrill (Saginaw).

28 1977 MASS POISONING

The worst outbreak of botulism in the nation's history occurred when fifty-nine people contracted the dread disease after eating food at a Pontiac Mexican restaurant. Though all but two of the victims were hospitalized — some in critical condition — quick identification of the toxin, one of the deadliest poisons known, prevented fatalities.

1950 HOCKEY STAR ESCAPES DEATH

The hockey world held its breath as Detroit Red Wing superstar Gordie Howe was taken off the ice unconscious after he and Toronto's Teeder Kennedy had smashed into the boards at Olympia Stadium during a Stanley Cup play-off game. But Howe recovered from a gash on his right eyeball, a fractured nose, facial lacerations and a severe brain concussion and went on to play another thirty years of professional hockey.

1926   FORMER GOVERNOR DIES
John T. Rich, Michigan's twenty-second governor, died. The Republican headed Michigan during the "Panic of 1893," a nationwide depression that closed Michigan banks and upper-peninsula mines and left thousands of Michigan residents without jobs. At the end of his second term, Rich served as customs collector and state treasurer. (See also April 23.)

1859   COLLEGE CHARTERED
A Wesleyan Methodist theological institute, founded at Leoni, Michigan in 1845 and later called the Michigan Union College, moved to Adrian and received a charter as Adrian College. Eight months later Adrian College opened.

1820   Though fewer-than-sixty families lived in the area, Oakland County was officially organized.
1820   St. Clair County was established.
1835   Genesee County was established.
VILLAGES INCORPORATED THIS DAY
1836   New Buffalo (Berrien County) which incorporated as a city March 8, 1965; Marshall (Calhoun County) which incorporated as a city February 14, 1859; and Adrian (Lenawee County) which incorporated as a city January 31, 1853.
1867   Houghton (Houghton County) which incorporated as a city November 4, 1969.
1873   Pierson (Montcalm County).
1883   Cass City (Tuscola County), Westphalia (Clinton County) and Breedsville (Van Buren County).

29 1979   ADOPTION FIRST
A childless Detroit couple adopted a baby born by a female friend whom they had inseminated with the husband's sperm. The adoption was the nation's first of a child born to a surrogate mother.

1935   SKATES SQUELCHED
The Detroit police commissioner ordered all members of his force to confiscate the roller skates of any children found skating in the streets. The commissioner said he took the action to safeguard young skaters against traffic accidents.

1929   FIREWORKS RESTRICTED
The state legislature passed a law, the nation's first, prohibiting the use of fireworks by the general public and allowing displays only by approved or licensed operators.

VILLAGES INCORPORATED THIS DAY
1869   Plainwell (Allegan County) which incorporated as a city March 12, 1934.
1877   Sheridan (Montcalm County).
1890   Stambaugh (Iron County) which incorporated as a city November 12, 1923.
1899   Camden (Hillsdale County).

30 1964   FIRST KIDNEY TRANSPLANTED
Michigan's first kidney transplant took place at the University of Michigan. The operation involved identical twins, both

female. Both women, now nurses, are married with children and lead normal lives.

1903   QUITE A SWITCH

Michigan Bell began installing central switchboards in Michigan cities and removing all bells and batteries from subscribers' homes. With the installation, Bell customers no longer had to ring a central office to place a call but only pick up the receiver.

1869   The city of Lapeer (Lapeer County) incorporated.
1869   The legislature changed the name of Crawville (Muskegon-Ottawa County) to Fruitport which incorporated as a village March 21, 1891.
VILLAGES INCORPORATED THIS DAY
1869   Milford (Oakland County); Leslie (Ingham County) which incorporated as a city December 12, 1967; Portland (Ionia County) which incorporated as a city December 9, 1968; and Union City (Branch-Calhoun Counties).
1885   Iron River (Iron County) which incorporated as a city January 11, 1926.
1887   Eagle (Clinton County).

31

1984   PISTONS PACK THEM IN

The largest crowd ever to attend a regular-season National Basketball Association game, 35,407, watched the Detroit Pistons beat the Milwaukee Bucks 107-105 at the Pontiac Silverdome.

1976   RIGHT TURN ON RED

A state traffic law went into effect making it legal to turn right at red lights after yielding to traffic or pedestrians.

1976   PLURAL PENALTIES

In an NHL game played at Detroit between the Detroit Red Wings and the Toronto Maple Leafs, referee Lloyd Gilmour handed out a record forty-eight penalties to both teams, most of them during a second-period bench-clearing brawl. The Leafs received twelve minors, seven majors, and four game misconducts while the Wings got fifteen minors, six majors and four game misconducts during the game which ended in a 4-4 tie.

1975   NO STUDS ALLOWED

Michigan banned the use of studded tires because the super-hard, tungsten-carbide studs inserted into the treads to improve traction and handling on snow were rapidly destroying road surfaces.

1818   FIRST PROTESTANT CHURCH BUILT

At River Rouge, the Society of Methodists erected the first Protestant church building in the Michigan territory.

VILLAGES INCORPORATED THIS DAY
1875   Mendon (St. Joseph County).
1871   Grass Lake (Jackson County).

APRIL

1 1978   EXPRESS DEBUT

At Tulsa, Oklahoma, Coach Ken Furphy's son Keith scored the winning goal as their Detroit Express professional soccer team played their first North American Soccer League game and beat the Roughnecks 2-1.

1963   CONSTITUTION ADOPTED

Michigan voters narrowly approved Michigan's fourth and latest constitution which streamlined and modernized the 1908 constitution (see October 22) and changed the term of governor from two to four years.

1906   LET YOUR FINGERS DO THE WALKING

The Michigan State Telephone Company issued at Detroit the state's first telephone directory that featured yellow-page classified business advertising.

COUNTIES ESTABLISHED THIS DAY
1840   Alcona, Alpena, Antrim, Clare, Crawford, Emmet, Huron, Iosco, Leelanau, Manistee, Mason, Mecosta, Missaukee, Montmorency, Newaygo, Ogemaw, Osceola, Oscoda, Otsego, Presque Isle, Roscommon, Tuscola and Wexford.
VILLAGES INCORPORATED THIS DAY
1850   St. Clair (St. Clair County) which on February 4, 1858, incorporated as a city.
1873   Byron (Shiawassee County).
1879   Unionville (Tuscola County).
1885   Metamora (Lapeer County); Newberry (Luce County); Frankfort (Benzie County) which incorporated as a city March 11, 1935; and Boyne City (Charlevoix County) which incorporated as a city March 5, 1907.
1887   Harrisville (Alcona County) which incorporated as a city May 18, 1905.
1963   Sanford (Midland County).
CITIES INCORPORATED THIS DAY
1963   Zilwaukee (Saginaw County) and Ferrysburg (Ottawa County).

2 1977   PLEASE EXTINGUISH ALL SMOKING MATERIALS

A new anti-smoking law took effect in Michigan that banned smoking in grocery stores and required restaurants seating fifty-or-more people to have designated nonsmoking areas.

1975   ICE CONQUERED

A 384-foot Canadian tanker *Saturn* fought its way through the ice-clogged St. Mary's River and passed through the MacArthur lock at Sault Ste. Marie, marking the first time in history that shipping on the upper Great Lakes completed 365 days without interruption.

1966   COHO COME TO MICHIGAN

Conservation Commissioner Carl T. Johnson upended a bucket and spilled the first of 850,000 six-inch Coho salmon into the Platte River. Though Coho had never been successfully planted anywhere outside of their native Pacific Coast, massive and continued releases successfully established the salmon as the backbone of Michigan open-water sport fishing.

1881   GIANT STARTS SMALL

Joseph Lowthian Hudson held a grand opening at a men's, boy's and furnishings store he had opened in leased space at the Detroit Opera House. By the late 1920s, Hudson's had become the third-largest department store in America and carried more than a half-million items displayed over forty-nine acres of sales space in a mammoth 25-story red-brick downtown Detroit building. On January 17, 1983, Hudson's closed that downtown store and in March 1984 the company announced it would move its head-quaters out-of-state. (Illustration following page.)

1962   The city of Walker (Kent County) incorporated.
VILLAGES INCORPORATED THIS DAY
1849   Port Huron (St. Clair County) which incorporated as a city February 17, 1857.
1850   Battle Creek (Calhoun Conty) which incorporated as a city February 3, 1859.
1869   Wayne (Wayne County) which incorporated as a city August 5, 1958.
1885   Brockway Center (St. Clair County) which changed its name to Yale March 6, 1889, and incorporated as a city June 7, 1905.
1891   Benzonia (Benzie County).
1923   Berkley (Oakland County) which incorporated as a city May 23, 1932.

3 1970   CHARITABLE DENTISTS

The first dental clinic in Michigan to be staffed entirely by volunteer dentists and dental assistants opened at Corunna to provide free dental care to low-income families.

1871   SOLE WOMAN VOTER

Almost fifty years before women were granted suffrage, Mrs. Nannette B. Gardner voted in a Detroit election. Gardner, a wealthy widow and a tax-payer, had convinced an alderman he should register her because she had no husband to protect her interests and, for as long as she lived, she was Detroit's only woman voter.

1869   FIRST FREE SCHOOLS

The state legislature established a free statewide school system supported by local taxes and state aid. Prior to the act, local governments had

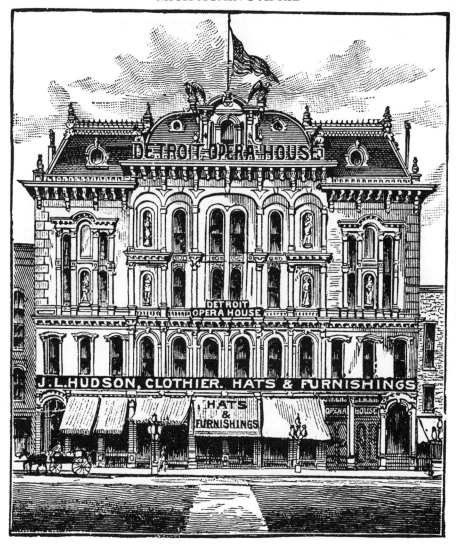

The modest beginning of a retail giant (see April 2).

issued rate bills (tuition charges) to the parents of children who attended primary schools that had opened in most settled parts of the state.

1838   CORRECTIONS CONSTRUCTION BEGINS

The governor appointed two commissioners to supervise the building of a prison, Michigan's first, at Jackson. Nine months later the prison, a plank building surrounded by a high fence of tamarack poles, received its first inmate. In 1841 stone walls were erected, and in the 1880s a massive medieval-like prison was built. The present facility, the world's largest

61

walled prison, was constructed during the 1930s.

1837   BUILDERS STRIKE

Detroit journeymen carpenters carrying signs saying, "Ten hours a day — two dollars for pay," walked off their jobs in Michigan's first organized protest against low wages and long hours.

1885   Iron County was created.
1848   The town of Michigan, Michigan, home of the state's new capital for a year, officially changed its name to Lansing.

VILLAGES INCORPORATED THIS DAY
1838   Originally called Bronson (Kalamazoo County), the village of Kalamazoo incorporated. On June 8, 1883, Kalamazoo incorporated as a city.
1869   Chesaning (Saginaw County); Benton Harbor (Berrien County) which incorporated as a city June 5, 1895; and Midland (Midland-Bay counties) which incorporated as a city February 21, 1887.
1879   Charlevoix (Charlevoix County) which incorporated as a city June 1, 1905.
1907   Stanwood (Mecosta County) and Freeport (Barry County).
1911   Grosse Pointe Shores (Macomb-Wayne counties).

4 1979   WHAT A DIVE

A TWA Boeing 727, carrying eighty passengers at 39,000 feet over Flint, suddenly swerved to the right, completed a 360-degree barrel roll, and nose-dived five miles at a speed the plane's instruments could not record. Harvey "Hoot" Gibson, the pilot, finally regained control by putting the landing gear down and made an emergency landing at Detroit Metro Airport.

1943   ACTOR BORN

Actor Max Gail, best known for his role as Sergeant Wojehowicz on television's "Barney Miller," was born at Detroit.

1825   DETROIT ELECTS FIRST MAYOR

John R. Williams became Detroit's first elected mayor receiving 102 votes to a total of eleven for the other candidates combined.

VILLAGES INCORPORATED THIS DAY
1873   Imlay City (Lapeer County) which incorporated as a city March 30, 1970.
1921   Lincoln Park (Wayne County) which incorporated as a city July 23, 1956.
1927   Allen Park (Wayne County) which incorporated as a city July 23, 1956.

5 1955   STREAK ENDS

The Detroit Red Wings won the last game in a National Hockey League-record fifteen-game winning streak beating Montreal 7-1 in the second game of a Stanley Cup championship series at Detroit. Two nights later, Montreal beat Detroit 4-2 at Montreal, but Detroit won the series and the Stanley Cup.

1941   ACTOR BORN

Theatre and film actor Michael Moriarity was born at Detroit. In 1974

Moriarity won a Tony Award for his role in the Broadway production of *Find Your Way Home* and an Emmy for his supporting role in *The Glass Menagerie.*

1920   ON THIN ICE

A Pere Marquette five-car steamer ferry got stuck in the ice off Pt. Sauble after leaving Ludington, and eleven passengers attempted to walk to shore. Suddenly the ice floe broke up and winds carried the piece holding the group out into Lake Michigan. Hundreds of spectators lined the shore and watched as the Coast Guard, with great difficulty, rescued the nearly frozen passengers.

1869   The city of Big Rapids (Mecosta County) incorporated.
VILLAGES INCORPORATED THIS DAY
1838   Grand Rapids (Kent County) which incorporated as a city April 21, 1850.
1869   New Haven (Macomb County) and South Haven (Van Buren County) which incorporated as a city March 10, 1902.
1871   Williamston (Ingham County) which incorporated as a city July 1, 1963.
1915   Powers (Menominee County).
1926   Huntington Woods (Oakland County) which incorporated as a city June 14, 1932.

6 1971   RECORD HOME OPENER

The Detroit Tigers, behind the pitching of Mickey Lolich, beat Cleveland 8-2 before the largest opening-day crowd, 54,089, in the team's history.

1958   WORST AIRLINE CRASH

A Capitol Airlines four-engine turbo jet slammed into a mucky cornfield and exploded while approaching Tri-City Airport near Freeland. Forty-four passengers, including twenty from Michigan, and three crew members died in the fiery crash, Michigan's worst airline disaster.

1937   CHRYSLER WORKERS REPRESENTED

The United Auto Workers became the sole bargaining agent at the Chrysler Corporation.

1917   U.S. JOINS WORLD WAR

The U.S. Congress declared war on Germany and a wave of anti-German sentiment swept across Michigan and the rest of the country. Seized with fear that the enemy might be close-at-hand, Michigan residents considered anything even remotely connected with Germany to be suspicious and evil. German foods such as sauerkraut and frankfurters were renamed "liberty cabbage" and "hot dogs." Many Michigan residents with German names Americanized them and the residents of Berlin, Michigan, changed their town's name to a more-suitable "Marne." (See also February 17.)

1900   FIRST CHAMPIONSHIP FIGHT

James Jackson Jeffries, 250 pounds, knocked out John Finnegan, 180 pounds, in fifty-five seconds of the first round at Detroit in the world's first heavyweight-title fight.

VILLAGES INCORPORATED THIS DAY
1838   Clinton (Lenawee County).
1877   Tekonsha (Calhoun County).
1925   Clarksville (Ionia County).
1926   Center Line (Macomb County) which incorporated as a city December 26, 1935.
1953   Cement City (Lenawee-Jackson counties).
1954   Wolverine Lake (Oakland County).

7 1984   TIGER THROWS NO-HITTER

Jack Morris became only the fourth Detroit Tiger pitcher and the first since 1958 to pitch a no-hitter as the Tigers shut out the Chicago White Sox 4-0 at Chicago.

1947   AUTO PIONEER DIES

Henry Ford, legendary automobile-industry pioneer, died at his Dearborn mansion at the age of eighty-three. (Photo following page.)

1939   DIRECTOR BORN

Francis Ford Coppola, Oscar-winning director of *The Godfather*, was born at Detroit.

1933   LIQUOR AVAILABLE BUT CONTROLLED

The state Liquor Control Commission was created, and three weeks later, after nearly fifteen trouble-filled years of prohibition, alcoholic beverages once again became legal in Michigan. (See also April 27.)

1929   WOMEN FLYERS ORGANIZE
The first meeting of the Women's National Aeronautic Association was held at the Hotel Statler (Detroit), and Mrs. Orra Heald Blackmore (Detroit) was elected president.

VILLAGES INCORPORATED THIS DAY
1930   Shoreham (Berrien County) and Parchment (Kalamazoo County) which incorporated as a city November 8, 1938.
1947   Prescott (Ogemaw County).

Henry Ford.

8 1984   ANOTHER ALL-AMERICAN

Traverse City became the most-recent Michigan city to win the National Municipal League's All-America Cities award for community improvement through citizen action. Other Michigan cities that have won are: Harbor Springs (1975), Pontiac (1974), Albion (1973), Saginaw (1968), Royal Oak (1967), Detroit (1966), Ann Arbor (1966), Port Huron (1955), Flint (1953), Kalamazoo (1951 and 1969), and Grand Rapids (1949, 1960 and 1961).

1931   STATE GETS A BIRD

The state legislature designated the Robin Red Breast as Michigan's official state bird. The Michigan Audubon Society had conducted a contest to choose a feathered mascot, and the robin had received nearly one-fourth of the 200,000 ballots cast, beating out the runner-up Chickadee by more than eight-thousand votes.

1889   The city of Ironwood (Gogebic County) incorporated.
VILLAGES INCORPORATED THIS DAY
1871   Grand Ledge (Eaton County) which incorporated as a city March 27, 1893, and Laingsburg (Shiawassee County) which incorporated as a city May 28, 1951.

9 1984   SCOUTS SUFFER

Three Saginaw-area residents reported finding pins in Girl Scout cookies they had purchased. The reports of tampering, similar to those from other areas of the country, caused a temporary halt in cookie delivery and damaged public trust in the organization's major fund-raiser.

1901   TURN OF THE CENTURY PRICES

A grocery-store advertisement in the *Flint Globe* featured eggs at twelve cents per dozen, butter at seventeen cents a pound, and rice at six cents a pound. The ad also advised customers to shop at the store because "we have no bad debts and therefore you do not have to pay for the losses of bad accounts."

1865   CIVIL WAR ENDS

General Robert E. Lee's army surrendered its guns and battle flags to two Michigan regiments, and the Civil War, in which 90,000 Michigan men fought and 14,000 died, ended.

VILLAGES INCORPORATED THIS DAY
1881   Traverse City (Grand Traverse County) which incorporated as a city May 18, 1955.
1891   Watervliet (Berrien County) which incorporated as a city December 4, 1924.

10 1922   FIRE HORSES RETIRED

Detroit's last horse-drawn fire wagon made a five-minute ceremonial final run.

1915   M*A*S*H C.O. BORN

Harry Morgan was born at Detroit as Harry Bratsburg. The character actor played villains and losers in films of the 1940s and 1950s before starring in television roles, most notably as M*A*S*H 's company commander, Col. Sherman Potter.

 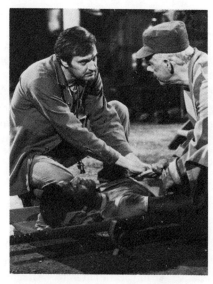

Detroit native Harry Bratsburg (Harry Morgan) portrayed Hawkeye Pierce's (Alan Alda) commanding officer, Colonel Sherman Potter, in television's hit series M*A*S*H.

1839   COLLEGE CHARTERED

The state legislature granted a charter for Michigan's first nonpublic, nonreligious college which the organizers planned to locate at Marshall. But because of objections to the proposed name, "Michigan College," the founders changed the name to "Marshall College" which gave it the appearance of being a minor local school and the enterprise failed.

1883   The village of Mackinaw City (Cheboygan-Emmet counties) incorporated.

11 1965   DEADLY TORNADO STRIKES

On Palm Sunday, three tornado systems ripped through central and southern Michigan killing forty-nine and injuring 732. The storm also destroyed or damaged nearly 2,500 buildings, and President Lyndon B. Johnson declared ten Michigan counties disaster areas.

1965   TWO-GOAL RECORD

Detroit Red Wing hockey-player Norm Ullman set a National Hockey League record for fastest-two play-off goals when he scored twice in five seconds during the second period of a game against Chicago at Olympia won by the Wings 4-2.

1936   FIRST CHAMPIONSHIP

The Detroit Red Wings defeated Toronto 3-2 to win their first National Hockey League Stanley Cup. The Wings went on to win the cup again in 1937, 1943, 1950, 1952, 1954 and 1955.

1884   TROUT FINDS AMERICAN HOME

J. F. Ellis, a member of the Northville, Michigan, fish hatchery, lugged a can containing five-thousand brown-trout fry to the banks of the Baldwin River near Baldwin and upended it. With a gurgle and a splash, Ellis unceremoniously dumped the first German brown trout ever released in American waters.

CITIES INCORPORATED THIS DAY
1873   Negaunee (Marquette County).
1971   Burton (Genesee County).

12   1865   MICHIGAN CAPTURES COMMANDER

The 4th Michigan Cavalry, commanded by Colonel Benjamin D. Pritchard (Allegan), surrounded the fleeing remnants of the Confederate government and captured Jefferson Davis, president of the Confederacy.

1859   FIRST BILLIARDS CHAMPIONSHIP

Michael Phelan (New York City) and John Seereiter (Detroit) played at Detroit the first billiard match to attain international prominence. Phelan won the world championship and a $15,000 purse by a score of 2,000-to-1,904. Exactly one year earlier, Phelan had defeated Seereiter in a 9½-hour match at Detroit's Fireman's Hall for the first U.S. billiards championship.

VILLAGES INCORPORATED THIS DAY
1827   Monroe (Monroe County) which incorporated as a city March 22, 1837.
1873   Reading (Hillsdale County) which incorporated as a city March 22, 1837.
1891   Clifford (Lapeer County).

13   1978   JUSTICE PREVAILS

Governor William G. Milliken denied an extradition request from Alabama authorities who had asked that a sixty-year-old Detroit woman be returned to serve the remainder of a 218-year prison term. The black woman, who had been sent to prison for lying to white authorities to protect her boyfriend from robbery charges, had escaped in 1951 after serving nine years. Her sister, whom she had lived with in Michigan since her escape, turned her in after a fight.

1890   GOVERNOR BORN

Frank Murphy, Michigan governor 1937-38, was born at Harbor Beach. The former Detroit mayor took office when the great General Motors sit-down strike was under way and played a decisive mediatory role that brought the strike to a peaceful end on grounds that paved the way for the UAW's subsequent growth. (See also July 19.)

1875   FIREMEN ORGANIZE

The Michigan State Firemen's Association was formed at Battle Creek "for the protection and promotion of the best interests of the firemen of Michigan."

1905   The city of Rose City (Ogemaw County) incorporated.
VILLAGES INCORPORATED THIS DAY
1871   Pewamo (Ionia County).
1886   Garden (Delta County).
1966   Rothbury (Oceana County).

14

1982   MICHIGAN GETS WELL-TRAVELED FLAG

Michigan astronaut Col. Jack Lousma presented Governor William G. Milliken with a small United States flag he had carried on an eight-day Columbia space shuttle that made 129 trips around the world and flew 3.8-million miles.

1982   STATE STAMPS ISSUED

The U.S. Postal Service issued simultaneously at Lansing and Washington, D.C., two twenty-cent stamps, one that featured the Michigan-state bird (robin) and the other the state flower (apple blossom).

1931   FORD PRESERVES A FORD

Henry Ford stepped behind the wheel of the twenty-millionth Ford to roll off his Detroit assembly line, drove the car to the Ford Museum at Greenfield Village, and placed it beside Ford car-number-one built in 1893.

1871   The village of Eaton Rapids (Eaton County) incorporated. On April 1, 1881, Eaton Rapids incorporated as a city.

15 1977 REN CEN DEDICATED

Detroit's glittering river-front Renaissance Center, a $337-million complex of towers and office buildings built to revitalize the city, was formally dedicated.

1876   HOLIDAY FIRST

Michigan celebrated its first Arbor Day, the tree-planters holiday, but most Michigan residents ignored the occasion.

1859   GOVERNOR BORN

Luren D. Dickinson, Michigan governor 1939-40, was born at Niagara County, New York. Dickinson was Michigan's longest-serving lieutenant governor, was the only lieutenant governor to succeed an incumbent who died in office (see March 16), and was the oldest governor, a month short of eighty, to take office.

VILLAGES INCORPORATED THIS DAY
1871   Fowlerville (Livingston County) and Rockford (Kent County) which incorporated as a city April 8, 1935.
1873   Deerfield (Lenawee County) and Morenci (Lenawee County) which incorporated as a city March 12, 1934.

16

1937   CHEAP MILK

A dozen Detroit milk retailers, who were engaged in a price war, slashed the price of milk to nine cents a quart.

1927   FIREWORKS RESTRICTED

The state legislature unanimously passed a ban on the sale of fireworks.

1913   FLY PAPER

The *Flint Journal* newspaper, writing that "the angel of death mounts the back of every fly," offered to pay residents of their area twenty-five cents for each one-thousand dead flies brought to their office in a campaign to "fight for a flyless Flint."

VILLAGES INCORPORATED THIS DAY
1875   Vandalia (Cass County); Casnovia (Muskegon-Kent counties); Mount Pleasant (Isabella County) which incorporated as a city March 22, 1889; and Zeeland (Ottawa County) which incorporated as a city May 29, 1907.
1889   Highland Park (Wayne County) which incorporated as a city October 31, 1917.
1891   Onekema (Manistee County).
1973   Barton Hills (Washtenaw County).

17

1979   BOUNTY ENDS

Governor William G. Milliken signed into law a bill repealing Michigan's long-standing bounty on coyotes, the last large animal in the state to carry a price on its head.

1963   LEAGUE SUSPENDS LION

The National Football League suspended Detroit Lion star Alex Karras and Green Bay's Paul Hornung for betting on NFL games and associating with gamblers. The league also fined five other Detroit players $2,000 each. Karras was reinstated eleven months later.

1893 RARE WAVE HITS ST. JOSEPH

A six-foot-high seiche, or tidal wave, surged from Lake Michigan and swept seven-hundred feet beyond the high-water mark at St. Joseph.

1871   The city of Norway (Dickinson County) incorporated.

VILLAGES INCORPORATED THIS DAY

1871   The town of Duncan (Cheboygan County) changed its name and incorporated as the village of Cheboygan. On March 13, 1889, Cheboygan incorporated as a city.

1907   Posen (Presque Isle County).

1972   Lennon (Shiawassee-Genesee counties).

18 1942 WAR PREPAREDNESS

Four months after the United States had entered World War II, Michigan's largest banks photocopied valuable documents and dispersed them among small rural banks not expected to be bombed; detailed inch-by-inch aerial photographic maps of Michigan showing the locations of all factories and other industrial centers were declared secret and made available only to a select few; and the city of Detroit purchased twenty new air-raid sirens.

1905 STRANGE COINCIDENCE

A Saugatuck undertaker dropped dead of a heart attack while conducting the funeral of a man who had died of a heart attack.

VILLAGES INCORPORATED THIS DAY

1873   L'Anse (Baraga County) and South Lyon (Oakland County) which incorporated as a city August 19, 1930.

1889   Laurium (Houghton County).

19 1973 CRATERS APPEAR; RESIDENTS DISAPPEAR

Residents of Williamsburg, a small town of three-hundred residents northeast of Traverse City, awoke to find hundreds of craters that had mysteriously appeared throughout their town. The craters, many of which spewed water, mud and volatile gas in three-foot geysers, forced virtually all residents to evacuate for nearly a month and turned the town into a moonscape. State geologists theorized that natural gas from an oil-company's well being drilled four miles south of town escaped through a hole in the casing, traveled through porous rock and subterranean water and burst through the earth's crust.

1912 SCIENTIST BORN

Glenn T. Seaborg, professor of chemistry at the University of California, Berkeley, chairman of the Atomic Energy Commission, and Nobel-prize winner, was born at Ishpeming.

1895 GOVERNOR BORN

Harry F. Kelly, Michigan governor 1943-46, was born at Ottawa, Illinois. The Republican lawyer and former Michigan secretary of state was the last statewide holder of elective office who had served in World War I. Kelly mobilized the state during World War II and also established a trust fund for veterans, expanded a building program for Michigan colleges and universities, and reorganized the state's mental-health program. (See also February 8.)

20
1952   PRISONERS RIOT

From behind the bars of the world's largest walled prison came the cry, "There's salt in the coffee," which signaled the start of the bloodiest riot ever to strike Southern Michigan Prison (Jackson). In the pitched battle that followed, one convict was killed, ten others and four state policemen were injured, nine guards were held hostage, and the prison laundry was destroyed.

1948   LABOR LEADER SHOT

Barely a year after his landslide victory for the presidency of the UAW-CIO, Walter P. Reuther was severely wounded but survived a shotgun blast that crashed through the window of his Detroit home and struck him in the right arm and shoulder. A year later, Reuther's brother Victor lost an eye in a similar attack. Neither of the would-be assassins was ever apprehended.

1940   UNIQUE HOMER

Rookie first-baseman George Vico stepped to the plate in the second inning of an opening-day game at Chicago and, with his first swing, became the only Detroit Tiger ever to hit a home run on the first pitch in his first major-league at bat.

1927   FIRST LIVE COVERAGE

The Detroit Tigers opened their American League baseball season at their home Navin Field and WWJ radio-announcer Ty Tyson, in the first broadcast of a sporting event by any Detroit station, gave fans at their sets a play-by-play account of the game direct from the field.

1909   CONCRETE FACTS

The three-year-old Wayne County Road Commission began work on the nation's first mile of concrete highway. The commission built the 17'8"-wide road on Woodward Avenue between Six and Seven Mile roads at a cost of $13,354. (See also July 4.)

21

1976   DETROIT HOLDS GARAGE SALE

The city of Detroit opened its first "world's-largest garage sale" at mammoth Cobo Hall. More than 75,000 shoppers bought $100,000 worth of fire hydrants, old street lamps, typewriters, used police cars, motorcycles, bedpans, old barber chairs, firemen's helmets, and other surplus items so fast that the city ran out of merchandise and had to close a day early.

1928   PLANE DEALING

The nation's first aircraft show, patterned after successful automobile shows, ended after more than a week in which forty manufacturers exhibited sixty-three different aircraft at Detroit's convention center.

1825   FIRST TAX-SALE LAW

A Michigan territorial law directed that, instead of jailing property owners for nonpayment of property taxes (see May 8), the territory would confiscate and sell the tax-delinquents' lands.

VILLAGES INCORPORATED THIS DAY
1883   Emmett (St. Clair County).
1891   Muskegon Heights (Muskegon County) which incorporated as a city March 13, 1903.

22

1976   MOON TREE

Governor William G. Milliken planted an unusual two-foot-high sycamore tree on the state capitol grounds. The tree had been grown from a seed carried to the moon by Apollo 14 astronauts.

1974   FIRST DEATH LEAP

A young Royal Oak man left his Chevrolet-van lights on and motor running and leaped to his death from the middle of the Mackinac Bridge. His was the first known suicide leap from the bridge.

1833   BAPTISTS START COLLEGE

The Michigan territorial governor signed a bill incorporating the "Michigan and Huron Institute," a college to be set up under Baptist control at Kalamazoo. In 1836 construction of a two-story frame building was completed and students admitted. In 1855 the school changed its name and received a charter as Kalamazoo College.

1958   A portion of Ecorse Township (Wayne County) incorporated as the city of Southgate.
VILLAGES INCORPORATED THIS DAY
1875   Clam Lake (Wexford County) which on March 20, 1877, changed its name and incorporated as the city of Cadillac.
1881   North Muskegon (Muskegon County) which incorporated as a city March 18, 1891.

23 1940   BIONIC MAN
BORN
Lee Majors, who starred in three television hit series, "The Big Valley," "Owen Marshall - Counselor at Law," and "The Six-Million-Dollar Man," was born at Wyandotte.

1859   FIRST HELP FOR MENTALLY ILL

The Michigan Asylum for the Insane (Kalamazoo), Michigan's first state institution for the treatment of the mentally ill, admitted its first patient. For many years, however, most families, rather than suffer the social disgrace of committing a relative, continued to confine mentally ill family members in attics, sheds or even backyard iron cages.

1841   GOVERNOR BORN

John T. Rich, Michigan governor 1893-96, was born at Conneautville, Pennsylvania. The former farmer, U.S. congressman, and Michigan state senator and representative was elected to his second term by the highest plurality in any Michigan gubernatorial election to that time. (See also March 28.)

VILLAGES INCORPORATED THIS DAY
1833   Ann Arbor (Washtenaw County) which incorporated as a city April 4, 1851.
1875   Hersey (Osceola County) and Fremont (Newaygo County) which incorporated as a city November 7, 1911.

24 1965   CARNIVAL TRAGEDY
At a carnival in a suburban Taylor Township shopping-center parking lot, five laughing children were riding in a "Flying Comet," a mechanical "maypole" whose arms and attached buckets whirled in circles ten to twelve feet above the ground. Suddenly, the arm holding their bucket collapsed, and the children were dragged around the center pole until the operator shut off the motor. Two died and three were critically injured in the tragedy which prompted the legislature to enact a safety-inspection law for such thrill rides.

1941   TANKS A LOT

The first M-3 28-ton General Grant tank was delivered from a Detroit Chrysler plant to the army. During the course of World War II, Chrysler produced more than 25,000 tanks.

1898   AT WAR

Governor Hazen Pingree ordered up the Michigan National Guard, and two days later, Michigan soldiers marched off to fight in the Spanish-American War. The role of Michigan regiments in the conflict was limited to road-building in Cuba as the soldiers were sent into the semitropical weather with wool uniforms, Civil War rifles, and inadequate medical supplies. Three Michigan men were killed in action, but another 698 died from dysentery, yellow fever, malaria and other illnesses.

VILLAGES INCORPORATED THIS DAY
1883   Hesperia (Oceana-Newaygo counties) and Montague (Muskegon County) which incorporated as a city March 22, 1837.

25 1981   MANNING A COMMISSION

Governor William G. Milliken named former Rep. Louis Cramton (Midland) as the first man to serve on the Michigan Women's Commission, a fifteen-member group established in 1968 to overcome discrimination in employment and recognize women's accomplishments in the state.

1959   MICHIGAN CONNECTED TO ATLANTIC

The St. Lawrence Seaway, a four-hundred-mile waterway that enabled large oceangoing vessels to reach Michigan ports on the Great Lakes, officially opened to shipping.

1901   TIGERS PLAY FIRST A.L. GAME

In the first American League game ever played, the Detroit Tigers rallied for ten runs in the bottom of the ninth inning to beat the Milwaukee Brewers 14-13 at Bennett Park. The Tigers' home field had been created by spreading two inches of loam over cobblestones that dated back to when the site had served as the town hay market.

26 1976   METRIC MOONSHINE

Michigan liquor stores first sold alcoholic beverages in metric-sized bottles.

1901   NO FREE LUNCH

Fifty Kalamazoo saloon keepers, who had been caught up in an expensive, out-of-control competition to attract customers by serving extravagant free lunches, signed an agreement to serve only cheese and crackers.

1775   EARLY LIQUOR CONTROL

Because of continual disturbances by intoxicated Indians, Detroit merchants agreed to put their liquor in one general store and sell to an Indian no more than one glass at a time.

27 1933   DAMPENING THE SPIRITS

Michigan dampened its nose slightly by allowing the sale of 3.2% beer, but waited until January 1934, three weeks after national prohibition had ended, to legally sell liquor.

1933   CELEBRATING YOUTH

In celebrating the end of prohibition, Governor William A. Comstock signed a law allowing persons 18-20 years of age to drink beer and wine but not hard liquor. Four years later, however, the legislature had second thoughts and on July 21, 1937, raised the age limit for all alcoholic beverages to twenty-one where it stayed until 1972. (See January 1.)

1833   LUXURY SHIP LAUNCHED

The steamboat *Michigan*, the first steamer built at Detroit and the most-advanced Great Lakes passenger vessel of its time, was launched at Detroit.

1764   MASONS FORM

The provincial grand master of the Free and Accepted Masons in New York issued a charter for a Masonic lodge at Detroit, and the "Lodge of Masons, No. 1," Michigan's first and the oldest west of the Alleghenies, organized.

28 1976   NO PUBLIC MONEY FOR SEX CHANGE

The Michigan attorney general ruled that the state was not obligated to pay for a prison inmate's sex-change operation.

1955   OFFICIAL TREE PLANTED

The planting of a white pine on the capitol lawn at Lansing marked public recognition of the tree, long-renowned in Michigan lumber industry, as Michigan's official state tree.

1910   VEHICLE BUILT FOR BAD GUYS

The Flint Police Department authorized the Buick Motor Company to build the city's first "paddy wagon." The specially built vehicle, when completed, carried a 4½- by 6½-foot wire cage equipped with curtains that could be drawn to keep prisoners from public view.

1897   OFFICIAL FLOWER
The state legislature, reasoning that Michigan's blossoming apple trees added much to the state's beauty and that Michigan apples had gained a worldwide reputation, adopted the apple blossom as Michigan's official state flower.

29 1970   FIRST BLACK GM DEALER
Clarence S. Carter, veteran of twenty-four years in the automobile business, was awarded a Detroit Chevrolet dealership and became General Motors' first black auto dealer in Michigan.

1911   FLAG APPROVED
The legislature adopted Michigan's current official state flag, a blue field upon which is delineated the state coat of arms.

1891   The village of Bellaire (Antrim County) incorporated.

30 1982   PRISON(H)ER SENTENCED
A 25-year-old transsexual was ordered to serve a one-to-five-year prison sentence at the Huron Valley Correctional Facility for women. The man, who had to undergo one final operation to complete a sex change to a woman, had caused a temporary judicial quandary over whether (s)he should be sent to a men's or women's prison.

1980   STATE BAILS OUT CHRYSLER
In hopes of saving tens-of-thousands of jobs within the state, the State of Michigan loaned the nearly bankrupt Chrysler Corporation $150 million. By 1983 the auto company, which had also received a $1.5-billion federal loan guarantee, had staged a remarkable comeback and paid back all loans ahead of schedule. During the first three months of 1984, Chrysler recorded the largest first-quarter profit in its history.

1977   RECORD ROCK CROWD
A world's record crowd of 76,229 paid to see the rock-group Led Zeppelin perform at the Pontiac Silverdome.

1954   FIRST MAJOR FLIGHT
Following several ceremonial speeches, a London-bound DC6B "Great Lakes Clipper" sped down a lone runway past a skinny control tower and climbed into sunny skies as the first passenger flight to lift off from Wayne Major (now Metropolitan) Airport.

MAY

1 1981   POLETOWN RAZED - GROUND BROKEN

General Motors held ground-breaking ceremonies for a controversial $600-million, 465.5-acre plant at Hamtramck's Poletown, one
of the Detroit area's oldest neighborhoods which was sacrificed for progress. Two-hundred-million dollars in federal funds were used to acquire the
neighborhood and uproot 3,500 residents whose small businesses, churches,
and schools were razed to make way for the plant.

General Motors' Detroit/Hamtramck Assembly plant, better known as the "Poletown Plant,"
spreads over 360 acres where some 1,320 homes once stood.

1975 "ONE-FOR-THE-HOUSE" ELIMINATED

A new state law prohibited beer salesmen from buying rounds for the house at bars and, instead, allowed them to buy a single beer of the salesman's company's brand for one person.

1918 ON THE WAGON

A year-and-a-half before national prohibition took effect, Michigan became dry after state voters approved a prohibition amendment by over 80,000 votes. Temperance forces rejoiced that "John Barleycorn was dead and buried," but until prohibition was repealed in 1933, "blind pigs," "speakeasies," and assorted forms of home brewing illegally provided beer and alcohol to Michigan residents who wanted it.

1912 SALOONS CLOSE

An act of the state legislature, which provided that the number of retail liquor dealers in each township, village, or city should not exceed one-to-every-five-hundred inhabitants, went into effect, and overnight, more than two-hundred upper-peninsula saloons were forced to close.

1910 EYE EXAMINERS EXAMINED

All persons beginning the practice of optometry in Michigan were required, for the first time, to pass an examination and be licensed.

1903 HOUSE BUILDS CHURCH

The first church built by a group of people claiming to be descendants of the scattered tribes of Israel and calling themselves the "House of David" opened at Benton Harbor. Led by Benjamin Purnell, the group built homes and communal industries while waiting for the end of the world. The House of David also fielded a bearded baseball team that traveled the country in search of hometown teams willing to pay for the privilege of getting trounced. The survivors of the House of David still live in communal obscurity near Benton Harbor.

1901 SOO STAMP ISSUED

The United States Post Office, as part of a Pan American Exposition commemoration, issued, at Buffalo, New York, an eight-cent violet-and-black stamp featuring the canals and locks at Sault Ste. Marie.

1901 MOST EMBARRASSING GAME

The Detroit Tigers committed an American League-record twelve errors in a game against the White Sox.

1818 FOR SALE BY OWNER

President James Monroe authorized the first public-auction sale of lands in Michigan. The sale took place July 6, 1818, with lands being sold for an average of $4 per acre.

1877   The village of Rogers (Presque Isle County) incorporated. In 1923 the village changed its name to Rogers City and, on October 2, 1944, incorporated as a city.

2 1983   HAIL OF A STORM

The worst property-damage storm in Michigan struck southeastern Michigan when hail caused an approximate $165.2 million in damage to homes and automobiles.

1976   SHAKY BUSINESS

An earthquake measuring 3.75 on the Richter scale shook ten southern Wayne County communities between Trenton and Rockwood.

1901   TIGERS WIN UNIQUELY

When rain began to fall at Chicago after the Tigers had taken the lead, the White Sox, in spite of the umpire's warnings, tried stalling to get the game washed out. Finally, the exasperated umpire declared Detroit the winner, and the Tigers won the first forfeit in American League baseball history.

1894   GOVERNOR BORN

Kim Sigler, Michigan governor 1947-48, was born at Schuyler, Nebraska. Sigler, a lawyer, skyrocketed to political heights quickly when his role in a grand-jury investigation of legislative graft gave him statewide recognition. But he plummeted just as dramatically, and his reelection bid resulted in one of the worst defeats in modern gubernatorial history. (See also December 1.)

1844   FIRST PUBLIC HIGH SCHOOL OPENS

The Detroit Board of Education appropriated $150 and opened a public high school, Michigan's first, in the second and third stories of the former University of Michigan building. The school, which admitted only males, operated only a short time.

3 1881   RAILROADS SEE THE LIGHT

Leonidas G. Woolley (Mendon) patented the nation's first electric locomotive headlight. Woolley suspended his polygonal lamp frame in position with opposing strings which neutralized jarring.

1820   MAIL ROUTES EXPAND

The second post road for delivery of mail in the Michigan territory was established between Detroit and Mount Clemens via Pontiac. "Postboys" carried mail in leather saddlebags and, from the time they entered a city until they reached the post office, blew horns which notified residents of the mail's arrival. (See also March 3.)

1893   The village of Warren (Macomb County) incorporated. On October 13, 1955, Warren incorporated as a city.

4

1939   SMASH HIT

Rookie Boston outfielder Ted Williams hit two home runs as the Red Sox beat the Tigers 7-6 at Briggs Stadium. Williams' fifth-inning blast was the first to ever clear the stadium's right-field double-deck roof.

1922   SECOND STATION'S FIRST BROADCAST

The Detroit Free Press radio station, now WJR, went on the air. Their first broadcast included the participation of the Honorable Alexander Groesbeck, governor of Michigan, and Edgar Guest, poet-humorist.

1846   LIFE FOR DEATH

The Michigan legislature passed a law making Michigan the first state in the union to limit the punishment for murder to life imprisonment. The law, which retained capital punishment for treason, went into effect March 1, 1847.

5

1831   BEGINNING OF A FREE PRESS

A four-page weekly known as the *Democratic Free Press and Michigan Intelligencer* began publishing from a log cabin at Detroit. The paper, which initially sold for $2 a year, later shortened its name to the *Detroit Free Press*.

1828   CAPITOL OCCUPIED

The territorial legislature met, for the first time, at Michigan's first capitol building constructed at Detroit at a cost of $24,500. The sixty-by-ninety-foot building served as the territorial and state capitol until 1847 when the seat of Michigan government moved to Lansing.

1824   FIRST MICHIGAN COPYRIGHT ISSUED

Philo E. Judd received a copyright, Michigan's first, for a map of the Territory of Michigan. Judd, however, submitted only the title to the Michigan court, District Court of the United States, and died before finishing the map itself.

1710   FIRST RECORDED MARRIAGE

Jean Baptiste Turpin and Margaret Fafard, both French, were married at St. Anne's Church (Detroit) in the first known Michigan wedding involving two white people.

6
1964 TORNADO HITS U.P.

A rare upper-peninsula tornado struck a farm near Sundell (Alger County) killing twenty-five head of cattle and wrecking two barns.

1945 ROCK SINGER BORN

Bob Seger was born at Ann Arbor. One of rock's great regional acts, Seger finally achieved national success with the release of his single and album, "Night Moves."

1903 COMEDY OF ERRORS

The Detroit Tigers and Chicago White Sox played a game in which they committed an American League-record eighteen errors (Detroit — six, Chicago — twelve).

1763 CANNIBALISM ALONG THE ST. CLAIR

Hundreds of Indians attacked two canoes carrying nine British soldiers and two sightseers up the St. Clair River to (present-day) Port Huron. The Indians captured or killed the Englishmen and roasted and ate the commander's body.

7
1977 ASTRONAUTS OPEN SPACE CENTER

Former astronauts James McDivitt, Alfred Worden and Jack Lousma, all University of Michigan graduates with childhood ties to Michigan, dedicated a $750,000 space-center museum at Jackson.

1922 COBB CAUSES TOO MUCH EXCITEMENT

A 65-year-old Detroit Tiger baseball fan, overcome, according to doctors, with the excitement of the moment, died of heart failure at the exact moment Ty Cobb hit a seventh-inning home run with two on in a game with the Chicago White Sox at Detroit.

1867 DRUG COMPANY BEGINS

The Duffield, Parke and Company organized at Detroit. In 1871 the company reorganized, changed its name to the Parke, Davis and Company, and over the next hundred years, became one of the world's largest pharmaceutical houses.

1763 PONTIAC'S CONSPIRACY

Chief Pontiac and sixty of his best Ottawa warriors, each concealing tomahawks, knives and muskets, approached the British fort at Detroit with the intention of capturing the stockade. Pontiac had requested a parley to gain entrance and planned, at a given signal, to attack the unsuspecting soldiers.

But an informer had warned the British commander, and his heavily armed soldiers immediately surrounded the Indians who then left without incident. Pontiac failed, but others, using his basic strategy, succeeded, and over the next month and a half, in the greatest Indian war in American history, Indians ravaged nine of twelve British forts throughout the East and Midwest including one at Mackinaw City. (See June 2.)

1957   The city of Wyoming (Kent County) incorporated.

8 1973   LITTLE LEAGUE TRAILBLAZER

Twelve-year-old Carolyn King (Ypsilanti), who had beat out three boys to win a spot on the Ypsilanti Orioles baseball team, took the field for the team's first game and became the first girl in the nation to play in the Little League. As a result, national Little League officials revoked the Ypsilanti chapter's charter, and the city of Ypsilanti, on behalf of Carolyn King, retaliated with a sex-discrimination suit. But before the case made its way through the legal system, the U.S. Division of Civil Rights ordered the national Little League to drop its boys-only policy which it did.

1954   BRIDGE BEGUN

A two-day ground-breaking ceremony at Mackinaw City, including parades, fireworks and choirs, marked the beginning of the construction of the Mackinac Bridge. Three-and-a-half years later, one of the world's most spectacular engineering achievements and one of the state's best-known attractions opened to traffic. (See November 1.)

1942   CARRIER PRODUCED

The first World War II amphibious cargo carrier to be constructed under navy contract was completed at the Ingersoll plant (Kalamazoo).

1927   KOP GOES THROUGH THE AIR

The Detroit Police Department installed radio-receiving sets in six of their cruisers and equipped their headquarters with a signal mast. The experimental use of radio to combat crime, the nation's first, succeeded, and a year later, the department created an unlicensed police-radio station, KOP. In 1929, the Michigan State Police installed the world's first licensed police-radio network.

1905   SPEED DEMON

Dwight B. Huss (Detroit) set the nation's first transcontinental automobile time record when he traveled in his Oldsmobile runabout from New York City to Portland, Oregon, in forty-four days.

1820   FIRST PROPERTY TAX

The territorial legislature levied, for the first time in Michigan, taxes on personal property and land and authorized the sheriff to imprison delinquents.

1907   The city of East Lansing (Ingham County) incorporated.

VILLAGES INCORPORATED THIS DAY

1896   Munising (Alger County) which incorporated as a city July 13, 1914.

1907   Grosse Pointe Park (Wayne County) which incorporated as a city March 13, 1950.

9 1972   ON THE SAME TRACK

Sue Parks (Ypsilanti) became the first girl to compete with and against boys in a Michigan high-school dual track meet. The sixteen-year-old daughter of Eastern Michigan University's track coach finished fifth in the 880-yard run.

1970   LABOR LEADER KILLED

A chartered plane carrying UAW President Walter P. Reuther, his wife, and four other persons clipped treetops and crashed as it approached the Pellston airport. The crash and explosion killed all passengers.

1941   FM FIRST

WWJ-FM (Detroit) became Michigan's first FM radio station.

1893   The village of Boyne Falls (Charlevoix County) incorporated.

10 1921   CLEANING UP SPORTS

The Michigan state legislature passed a law making it illegal to "fix" any professional sporting event and provided for a fine of not-more-than $500 or five years in prison for anyone convicted of trying to bribe an athlete.

1919   AMERICAN LEGION FOUNDED

Following the first regular national meeting of the American Legion at St. Louis, Missouri, Michigan delegates met and formed the Department of Michigan of the American Legion. By July, forty-five posts had been granted charters and were forming throughout the state.

1803   FIRST FUTURE PRESIDENT VISITS

William H. Harrison, governor of the Indiana territory and the first future president to visit Michigan, arrived at Detroit. Harrison came to Michigan three more times before becoming president in 1841.

VILLAGES INCORPORATED THIS DAY

1877   Manton (Wexford County) which incorporated as a city December 11, 1923.

1954   Gibraltar (Wayne County) which incorporated as a city January 10, 1961.

MICH-AGAIN'S MAY

11 1983   FIRST BRIDGE BIRTH

A Kinross (Chippewa County) woman, while traveling by ambulance to a Petoskey hospital, began giving birth, prematurely, as the vehicle crossed the Mackinac Bridge. The ambulance stopped in the middle of the bridge and the woman completed the birth of a boy.

1978   GENERALLY SPEAKING

Margaret Ann Brewer (Durand) became the Marine Corps' first woman brigadier general.

1964   A portion of Nankin Township (Wayne County) incorporated as the city of Westland.
1885   The village of Hart (Oceana County) incorporated. On November 5, 1946, Hart incorporated as a city.

12 1970   THE NOT-SO-GREAT TRAIN ROBBERY

Three young bandits boarded a freight train as it pulled into a west-side Detroit freight yard, held a conductor at gunpoint, and broke into two freight cars. The bandits, in what was believed to be the first train robbery in Detroit's history, then made off with several items of the contents — baby strollers, bassinets and rattles.

1965   SAY "CHEESE"

The Lansing Police Department installed the state's first camera used to produce Michigan's first color-photo drivers' licenses.

1934   FORMER GOVERNOR DIES

Albert E. Sleeper, Michigan governor 1917-20, died. During his first term, the former banker/businessman mobilized the state for World War I. Sleeper, a Republican, also inspired the postwar state-park plan that has provided Michigan with its nation-leading park system. (See also December 31.)

1781   MACKINAC SOLD

The Chippewa Indians ceded the Island of Michilimackinac (Mackinac Island) to the British for five-thousand pounds.

1953   The city of Lathrup Townsite (Oakland County) incorporated. Seven months later the city changed its name to the City of Lathrup Village.

13 1980   TORNADO STRIKES

Kalamazoo office workers had started their daily trip home when a tornado ripped through the downtown area. The twister left five dead, almost eighty injured, forced 1,200 from their homes, and damaged or destroyed $50-million worth of buildings and homes.

86

1971   BLOODLETTING

Governor William G. Milliken signed into law a bill which lowered the age, from twenty-one to eighteen, at which persons could donate blood without permission from parents.

1950   MUSICAL GENIUS BORN

Recording-artist Stevie Wonder was born at Saginaw as Steveland Morris Hardaway. Blind at birth, Wonder became a virtuoso on piano, bongos, guitar, and harmonica by the time he was ten. At twelve he had recorded "Fingertips" and began cranking out top-forty hits at the rate of one a year. Wonder has won several Grammys for his albums which cover the musical spectrum — rock, jazz, reggae and soul.

1857   FARM COLLEGE OPENS

The nation's first state college of agriculture, the Michigan Agricultural College, opened at Lansing with seventy-five students. The school later changed its name to Michigan State University.

14
1970   FIRST BLACK-OWNED BANK

At 10:00 a.m. the First Independence National Bank, the first bank in Michigan to be owned and operated by blacks, opened its doors at Detroit.

1930   TROOPERS AID VICTIMS

The Michigan State Police equipped their cars and motorcycles, for the first time, with medical kits, and the troopers, who were required to take first-aid courses, were directed to administer medical aid upon arriving at an accident scene.

1898   BREAD PRICES SOAR

A month after the outbreak of the Spanish-American War, bread rose to the unheard-of price of ten cents for a two-pound loaf prompting the *Detroit Free Press* to observe, "War has . . . (caused) a material rise in the price of flour. The bakers clung to the customary prices of the one- and two-pound loaves until the substantial material of the staff of life assumed its present costly standard."

1866   COLLEGE CHARTERED

The Holland Academy, created in 1851 by the Holland, Michigan, Dutch and supported by the Dutch Reform Church, chartered as Hope College.

15 1973 MAN WITH ANOTHER'S HEART DIES

Donald Kaminski (Alpena), Michigan's longest- and the world's second-longest-living heart transplant died. Kaminski had received the heart of an auto-accident victim December 2, 1968, at the University of Michigan and lived an active life hunting, fishing and boating until his death from chronic rejection of his transplanted heart.

1912 COBB HITS — TIGERS STRIKE

The American League suspended Ty Cobb who had assaulted a heckling New York fan. Three days later, in support of their teammate, the rest of the Tigers refused to play but, faced with a $100-per-day fine and at the request of Cobb, ended baseball's first strike after missing one game and forcing the re-scheduling of another. Cobb returned to play May 26.

16 1972 STATE-RUN GAMBLING APPROVED

Michigan voters, by a 3-1 margin, wiped out a 137-year-old constitutional ban on lotteries, paving the way for the state to become the seventh in the nation to adopt this form of gambling and state-government financing.

1968 FORMER PROF LOOKS AFTER NATION'S WELFARE

Wilbur J. Cohen, former University of Michigan professor, became secretary of Health, Education and Welfare (HEW) in the Cabinet of President Lyndon B. Johnson.

1861 MICHIGAN ENTERS CIVIL WAR

The 1st Michigan Infantry arrived at Washington, D.C., and President Abraham Lincoln, pleased with the first tangible western support for the Civil War, tearfully exclaimed, "Thank God for Michigan."

1842 FIRST PUBLIC SCHOOL BEGINS

Michigan's first free tax-supported schools opened at Detroit. A twelve-member board of education controlled the schools which, by November, had enrolled five-hundred students. Male teachers, who earned $30 a month, taught middle schools and female teachers, who received $18 per month, taught primary grades.

1826 GOVERNOR BORN

Edwin B. Winans, Michigan governor 1891-92, was born at Avon, New York. Voters elected Winans, a farmer, mainly because they intensely disliked his opponent, a Republican railroad baron.

1972 Farmington Township and the villages of Quakertown and Woodcreek Farms incorporated as the city of Farmington Hills (Oakland County).

VILLAGES INCORPORATED THIS DAY
1883   Sparta (Kent County).
1922   Ravenna (Muskegon County).

17 1928   STUDENT FLIPS OUT

A flying student grabbed a hammer and suddenly attacked his teacher who was piloting a plane two-thousand feet over Oakland County. The pair struggled as the plane spun wildly out of control, but the pilot briefly overcame the attacker, barely gained control of the small plane, crash-landed, and flipped them both onto the grounds of the Pontiac State Hospital for the Insane.

1881   THAR'S GOLD IN THEM THAR HILLS

Julius Ropes, a Marquette chemist and geologist, struck his exploring pick into some moss-covered rock near Ishpeming, analyzed it, and discovered that it contained gold. Two years later, Ropes opened a mine, the only gold mine east of the Mississippi River, and hauled out $703,000 worth of gold and silver before labor disputes forced him to close in 1897.

18 1929   TULIP FEST BLOSSOMS

Holland opened its first Tulip Festival. The colorful festival grew to become Michigan's largest and ranks just behind the Mardi Gras (New Orleans) and Rose Parade (Pasadena) in national popularity.

1927   THE MAD BOMBER OF BATH

Albert Kehoe, a disgruntled citizen of Bath (Clinton County), bombed the village's schoolhouse killing himself, thirty-eight students and teachers, and six bystanders in Michigan's worst mass murder.

1879   AN ILLUMINATING AD

The *Detroit Post and Tribune* carried Michigan's first advertisement for an electric light. The four-column ad announced the coming of a circus and promised that tents would be "lighted with wondrous arc lights, worth traveling five-hundred miles to see."

1868   COLLEGE FOUNDED

The Detroit Medical College, forerunner of Wayne State University, organized at Detroit and, the following February, opened for students.

1675   MARQUETTE DIES

After returning from a visit with Indians in Illinois, 37-year-old Father Jacques Marquette, Michigan explorer and missionary, died of a lingering illness on Michigan's west coast. Two years later, Christian Indians removed his remains and buried them at his mission at St. Ignace. (See also June 1.)

19

Nothing of any interest, importance or significance ever happened in Michigan on this day.

20

1980   NO BONES ABOUT IT

The nation's and perhaps the world's first arthroscopic surgery center opened at Lansing's Ingham Medical Center. There, surgeons insert miniscule vacuums and motorized files through tiny punctures and, by watching the tools on a small television screen, repair the human body's most hidden bones without making incisions.

1979   FATAL FLUID

Three Southern Michigan Prison (Jackson) inmates stole three gallons of copy-machine fluid from a supply room and sold it to 150 fellow inmates as moonshine. Two of the inmates, who drank the fluid which contained methyl alcohol, died, and several others suffered stomach cramps and temporary blindness.

1943   GREENVILLE HONORED

The U.S. Treasury Department presented a distinguished-service award, the first of its kind, to Greenville High School students, who had purchased a World War II glider by selling war bonds. (See also June 6.)

1929   PILOT PROGRAM

The legislature created the Michigan Board of Aeronautics to regulate licensing of pilots, standardize aviation schools, investigate air accidents, and control airport construction and operation.

1927   LUCKY LINDY LANDS

Detroit-native Charles A. Lindbergh completed the first nonstop solo flight across the Atlantic Ocean flying 3,610 miles in the "Spirit of St. Louis" from New York to Paris in thirty-three hours.

1835   DETROIT HAS A SWILL TIME

A committee of the Detroit Common Council recommended that a stone-and-brick "grand sewer" be built to replace an unsightly and unsanitary series of open ditches that ran through the city. The full council agreed, and a year later, Michigan's first underground sewer was built at a cost of $22,607.

VILLAGES INCORPORATED THIS DAY
1879   Grosse Pointe (Wayne County) which incorporated as a city March 12, 1934.
1891   Hillman (Montmorency County).
1893   Grosse Pointe Farms (Wayne County) which incorporated as a city March 14, 1949.

21 1941   FORD UNIONIZED

Seventy percent of the Ford Motor Company's workers voted to have the UAW-CIO represent them, and the automobile giant became the last of the Big Three automakers to recognize the UAW.

1928   SAFETY FIRST

The state highway department through local committees in more-than-one-hundred cities and towns began Michigan's first statewide traffic-safety program. State-approved garages checked, at no charge, brakes, lights, warning signals, and steering gears, then marked inspected vehicles with a red sticker.

1892   MICHIGAN CAR FEATURED

The *Scientific American*, in the first national notice given to a mechanically driven vehicle made in Michigan, featured an article about a sophisticated steam-engine automobile developed by Ransom E. Olds.

1891   Dickinson County was established.

22 1936   UNDERGROUND TERRORISTS EXPOSED

A 22-year-old Detroit WPA worker was kidnapped, shot ten times, and his body left lying on a rural road. The murder investigation exposed and destroyed a statewide organization called the "Black Legion," an underground society that used guns, group vengeance and terrorism against those who opposed their anti-Jew, antiblack, anti-communist, anti-Catholic philosophy.

1926   MILLIONTH CAR LICENSED

Michigan became the nation's sixth state to register and license more-than-a-million automobiles.

1900   MAKING MUSIC

E. S. Votey (Detroit) patented the nation's first pneumatic player piano.

1837   GOVERNOR BORN

Aaron T. Bliss, Michigan governor 1901-04, was born at Smithfield, New York. The wealthy Republican lumberman's years in office saw great industrial progress with the organization of Cadillac in 1901 and Ford in 1903 and the beginnings of Buick at Flint.

23

1970   TRACK SPECTATORS SURPRISED

One-thousand people were watching a state Class A high-school championship track meet at the University of Michigan's Perry Field when a 150-foot section of bleachers suddenly collapsed and threw fans into a jumble of steel, wood and mud. Twenty-five spectators were hospitalized but suffered no serious injuries.

1941   BOMBER BOXES BAER

Joe Louis successfully defended his heavyweight boxing crown for the seventeenth time when challenger Buddy Baer was disqualified at the start of the seventh round after his manager refused to leave the ring. (See also March 1, June 22, June 25 and September 27.)

1893   THE CORUNNA LYNCHING

An angry mob rushed into a Corunna jail, looped a rope around the neck of an accused murderer, and jerked the man into the street. After hanging him from a nearby tree, the mob dragged the body over Corunna's streets before finally cutting up the rope and man's clothes and passing them out as souvenirs.

1934   The village of Grand Beach (Berrien County) incorporated.

24

1981   RESCUERS RESCUED

A crowd of forty angry people attacked two Detroit Emergency Medical Services (EMS) technicians because they had taken sixteen minutes to arrive at an accident scene. The accident victims went unattended for another thirty minutes while police restored order and protected the EMS men.

1918   FIRST CASUALTY

German machine-gun fire killed private Joseph W. Guyton (Evart), making him the first American soldier to be killed on German soil during World War I.

1904   GOVERNOR BORN

Henry H. Crapo, Michigan governor 1865-68, was born at Dartmouth, Massachusetts. The former Flint mayor's most significant and controversial achievement as governor was to prevent local communities from jeopardizing their fiscal solvency by undertaking bonding schemes to finance internal improvements.

1825   HIGHWAY BEGUN

Surveyors began laying out a military road from Detroit to Chicago. The crude road followed the path of the Old Sauk Trail (approximately present-day U.S. 12), and upon its completion, two stagecoaches a week operated between Detroit and Fort Dearborn (Chicago). (See also March 2.)

1749 FIRST "SAY-'YES'-TO-MICHIGAN" CAMPAIGN

The governor general of Canada, in an attempt to attract people to France's new settlement at Detroit, offered to every man who would settle there a spade, an axe, a ploughshare, one large and one small wagon, a cow, a sow, seed, and family support for one year. Over the next two years, 103 persons accepted the offer and came to Michigan.

25 1979 MICHIGAN PASSENGERS DIE

Eight Michigan passengers were among 271 killed when a DC-10 American Airlines jet crashed on takeoff from Chicago's O'Hare International Airport. The wide-bodied jet lost one of its three engines, rolled, and crashed nose first in the worst air accident in U.S. history.

1909 AN ICY RELATIONSHIP

When Howell ice dealers raised the price of block ice 1/25th of a cent per pound, angry meat dealers protested the "exhorbitant" increase by temporarily raising the price of their best cuts fifteen cents and eighteen cents a pound.

1822 A SUPERIOR VOYAGE

The *Superior*, only the second steamboat on the Great Lakes, arrived at Detroit with ninety-four passengers on her first trip from Buffalo. The *Superior*, which made the Detroit-Buffalo trip every two weeks, had replaced the Lakes' first steamer, *Walk-In-The-Water*, which had been wrecked in a Lake Erie storm.

26 1967 WOMEN JOIN TROOPERS

The Michigan State Police swore in Kay E. Whitfield (Pontiac) and Noreen E. Hillary (Grand Rapids) as their first women officers.

1937 BATTLE OF THE OVERPASS

Members of the Ford-factory police brutally beat Walter Reuther and Richard Frankensteen at a bridge leading to the company's River Rouge plant where the two UAW officials were supervising the distribution of a union pamphlet. Newspaper photographers recorded the bloody attack, and from that day forward, public opinion shifted away from the company and toward the UAW.

1927   END-OF-THE-TIN LIZZIE

Henry Ford, with his son Edsel at the wheel, rode in his company's fifteen-millionth production Model T. After introducing the affordable "farmer's car" in 1908, Ford had controlled over half of the automobile-sales market selling 1,871,891 Model Ts in 1923 alone. But by 1926, as roads improved, the "Tin Lizzy's" sturdy construction became less important to drivers, and purchasers began to look for luxury and style. So later this day, Ford assembled the last Model T and began to manufacture the Model A.

A 1921 Ford Model T Touring Car.

1913   ROOSEVELT FIGHTS MICHIGAN PAPER

Theodore Roosevelt sued a Marquette newspaper for libel after the editor had charged that the former president was habitually drunk. Roosevelt traveled to Marquette to testify in person, and after he had also produced a parade of character witnesses that attested to his temperance, the jury awarded the former president six cents in damages, and the editor made a public retraction.

1927   The village of Bridgman (Berrien County) incorporated. On September 12, 1949, Bridgman incorporated as a city.

27 1979   RECORD FISH CATCH

Warren Dellies caught a world-record seven-pound, fifteen-ounce splake at Crystal Falls, Michigan.

1947   SECRET INFLUENCE-PEDDLING ENDS

The legislature sent to Governor Kim Sigler for his signature a bill that required, for the first time in Michigan history, lobbyists to publicly register their names and connections before attempting to influence state lawmakers.

28 1922   LIVE MUSIC BROADCAST

The nation's first radio orchestra, a sixteen-piece symphonic ensemble composed principally of members of the Detroit Symphony Orchestra, played over the airwaves of Detroit's WWJ as the Detroit News Orchestra.

1913   HISTORIANS ORGANIZE

The Michigan Historical Commission organized at Lansing. The organization succeeded the Michigan Pioneer and Historical Society which itself had succeeded the Historical Society of Michigan. (See July 3.)

1903   Michigan's smallest city, Omer (Arenac County), incorporated.
VILLAGES INCORPORATED THIS DAY
1879   Clare (Clare-Isabella County) which incorporated as a city March 12, 1891.
1917   Sterling (Arenac County).

29 1931   ENDURING RECORD

Detroit aviators Walter Lees and Frederick Brossy landed a diesel-motored monoplane at Jacksonville Beach, Florida, after staying aloft a world-record eighty-four hours and thirty-three minutes without refueling.

1879   DETROIT BECOMES CITIFIED

Although Detroit had become the nation's seventeenth-largest city, many residents still treated parks as pastureland and streets as herding areas, so the Detroit City Council passed an ordinance forbidding the "running at large of cattle in public places."

1869   HOLIDAY FIRST

Michigan observed Memorial Day for the first time. The origin of the holiday is disputed but most versions agree that it began in the South in 1866 when Civil War widows gathered to place flowers on their husbands' graves.

1848   MICHIGAN'S FIRST PRESIDENTIAL CANDIDATE

The Democratic party nominated Lewis Cass, former Michigan territorial governor and U.S. senator, as their candidate for U.S. president. But because of the presence of a third party, the Free-Soil party, Michigan's first presidential candidate lost the election to Zachary Taylor.

VILLAGES INCORPORATED THIS DAY
1879   Sault Ste. Marie (Chippewa County) which incorporated as a city June 21, 1887.
1889   Davison (Genesee County) which incorporated as a city December 5, 1938.
1907   Lincoln (Alcona County).

30 1976   A GRAPE ACHIEVEMENT

Jim Ellis (Montrose) set a Guinness Book world record by eating three pounds, one ounce of grapes in 74.6 seconds.

1928   CHRYSLER BUYS DODGE

The Chrysler Corporation purchased the Dodge Brothers automobile company and became the third-largest automobile manufacturer behind Ford and General Motors.

1911   FIRST THEATRE

Sarah Bernhardt performed *Camille* in French at the Calumet Theatre, the first municipal theatre in America.

31 1975   WOMAN TAKES COMMAND

Mattie V. Parker assumed command of the Armed Forces Examining and Entrance Station at Detroit and became the nation's first woman recruiting station commander.

1942   YOU'RE IN THE ARMY NOW

The last civilian truck was assembled at Detroit as the state's automobile plants completed their conversion to the production of war materials. Michigan received over $20 billion in World War II contracts, and General Motors symbolized the unity of the auto-industry's war effort with its slogan, "Victory is our Business."

1855   SOO CANAL COMPLETED

A one-mile-long canal and two solid masonry locks at Sault Ste. Marie officially opened and marked the completion of one of the most spectacular engineering feats of the era. The $999,802 two-year project conquered the rapids that drop twenty-two feet from Lake Superior to Lake Huron and removed the last barrier to development of the Upper Peninsula's mining resources. On June 18, 1855, the side-wheeler *Illinois*, flags flying and whistle blowing, made the first passage through the canal and locks.

VILLAGES INCORPORATED THIS DAY
1905   Belleville (Wayne County) which incorporated as a city July 23, 1946.
1921   Sylvan Lake (Oakland County) which incorporated as a city March 20, 1946.

JUNE

1 1967   RUSSIAN VISITOR FOLLOWED

A U.S. Coastguard patrol boat and a helicopter shadowed the first Soviet freighter to ply the Detroit River, the 3,725-ton *Syktyvar*, as it made its way toward Sarnia, Ontario.

1933   TAX INCITES RESIDENTS

The legislature eliminated a state tax on real estate and, in its place, enacted an unpopular three-percent sales tax to get the state out of debt. Most Michigan residents blamed Governor William Comstock for the measure, and sales personnel often told the customers, "That will cost you $1.00 plus three cents for Comstock." Rumors spread that Comstock might even be personally profiting from the tax and didn't stop until he finally offered a cash reward to anyone who could prove them.

1912   FIRST BOMBER PILOT DIES

Philip Orin Parmelee (Matherton), who held many world aviation endurance, speed, and altitude records, died at North Yakima, Washington, during a flying exhibition. Parmelee learned to fly at a school run by Orville and Wilbur Wright and later became the nation's first pilot to transport merchandise, drop live bombs from a plane, and search from the air for criminals.

1879   WOMEN TAKE OVER SWITCHBOARDS

Grand Rapids established a telephone exchange which later became the first in the state to regularly employ women as operators. The company hired the women when delivery boys, who were originally given the job, were discovered shooting marbles instead of tending switchboards.

1637   PRIEST BORN

Jacques Marquette, Michigan explorer and missionary, was born at Laon, France. The Jesuit priest founded Michigan's oldest settlement, Sault Ste. Marie, in 1668. (See also May 18.)

1927   The village of Garden City (Wayne County) incorporated. On October 28, 1933, Garden City incorporated as a city.

1966   A portion of Sterling Township (Macomb County) incorporated as the city of Sterling Heights.

2 1983   YOUTH BEAUTIFIES MICHIGAN

Governor James Blanchard signed into law a bill creating a temporary Michigan Youth Corps which created jobs for 25,000 unemployed youths ages eighteen to twenty-one. The corps cleared litter from 14,444 miles of road and landscaped 20,000 square feet of park and recreation areas as just a few of their projects.

(Left) Members of the Michigan Youth Corps relax on one of hundreds of picnic tables they built and (right) clear brush in the Davison Regional Park.

1763   BLOOD SPORT

A group of Chippewa and Sac Indians, using a game of lacrosse as a ruse, entered Fort Michilimackinac (Mackinaw City) and massacred twenty-two English soldiers and traders.

3 1983 $2 MILLION RICHER

A telephone operator from Traverse City became the biggest winner in the history of the Michigan state lottery when she drew an envelope containing a slip for $2 million.

1980   REPRESENTATIVE RESIGNS

Rep. Charles Diggs Jr., who had served Detroit's 13th Congressional District for twenty-six years, resigned his congressional seat after his colleagues censured him for his 1978 conviction on a payroll kickback scheme.

On June 24, 1980, Diggs began serving a jail term at a federal correctional facility at Arkansas and was paroled after serving fourteen months.

1965   MICHIGAN'S FIRST ASTRONAUT

James McDivitt (Jackson) became the ninth American and the first from Michigan to go into outer space. During the four-day flight, Edward White took the first American "space walk."

1964   SMILE

Governor George Romney signed into law a bill requiring, for the first time, photographs of Michigan drivers on their licenses.

1815   GOVERNOR BORN

Moses Wisner, Michigan's eleventh governor, was born at Springport, New York. The former lawyer and Lapeer County prosecutor served only a one-year term as governor before returning to his Pontiac law practice. (See also January 5.)

1929   Grand Blanc (Genesee County) incorporated as a city.

4 1982   PIZZA MAN BUYS TEAM

Mike Ilitch, a fast-food entrepreneur, purchased the Detroit Red Wings National Hockey League club from longtime owner Bruce Norris for a reported $10 million.

1906   REMARKABLE THEFTS

Third-baseman Bill Coughlin became the first Detroit Tiger to steal second, third and home in the same inning. The base-running feat occurred during the seventh inning of a game against the Washington Senators.

1896   A SMASHING START

Having built his first gasoline-powered "quadricycle" too wide for the door, Henry Ford broke out part of a brick wall of an old storage shed in what is now downtown Detroit, then drove the vehicle around the darkened streets in a successful trial run.

1853   DIGGING THE SOO

Excavation began on the canal and locks that would eventually connect Lake Superior and Lake Huron at the rapids of the St. Mary's River near Sault Ste. Marie. (See also May 31.)

VILLAGES INCORPORATED THIS DAY
1885   Tawas City (Iosco County) which incorporated as a city March 20, 1895.
1903   Twining (Arenac County).

5 1972 TRANSPLANTS BECOME COMMONPLACE

University of Michigan surgeons peformed their two-hundredth kidney transplant when they placed the kidney of a four-year-old boy into a 23-year-old woman.

1946 FIRST SYNTHETIC HOSPITAL SPONGE

Parke, Davis and Company (Detroit) marketed the nation's first oxidized cellulose sponge for medical and surgical use.

1896 FORMER GOVERNOR DIES

Josiah W. Begole, Michigan's eighteenth governor, died at Flint. Begole won the governorship in a very close election then lost his reelection bid in an even-closer race. (See also January 20.)

1866 DOCTORS ORGANIZE

About one-hundred physicians from all areas of Michigan met at Detroit's Odd Fellows Hall, adopted the code of ethics of the American Medical Association, and formed the Michigan State Medical Society.

VILLAGES INCORPORATED THIS DAY
1907   Pellston (Emmett County).
1911   Edwardsburg (Cass County).

6 1975 THE GREAT ESCAPE

A convicted hog thief and rubber-check artist hid between two buildings at Southern Michigan Prison (Jackson) as a friend, who had hijacked a helicopter at knife-point, swooped over the prison walls and landed out of the guards' firing range. The prisoner darted aboard and escaped only to be captured thirty hours later.

1968 LICENSED FOR SNOW

Governor George Romney signed into law a bill requiring registration of snowmobiles. The law took effect September 1.

1961 HERO DIES AT ZOO

G.I. Joe, a pigeon credited with saving the lives of one-thousand Allied soldiers during World War II, died of old age at the Detroit Zoo. In October 1943 a note was attached to one leg of G.I. Joe ordering that a raid by British planes which would have unknowingly killed their own soldiers be called off, and he successfully delivered the message twenty miles. The pigeon later received a medal of gallantry from London's mayor and recognition from the U.S. Congress before retiring to his home at the Detroit Zoo.

1944   MICHIGAN FIRST ON D-DAY

The first glider to land on Normany on D-Day was built by the Gibson Refrigerator Company (Greenville) and was purchased by Greenville High School students through a sale of $72,000 in war bonds. (See also May 20.)

1822   THE MAN WITH THE WINDOW IN HIS STOMACH

Dr. William Beaumont, an army surgeon at Fort Mackinac, was called to treat Alexis St. Martin, a trapper who had accidentally been shot in the stomach. St. Martin recovered, but his abdominal wound failed to heal, leaving an opening through which his stomach could be seen. Dr. Beaumont persuaded St. Martin to cooperate, fed him various foods over a period of years in order to watch the course of digestion, and later wrote a book reporting his conclusions which remain accurate to this day. St. Martin, except for his unusual wound, remained healthy and lived to the age of seventy-six.

7 1983   A MATTER OF DEGREE

The Michigan Court of Appeals at Lansing ruled that a woman who was divorced after helping pay for her husband's schooling owned part of his law degree and ordered the man to pay his ex-wife $2,000 a year for ten years.

1977   HORSING AROUND COSTS STATE

On the second day of a new daily lottery game, a Lansing TV station interviewed a new lottery agent who joked that 137 was a good bet since it was his favorite at horse tracks. Hundreds took his advice and when, incredibly, the number was drawn, the state paid out $25,000 more than was bet on the number.

1824   LAWMAKERS FIRST MEET

The first legislative council of the Territory of Michigan convened at Detroit. Father Gabriel Richard opened the session by praying that "the legislators may make laws for the people, and not for themselves."

1905   The city of Au Gres (Arenac County) incorporated.
1955   The village of Bingham Farms (Oakland County) incorporated.

8 1953   WORST TWISTER STRIKES

Michigan's worst tornado hit the Beecher area north of Flint killing 116, injuring nearly nine hundred, and destroying or damaging more-than-five-hundred homes and businesses. (Photo following page.)

Michigan's worst tornado ravaged Flint (see June 8). - *Flint Journal* photo -

1930   FRUIT STAND OPENS
     A new $40,000 municipal fruit-and-vegetable market, the largest open-air market in the world, opened at Benton Harbor.

1905   NEVER ON SUNDAY
     Marshall milkmen, meat sellers, and ice dealers joined forces and refused to make door-to-door Sunday deliveries.

9
1982   BIGGEST THEFT
     A lone gunman escaped with about $500,000 in cash from an Ecorse bank in the largest bank holdup in Michigan history.

1881   MICHIGAN GIVES AWAY SOO LOCKS
     The State of Michigan turned over ownership of the Soo locks and canal to the United States and made passage free to all vessels. From the locks' opening in 1855 until 1877, Michigan had collected first a four-cent- then a three-cent-per-ton toll except from U.S.-government ships.

1845   FIRST HOSPITAL OPENS
     The Sisters of Charity, a Catholic order of nuns, opened Michigan's first hospital, St. Vincent's, in an old log building at Detroit. Five years later, the facility, which for many years was the only hospital to admit persons with contagious diseases, changed its name to St. Mary's and moved.

MICH-AGAIN'S JUNE

1908   The village of Breckenridge (Gratiot County) incorporated.
VILLAGES INCORPORATED THIS DAY
1899   Mackinac Island (Mackinac County).
1954   Walled Lake (Oakland County).

10   1930   BLACK HOUSEWIVES ORGANIZE

To minimize the effect of the depression on black business people, Mrs. Fannie Peck started a Housewives League at Detroit, the first such organization among black women in the country. Later, a national housewives association formed with Mrs. Peck as its president.

1929   SEEING MICHIGAN BY AIR

Forty-two planes carrying 125 people left Pontiac for a five-day trip to thirty-two Michigan cities in the state's first organized Michigan Air Tour.

1919   MICHIGAN APPROVES WOMEN'S VOTE

Five days after the U.S. Congress passed the nineteenth constitutional amendment, Michigan became the first state to ratify the women's suffrage amendment which was ultimately ratified by the necessary three-fourths of the states August 1920.

1866   VETERANS RETURN

The last Michigan Civil War regiment returned to the state.

1828   DETROIT LANDS BAPTISTS

The city of Detroit donated a lot on the northwest corner of Fort and Griswold streets to the Baptist Society who, two years later, built Michigan's first Baptist church at that site.

11   1966   WHERE'S THE BEEF

For the first time in history, a herd of cattle set hooves on Mackinac Island. The twenty-one head, brought by boat for a "world-championship livestock-market auctioneer contest," were penned in the Grand Hotel's tennis courts, and the auction was conducted on the hotel's spacious lawn.

1961   SMASH BY CASH

Norm Cash blasted a pitch from Joe McLain of the Washington Senators over the right-field wall and became the first Detroit Tiger ever to hit a ball out of Tiger Stadium. The sixth-inning home run was Cash's second of the game won by the Tigers 7-4.

1805   FIRE DESTROYS DETROIT

A sudden gust of wind blew sparks and burning tobacco from a baker's pipe into a nearby barn of hay setting it on fire, and the resulting blaze practically leveled the entire town of Detroit. When Detroit was rebuilt, it was laid out with streets that radiate from the spokes of a hub on a wheel with a number of circular parks ("circuses") along the spokes.

1915   The village of Freesoil (Mason County) incorporated.

12 1979   CARD TRICK

Kevin St. Onge (Dearborn) set a Guinness Book world record by throwing a standard playing card 185 feet, one inch.

1964   DON'T BANK ON IT

At the close of an open house to celebrate the Ionia County National Bank's (Ionia) 30th anniversary, an employee wound the vault's time clock so tight the massive door couldn't be opened for thirty-six hours. As a result, the bank had to start its thirty-first year by asking customers to bring in some cash and arranging for a 36-hour loan from a competing bank across the street.

1907   The village of Barryton (Mecosta County) incorporated.

13 1964   FANTASTIC VOYAGE

Tony Calery, a 45-year-old, 200-pound bachelor lumberjack, left his hometown Sault Ste. Marie alone in a fifteen-foot rowboat and, seventy-five days and 2,200 miles later, arrived at the World's Fair in New York.

1924   WON THE FIGHT — LOST THE GAME

Tiger pitcher Bert Cole hit Yankee Bob Meusel with a pitch, and Meusel charged the mound precipitating an on-the-field brawl that incited the 18,000 Detroit hometown fans to riot and caused the Tigers to lose by forfeit.

1955   The city of Troy (Oakland County) incorporated.

14 1976   LARGEST FLAG RETIRED

The J. L. Hudson Company unfurled, for the last time, the world's largest flag in front of their downtown Detroit store. The company then donated the 235- by 104-foot flag, made in 1949 from 2,038 yards of shrink-proof wool, 5,500 yards of thread, fifty-seven yards of heavy canvas and over a mile of rope, to the Smithsonian Museum. (See also November 11.)

1929   COMMISSION HAS A FIELD DAY

The newly created state Aeronautics Commission (see June 14) dedicated its first county field, the Emmet County airport.

1671   PAGEANT OF THE SAULT

At a new mission built by French priests near the rapids at Sault Ste. Marie, French commander Simon Francois, Sieur de St. Lusson, raised a huge cross in front of a vast assemblage of Indians, warned them to trade only with the French, and, while raising a piece of sod three times, claimed most of North America, including Michigan, for France.

15

1971   BLACK HEADS STATE GOVERNMENT

For the first time in Michigan history, a black man held the reins, briefly, of state government. Secretary of State Richard Austin, third in line under the state constitution, filled in while both Governor Milliken and Lt. Governor James Brickley attended out-of-state functions.

1968   WET WEDDING

Penny Amos and Robert Cooley, two members of a Detroit diving club, gurgled vows at the bottom of Higgins Lake in Michigan's first underwater wedding.

1948   UNDER THE LIGHTS

The Detroit Tigers beat Philadelphia 4-1 at Briggs Stadium in the first night professional-baseball game every played at Detroit.

1920   WIRELESS WEDDING

From the First Presbyterian Church (Detroit), Mabelle E. Ebert pronounced her wedding vows into a telephone connected to the local telegraph office. The telegrapher then wired the ceremony to the Great Lakes Naval Training Station near Chicago who, in turn, sent it by wireless radio to the *U.S. Birmingham* in the Pacific Ocean. There, Seaman John R. Wichman said "I do," and completed the world's first radio wedding.

1905   DISASTER-RELIEF GROUP ORGANIZES

Nine Detroit citizens and one delegate from Kalamazoo met at Detroit and formed the Michigan branch of the National Red Cross. The first recorded activity of the group was the collection and donation of $65,107.87 to the victims of the great 1906 San Francisco earthquake.

16

1981   YOUNG MARRIAGE PERMITTED

Governor William G. Milliken signed into law a measure allowing sixteen-year-old boys to marry with their parents' permission. Previously, boys could not marry under any circumstances until the age of eighteen while girls could, with their parents' permission, marry at age sixteen.

1949   FORMER GOVERNOR DIES

William A. Comstock, Michigan governor 1933-34, died. The former Alpena mayor ordered a bank "holiday" during his term as governor and also initiated an unpopular sales tax to get the state out of debt. (See also July 2.)

1903   AUTO GIANT BEGINS

The Ford Motor Company incorporated.

1856   ASSASSINATING THE KING

Two disgruntled "subjects" assassinated James Jesse Strang, self-proclaimed king of a Mormon group on Beaver Island. (See also July 8.)

1828   BOOKED UP

The territorial legislative council established the Library of Michigan and later appointed William B. Hunt, at a $100 annual salary, as the first librarian.

1820   CASS COMMANDS RESPECT

At Sault Ste. Marie, Michigan territorial Governor Lewis Cass angrily lowered and removed the last British flag to fly over the United States and, though alone in the presence of a large band of hostile Chippewa Indians, forcefully demanded their respect of U.S. sovereignty over the territory.

1806   SKIES DARKEN

Lower Michigan residents witnessed a total eclipse of the sun.

17

1967   DOUBLE TROUBLE

The Detroit Tigers played at Detroit the longest doubleheader, nine hours and five minutes of playing time, in the club's history. The Tigers beat Kansas City 7-6 in the first game which was rain-delayed, then lost 6-5 in a nineteen-inning second game.

1966   KALINE MILESTONE

Al Kaline rapped out his 2000th major-league base hit, a two-run homer in the eighth inning of a 5-2 loss to New York at New York.

1925   TIGERS RUN YANKEES

The Detroit Tigers scored thirteen times in the sixth inning, the highest single-inning scoring in their history, en route to beating the New York Yankees 19-1 at Yankee Stadium.

1912   AERIAL DEVELOPMENT

Detroit News photographer William A. Kuenzel, riding in a hydro aeroplane piloted by Walter Brookens, took pictures of the Detroit River. The *News* then printed Michigan's first newspaper aerial photographs.

The Detroit River and a section of the city of Detroit's waterfront area as they appeared in Michigan's first newspaper aerial photograph - *Detroit News* photo -

1866   CASS DIES

Lewis Cass, one of Michigan's most eminent and successful statesmen, died at Detroit. (See also March 6, May 29 and October 9.)

1952   The city of Springfield (Calhoun County) incorporated.

18

1977   A CEREMONIAL FIRST

The Rev. Meredith Hunt became the first woman ordained to the Episcopal priesthood in a Michigan ceremony. Three months earlier, Rev. Georgia Helen Shoberg had become the first Michigan woman to be ordained but in a Alexandria, Virginia, ceremony.

1965   SOMETHING FISHY

Governor George Romney signed a bill designating the trout as Michigan's official fish. The bill, however, neglected to specify what kind of trout, and Romney later had to direct the conservation department to choose. Their choice — the brook trout.

1953   SOX GET MANY RUNS

At Boston, the Red Sox scored seventeen times in the bottom of the seventh inning, the most runs ever scored in one inning against the Tigers, and went on to pound Detroit 23-3.

1901   FORMER GOVERNOR DIES

Hazen Pingree, Michigan's twenty-third governor, died at London, England. After completing a stormy and tempestuous two terms, Pingree was urged by his physician to take a long rest. He traveled to South Africa then to England where he died prematurely. (See also August 30.)

1946   The city of Roosevelt Park (Muskegon County) incorporated.

19 1934   A STAR IS FILMED

Robert R. McMath (University of Michigan) took the world's first motion pictures of the sun. His films, taken at Lake Angelus (Pontiac), showed sunspots in motion.

1932   FIRST FEMALE FLIES

Aviator Frank Coffyn, on one of the first of his forty-five passenger-flying demonstrations from the Grosse Pointe Country Club golf course, took up Mrs. Russel A. Alger and made her the first Michigan woman to ride in an airplane.

1881   The village of Baraga (Baraga County) incorporated.

20 1943   THE WAR WITHIN DETROIT

During a blistering heat wave, blacks and whites began fighting on a bridge connecting Detroit's Belle Isle and the mainland. False rumors about the extent of the altercation incited twenty-four hours of shooting, stoning, knifing, bludgeoning, arson and looting that left thirty-five dead and seven hundred injured.

1913   CLOSING THE COMMUNICATION GAP

The Ford Motor Company hired a crew of linguists to help convey orders and requests to its 16,000-member workers who spoke ten different languages and fifteen different dialects. A young German, fluent in eight languages, supervised nine other men who spoke one or two languages each.

1898   FIRST BOB-LO VISIT

The first excursion steamer from Detroit arrived at Bois Blanc (Bob-Lo Island).

1887   The village of Pinconning (Bay County) incorporated. On February 16, 1931, Pinconning incorporated as a city.
1960   The city of Dearborn Heights (Wayne County) incorporated.

108

21
1972   BAR TILT APPROVED
Governor William G. Milliken signed into law a bill allowing pinball machines in liquor establishments.

1971   PICTURE-PERFECT PLASTIC
James E. Olterman (Detroit) and Mrs. George Seal (Detroit) received the first all-plastic Michigan drivers' licenses. The new licenses, which replaced paper licenses, were made of polycarbonate plastic treated with photosensitive material that allowed drivers' pictures to be photographed directly onto the plastic.

1965   HIGH-RISE LANDING
A helicopter carrying Lt. Governor William G. Milliken and James Ramsey, director of the state Department of Aeronautics, made the first landing on a heliport, Michigan's first, located on top of the National Lumberman's Bank Building, Muskegon. (*Muskegon Chronicle* photo.)

1948   FIRST KNAPP
The nation's first Bill Knapp's restaurant opened on Capital Avenue in Battle Creek. Knapp's later expanded to open more-than-thirty restaurants throughout Michigan, Ohio and Indiana.

1898   SAFE LANDING
Brig. General William Rufus Shafter (Galesburg), as commander of land operations in Cuba for the United States during the Spanish-American War, led the successful landing of sixteen-thousand men at Daiquiri, Cuba, over a twelve-hour period without suffering one casualty.

1832   PROFESSIONAL PERFORMANCE

Mr. Blisse, a Tyrolese singer, presented a formal concert, Michigan's first, at Detroit. Admittance to the performance at the Capitol building was twenty-five cents.

22 1937   LOUIS WINS FIRST CROWN

A year and three days after losing to Nazi Germany's Max Schmeling, Joe Louis knocked out defending heavyweight champion James Braddock in the eighth round to win his first heavyweight championship. Exactly one year later, in a fight Hitler aides said would prove Aryan supremacy forever, Louis pummeled Schmeling unmercifully before knocking him out in 2:04 minutes of the first round.   (See also March 1, May 23, June 25 and September 27.)

Joe Louis - a product of Detroit's black ghetto - was the world's longest-reigning heavyweight boxing champion and America's first black hero (see March 1, May 23, June 22, June 25 and September 26). - *Detroit Free Press* photo -

1933   GREENFIELD OPENS ITS DOORS

Greenfield Village, at a charge of twenty-five cents for adults and ten cents for children, admitted the general public for the first time. Though the village and museum had been dedicated nearly four years earlier, only tour groups, and by appointment only, had been allowed inside.

1896   FIRST ORIENTAL FEMALE PHYSICIAN

Mary Stone (Shih Mai-yu) graduated from the University of Michigan and became the first Chinese woman in the nation to receive a Doctor of Medicine degree. Dr. Stone, under the auspices of the Methodist Foreign Mission, then founded the Women's Hospital at Kiukiang, China, and served as its head for twenty-five years.

1835   LEGISLATURE GIVES
SEAL APPROVAL

The legislature adopted the first official Michigan state seal.

1965   The city of Kentwood (Kent County) incorporated.

23 1967 ALEWIVES RAISE A STINK

The rotting carcasses of billions of alewives, a small, oily "trash" fish that invaded the Great Lakes through the St. Lawrence Seaway, began littering four-hundred miles of Lake Michigan shoreline from Benton Harbor to Petoskey and, over the next month, cost tourist-related businesses an estimated $50 to $100 million. To control the exploding alewife population, the state imported coho and chinook salmon which gorged on the nuisance fish and grew to tremendous size.

1963 DETROIT WALKS TO FREEDOM

On the twentieth anniversary of the end of Detroit's World War II race riot, Martin Luther King Jr., national civil-rights leader, led 125,000 marchers down Detroit's Woodward Avenue in a "Walk-to-Freedom" demonstration.

1913 SHOCK THERAPY

A Saginaw farmer who suffered from a mild nervous disorder was struck by lightning while standing next to his chicken coop. The bolt knocked him unconscious and, according to a newspaper report of the incident, when he recovered, his nervous tic was gone.

1894 GOVERNOR BORN

Wilbur M. Brucker, Michigan governor 1931-32, was born at Saginaw. During the depression years, forty-three percent of working men in Michigan cities were unemployed yet Brucker opposed state aid to the jobless and, as a result, lost in his bid for reelection.

24 1968 POWER DISPLAY

Detroit Tiger Jim Northrup hit a major-league-record two grand-slam home runs in consecutive times at bat as the Tigers beat Cleveland 14-3 at Cleveland.

1966 WILLOW RUN RUNS OUT

Willow Run airport stopped passenger service and ended the facility's twenty-year career as a major Michigan airport.

1962 MARATHON BASEBALL GAME

The Tigers played the longest game in baseball history, a 22-inning game against New York that took seven hours to play. Yankee outfielder Jack Reed hit a two-run homer, the only one of his 222-game major-league career, in the top of the twenty-second inning to beat the Tigers 9-7.

1937　BRIDGE BEGUN
Construction began on the Blue Water Bridge which crosses the St. Clair River between Sarnia and Port Huron. (See also October 8.)

1824　A LAW-AND-ORDER FIRST
There was not a single person in the entire Michigan territory, which then included the present states of Michigan and Wisconsin, in prison for crime or debt. As a later observer said, "Either the officials were very lax or the inhabitants were a remarkably law-abiding people."

1924　The village of Melvindale (Wayne County) incorporated. On April 11, 1932, Melvindale incorporated as a city.

25 1958　BRIDGE STAMPED
The U.S. Post Office issued a three-cent bright greenish-blue stamp at St. Ignace and Mackinaw City (but postmarked "Mackinac Bridge, Michigan) to commemorate the dedication of the Mackinac Bridge.

1948　FINAL KNOCKOUT
Joe Louis knocked out Joe Walcott in the eleventh round to win his last heavyweight-championship bout. Eight months later, Louis retired as the world's longest-reigning heavyweight champion.　(See also March 1, May 23, June 22 and September 27.)

1930　FAMOUS AVIATRIX SETS RECORD
Amelia Earhart, flying a Lockheed "Vega," set a women's speed record, 174.9 miles per hour at Detroit. Seven years later, Earhart disappeared while attempting an around-the-world flight.

1901　The village of Vanderbilt (Otsego County) incorporated.

26 1982　ROYAL VISIT
Beatrix Wilhelmina Armgard, Queen of the Netherlands, visited Holland, Michigan, and Grand Rapids.

1978　WATCHING HIS STEP
Dennis Martz set a Guinness Book world record by running up the stairs of the 73-story Detroit Plaza Hotel in eleven minutes, 23.8 seconds.

VILLAGES INCORPORATED THIS DAY
1896　Ubly (Huron County).
1914　Alpha (Iron County).

27
1947   RETIRING IDEA

The Ford Motor Company began the automobile industry's first pension program by agreeing to contribute an initial $200,000 plus $15,000,000 million a year thereafter to a retirement plan for their workers.

1929   CONFIRMING RESERVATION

The Detroit Auto Club opened Michigan's first consolidated-air-travel ticket office.

VILLAGES INCORPORATED THIS DAY
1961   Woodhaven (Wayne County) which incorporated as a city June 21, 1965.
1967   Lakewood Club (Muskegon County).

28
1965   NOTABLE BREW

Frankenmuth's mayor tapped the ten-millionth barrel of beer produced at his city's Carling brewery.

1955   STAMP HONORS SOO

The U.S. Post Office issued a three-cent stamp at Sault Ste. Marie to commemorate the one-hundredth year of operation of the Soo locks.

1948   AIR RAIDS

Nine months after they received their first airplane, the Michigan State Police began patrolling airways over Detroit to control "wild city fliers."

1946   COMEDIENNE BORN

Gilda Radner was born at Detroit. Radner soared to fame by playing characters such as Baba Wawa, Emily Litella, and Roseanne Rosanadana on NBC's original "Saturday Night Live."

1907   GOT YOU COMING OR GOING

The state required, for the first time, two license plates — one on the front and one on the rear — of automobiles.

1948   The village of New Era (Oceana County) incorporated.

29
1928   WASTE NOT

The Michigan Conservation Department and Department of Health launched a joint program of pollution control, the state's first concerted attempt at eliminating human and industrial waste in Michigan's lakes and streams. The two departments combined because, under existing laws, the conservation department had more power to protect fish from contamination than the health department had to protect people.

1863   CUSTER'S FIRST STAND

The Michigan Cavalry Brigade organized under the command of Monroe's General George Armstrong Custer. Custer and his unit, identified by their bright-red neckties and flamboyant manner, became so popular that men in other Civil War units deserted to try to join them.

VILLAGES INCORPORATED THIS DAY
1832   Ypsilanti (Washtenaw County) which incorporated as a city February 4, 1858.
1925   St. Clair Shores (Macomb County) which incorporated as a city September 12, 1950.

30
1979   MISTAKEN IDENTITY

The Cuban government sent a $41.67 bill to a Frankfort aviation club with a note saying that one of their aircraft, identified as a Boeing 747, had flown through Cuban airspace. The Frankfort club, at the time, owned only two aircraft, both gliders.

1973   SPECIAL CROSSING

An Amish family crossed the Mackinac Bridge in horse and buggy on their way from Maine to Colorado. Bridge officials, who had given special permission for the trot across, closed one lane of the five-mile span during the one-hour, one-of-a-kind crossing.

1968   WAVE OVER KEWEENAW

An extremely strong low-pressure cell that moved very rapidly over Keweenaw Bay from L'Anse created a rare seven-foot tidal wave that damaged boats and flooded basements along the Keweenaw Bay shoreline.

1953   CHEVY SPORTS PLASTIC

The first Chevrolet Corvette, the nation's first plastic-laminated fiberglass-body sports car, rolled off the assembly line at Flint with a $3,250-price sticker.

1934   SPARTANS BECOME LIONS

G. A. Richards purchased a Portsmouth, Ohio, professional-football franchise called the Spartans, moved the team to Detroit, and re-named them the Lions.

1897   FIRST ALUMNI SECRETARY

The University of Michigan's alumni association became the first in the nation to hire a full-time paid secretary.

JULY

1 1974   YOUNG HOUSE ENTERS HOUSE
Twenty-two-year-old Colleen House (Bay City) was sworn in as the youngest female member in the history of the Michigan House of Representatives.

1971   CHECK IT OUT
Michigan motorists were able to pay for their automobile license plates with personal checks for the first time.

1961   BUMMED OUT
The Hoboes of America opened their international convention at Kalamazoo.

1917   AIR BASE OPENS
Selfridge Field (Mt. Clemens), named for Lt. Thomas E. Selfridge, the first casualty of powered flight, began operation as Michigan's foremost military aviation base.

1917   FIRST TRANS-LAKE FLIGHT
Jack Vilas made the first airplane flight across Lake Michigan, traveling from St. Joseph to Chicago in a Curtiss flying boat in one hour, ten minutes.

1905   ROAD AGENT
Michigan became the eighteenth state to establish a state agency, the state highway department, to supervise road improvements.

1863   MICHIGAN AT GETTYSBURG

The Twenty-Fourth Infantry, composed almost entirely of Detroit and Wayne County volunteers, opened the battle of Gettysburg and was almost completely destroyed while holding up the Confederate advance until the mass of the Army of the Potomac could get into position. Its casualty rate was the highest of any union regiment in the battle.

2 1980   UNDERWATER PARKS POSSIBLE

Governor William G. Milliken signed a law giving the Department of Natural Resources (DNR) authority to establish underwater parks and preserves. The law was enacted to give the state a method of controlling, if necessary, the exploration and pilfering of the hundreds of shipwrecks that lie in Michigan Great Lakes' waters.

1972   LOTTERY ESTABLISHED

The state legislature established a lottery to provide additional revenues for the state.

1966   FOR THE BERRIES

Manistee began its first national Strawberry Festival.

1877   GOVERNOR BORN

William A. Comstock, Michigan's 32nd governor, was born at Alpena. The three-time losing Democratic gubernatorial candidate during the 1920s was finally elected in 1932 by a Democratic landslide precipitated by the effects of the depression. (See also June 16.)

1824   GOVERNOR BORN

Cyrus G. Luce, Michigan governor 1887-90, was born at Windsor, Ohio. The former Republican state senator and representative served two terms. (See also March 18.)

3 1973   BROTHERS DUEL

At Cleveland, for the first time in American League history, two brothers, Jim Perry (Detroit) and Gaylord Perry (Cleveland) started a regular-season game as opposing pitchers. Neither finished the game won by the Tigers 5-4.

1936   FORD MAKES WRIGHT PURCHASE

Henry Ford purchased the Wright brothers' Dayton, Ohio, bicycle shop and later moved the birthplace of the world's first successful airplane to Greenfield Village.

1828   HISTORY BUFFS ORGANIZE

The Historical Society of Michigan was organized at Mansion House in Detroit. The first president and lecturer before the society was territorial Governor Lewis Cass.

1819   DOCTORS REMAIN UNORGANIZED

The territorial legislature authorized a meeting of physicians and surgeons at Detroit for the purpose of founding a medical society; but no meaningful society organized for twenty years.

4 1983   URBAN MOUNTAINEERS SCALE MICHIGAN PEAK

Two "human flies," using special gripping devices, scaled the outside of the 73-story Westin Hotel at Detroit's Renaissance Center. At the conclusion of the 6½-hour climb, police arrested the two young men for trespassing and disorderly conduct. (See photo opposite page 1.)

1909   SMOOTH ROAD AHEAD

The first mile of concrete road pavement in the nation opened on Woodward Avenue from Six Mile to Seven Mile roads.(See also April 20.)

1906   FIRST AIRSHIP BUILT

L.M. Driver constructed a 78-foot-long, 17-foot-diameter dirigible, the first built in Michigan, at the Drihopa Airship Company (Detroit).

1876   LUMBERJACKS GET FREEBEE

As part of a Fourth of July centennial celebration, "Big Delia," a six-foot two-inch 225-pound tobacco-chewing madam, and her employees built a huge pavilion near Muskegon, hired two bands, invited their "sisters" from Chicago and Milwaukee, provided free beer, and threw a free party for more-than-a-thousand lumberjacks.

1866   VETERANS DONATE MOMENTOES

General O. B. Willcox and a procession of the survivors of decimated Michigan Civil War regiments formally presented twenty-three battle-stained and bullet-marked flags to Governor H. H. Crapo.

1866   MONUMENTAL FIRST

Michigan's first Civil War monument, a simple sandstone shaft costing $1,500, was placed in the cemetery at Tipton (Lenawee County) and dedicated.

1845   FROM HOGS TO BEAUTIES
Fourth of July celebrants attending a picnic on Hog Island in the Detroit River voted to re-name the popular, lushly wooded escape spot "Belle Isle" in "honor of all the ladies who frequently patronized it." Thirty-four years later, the city of Detroit purchased the island for use as a park. (See September 25.)

1832   MICHIGAN'S FIRST CHOLERA EPIDEMIC
A transport ship carrying U.S. soldiers, sent to help defend against a threatened Indian war, docked at Detroit. Overnight a number of soldiers were stricken with cholera, and eleven died. The dread disease then swept through Detroit, killing twenty-eight of the city's residents, and on to other Michigan cities.

5 1980   RECORD-BREAKING SPIT
Rick Krause (Eau Claire) set a Guinness Book world record by spitting a cherrystone sixty-five feet, two inches.

1953   NAME CHANGE
Oscoda Air Force Base was renamed Wurtsmith Air Force Base in memory of the late World War II hero Maj. Gen. Paul B. Wurtsmith (Detroit).

1942   ACTING RATIONALLY
A news dispatch from Detroit reported that Edsel Ford, whose family had manufactured 30,000,000 automobiles since 1903, had to wait to get a new car until a local World War II rationing board approved his application.

World War II rationing policies were so strict that a Ford family member had difficulty obtaining one of his company's automobiles (see July 5).

6 1956 DEATH PLUNGE

Two ironworkers, working on the Mackinac Bridge, fell 540 feet to their deaths when a catwalk snapped.

1932 SINGER BORN

Recording-artist Della Reese was born at Detroit. Reese has recorded more than fifty gospel, jazz and popular record albums and has appeared on nearly every major television variety show.

1854 NEW PARTY FOUNDED

At an oak grove in Jackson, 1,500 Michigan Whigs, Democrats and Abolitionists, rebelling against slavery and other prevailing policies of their day, organized the nation's first Republican party.

1822 AUTHORITY FIGURES

Nearly forty years after Michigan had become a part of America, a battalion of federal troops reached Sault Ste. Marie and built Fort Brady, which finally convinced the French and Indian residents that their remote little village was truly a part of America.

7 1916 LAW AND ORDER

The Michigan attorney general reported that Oscoda County had neither arrested nor prosecuted anyone in their county for the first six months of 1916, a record never before set by any Michigan county.

1852 FIRST ORE TRAVELS LAKES

The Marquette Iron Company shipped six barrels of iron ore down the Great Lakes to New Castle, Pennsylvania. The upper-peninsula ore was the first to reach the Lake Erie smelters via the Great Lakes.

8 1950 GOVERNOR HOSTAGE IN ESCAPE ATTEMPT

As Governor G. Mennen Williams stepped into Marquette prison's kitchen while inspecting prison conditions, an inmate suddenly grabbed him by the arms as another lunged for a large kitchen knife. A guard quickly jerked Williams away from the prisoner as another guard shot the knife-wielding man who died two days later.

1941 DETROIT SEES FIRST STARS

More-than-54,000 fans watched the American League win the first major-league all-star game ever played at Detroit. The major leagues held the mid-season event at Detroit again in 1951 and 1971.

1938   MICHIGAN'S LAST HANGING

Anthony Chebatoris was hanged at Milan for shooting and killing a bystander while robbing the Chemical State Savings Bank in Midland. Though Michigan had abolished capital punishment for murder nearly one-hundred years before, Chebatoris was sentenced and executed under a stringent federal law, the National Bank Robbery Act. Chebatoris was the first person in the United States to be sentenced to death under the act and was the last person executed in Michigan.

1909   FIRST UNDER THE LIGHTS

Grand Rapids and Zanesville of the Central Baseball League played the nation's first regularly scheduled night baseball game. Grand Rapids won the game, played at Grand Rapids, 11-10.

1907   GOVERNOR BORN

George W. Romney, Michigan governor 1963-69, was born at Chihuahua, Mexico. The former American Motors Corporation chairman and president became the state's first gubernatorial candidate to be elected to a four-year term. Romney lost a bid for the 1968 Republican presidential nomination but, in 1969, became secretary of Housing and Urban Development (HUD) in the administration of President Richard M. Nixon.

1850   MICHIGAN ROYALTY CROWNED

James Jesse Strang, leader of a group of Mormons who had settled on Beaver Island, declared himself king of the island and, for the next six years, served as the only absolute monarch in America's history. (See also June 16.)

1836   STEAMING ALONG

The first regular steamer service from Detroit to Saginaw began.

9   1921   PRISON INDUSTRY

Jackson prison warden Harry L. Hulbert returned after a three-week trip through the West during which he sold a million pounds of binder twine produced by his inmates.

1906   COVERING A FAD

Father Timothy Murphy of St. Joseph's Catholic Church (St. Joseph) issued an ultimatum that women must wear hats to church. Father Murphy's directive opened a statewide crusade to keep the burgeoning fad of hatless women from invading the church.

1805   FIRST LAW

A governing body composed of a governor and three judges passed and published the new Michigan territory's first law. The act described and adopted an official territorial seal.

10
1928   FIRST GREAT-LAKE SHUTTLE

Arthur A. Billings and George Frers flew from Muskegon to Milwaukee then, by returning to Muskegon, completed the first round-trip airplane flight across Lake Michigan.

1889   SHOOTING STAR HITS ALLEGAN

Accompanied by thunderous rumbling sounds, a seventy-pound meteorite crashed into the streets of Allegan with such force that it buried itself one-and-a-half feet in the ground.

1887   GRAND OPENING

Mackinac Island's Grand Hotel, built by the Mackinac Island Hotel Company composed of two railroads and a navigation firm, opened and quickly became the most-fashionable resort in the Middle West.

1845   BAVARIANS SETTLE

After an eleven-week voyage from Germany, a small company of immigrants arrived at Saginaw then traveled twelve miles southeast to the banks of the Cass River where they built a church and established Michigan's first German community, Frankenmuth.

1838   ETHNIC FIRST

Ludwik Wesolowski, a draftsman on the Clinton and Kalamazoo Canal (see July 20) began building a house on a lot he had purchased in the village of Marcellus (Macomb County). His recorded purchase made him, according to author Harry Milostan in *Enduring Poles*, the first recorded property owner of Polish lineage in the new state of Michigan.

1796   FIRST U.S. FLAG REACHES MICHIGAN

American troops, sent to occupy former British forts in the Northwest Territory, raised at Monroe the first American flag to fly over Michigan.

11

1964   THE BERRY FIRST

Kalkaska began its first annual Blueberry Festival.

1939   DEPRESSING BUSINESS

The Grand Hotel (Mackinac Island), with a staff of 411 paid employees, registered only eleven guests as a second wave of financial depression washed over Michigan.

1923   FIRST EXTRA JUROR

A thirteen-member jury, the first in Michigan judicial history, heard evidence at a Hart murder trial. The extra juror was impaneled to fill in if one of the regular twelve couldn't complete the lengthy trial.

12

1979   FANS ROCK CHICAGO

The Detroit Tigers won the second game of a doubleheader against the Chicago White Sox at Chicago by forfeit when an estimated 5,000 to 10,000 people swarmed out of the stands during a between-games, anti-disco-music promotion and made the field unplayable.

1974   FIRST COMBAT WOMEN

Four Flint-area women became the first in Michigan to enlist in a National Guard infantry unit. Women had served with other guard units but only in administrative or other noncombative units.

1920   The village of Clawson (Oakland County) incorporated. On January 30, 1940, Clawson incorporated as a city.

MICH-AGAIN'S JULY

13
1980   SOO SLOWS

Because of shipping slowdowns caused by an economic downturn, two of the four Soo locks were temporarily closed, the first time in history more-than-one lock was closed.

1936   SCORCHER

Michigan recorded its hottest temperature, 112°F., at Mio.

1897   WEDDED BLISS BEGINS

Emma (17) and Azarie Hamel (20) were married at Lowell, Massachusetts, shortly before moving to Michigan. The couple renewed their vows on their 50th, 60th, 70th and 75th anniversaries, but after their 80th anniversary, Emma died at Warren, and the longest marriage in Michigan history finally ended.

14
1980   DETROIT BECOMES CONVENTIONAL

The thirty-second Republican National Convention opened at Detroit and, before nominating Ronald Reagan as its presidential candidate, brought twenty-thousand delegates, eight-thousand journalists, and almost $40 million to the city.

1975   MICHIGAN DEFINES DEATH

With little fanfare Governor William G. Milliken signed a law that stipulated that death has occurred in Michigan when no brain waves show on encephalographs taken twice within a 24-hour period. A group of religious, medical, legal and legislative leaders wrote the law because technological advances had made traditional criteria (heartbeat and lack of breathing) meaningless as physicians using machines can continue those functions almost indefinitely.

1968   SUNDAY LIQUOR RESUMED

For the first time in over fifty years, bars were able to legally serve liquor on Sunday.

1913   PRESIDENT BORN

Gerald R. Ford, 38th president of the United States, was born at Omaha, Nebraska, as Leslie King Jr. When he was two years old, King's parents were divorced and his mother moved to Grand Rapids, Michigan. There she met Gerald R. Ford Sr. who formally adopted the boy and gave him his name.

1910   FIRST DETROIT FLIGHT

An airplane flew in Detroit skies for the first time.

1817   Monroe County was established

125

15

1975   NAME CHANGE RULED OPTIONAL

The Michigan attorney general ruled that a woman's surname does not automatically change when she marries, she is not required to adopt her husband's name, and she may resume her maiden name at any time without court action.

1952   BELL MILESTONE

Michigan Bell installed its two-millionth Michigan phone on a farm near Holt.

1929   ATTORNEY GENERAL EXPOSES PASSENGERS

State Attorney General Wilbur M. Brucker ruled that, since control over highways was vested in the state highway commission, Livingston County did not have the authority to prohibit women in bathing suits from riding in cars.

16

1964   GO FLY A KITE

Eighteen-year-old David Rude (Muskegon) traveled eighty-one miles from Grand Haven across Lake Michigan to Milwaukee, Wisconsin, while hanging from a kite. A seventeen-foot boat with a 200-horsepower engine towed Rude, suspended below a fourteen-by-sixteen-foot kite on the three-and-one-half-hour journey.

1943   BOATING TRAGEDY

Nine young people attending a church camp near East Tawas drowned in Lake Huron when they leaped from an excursion boat they mistakenly thought was sinking.

1909   SCORELESS TIE SETS RECORD

At Detroit, the Tigers and Senators battled for eighteen scoreless innings before darkness called a halt to the longest-scoreless game in American League history.

1857   UNDERWATER COMMUNICATION

The world's first successful underwater telegraph cable was laid across the Detroit River from Detroit to Windsor.

1792   MICHIGAN'S FIRST U.S. ELECTION IS CANADIAN

Though Michigan had, by treaty, become a part of the United States nine years earlier, the British, who still occupied Michigan forts, included Michigan in a scheduled legislative session of the Provincial Assembly of Upper Canada. In August, in the first elections ever held in (present-day) Michigan, voters selected representatives to that English assembly.

17

1983   PANTHERS WIN TITLE

The Michigan Panthers won the United States Football League's first championship game, beating the Philadelphia Stars 24-22 at Denver.

1875   FATAL FIRST FLIGHT

Prof. Washington H. Donaldson, a professional aeronaut, and N.S. Grimwood, a newspaper reporter, set out from Chicago on the first balloon flight over Lake Michigan. A month later Grimwood's body washed ashore at Stony Creek, Michigan, and on August 24 Donald crash-landed his balloon in Canada. Just before Donaldson died of injuries suffered in the crash, he confessed that, after dumping all of his ballast, he had thrown Grimwood overboard into Lake Michigan in a desperate and successful attempt to raise the balloon above an approaching storm.

1812   BRITISH CAPTURE MACKINAC

During the War of 1812, a British force landed on the northwest shore of Mackinac Island and, though they had to slowly drag an artillery piece into position on a hill, surprised American soldiers stationed at Ft. Mackinac who surrendered without firing a shot.

1950   The village of Allen (Hillsdale County) incorporated.

18

1936   TRAGIC AUTO ACCIDENT

An Ann Arbor passenger train smashed into a sedan carrying nine members of two Pennsylvania families who had visited with Dundee relatives, dragged the vehicle seventy-five feet to a trestle, and hurled the bodies of all nine victims thirty feet into the shallow water of the Raisin River.

1921   ESCAPEES PREVENT ESCAPES

Inmates who had attempted ingenious or daring escapes began designing a new $80,000 escape-proof cell block at Marquette prison. The escape artists prepared, in exchange for reductions of their sentences, almost all of the plans and specifications of the special wing, and their fellow inmates carried out most of the construction work.

19

1976   NORSEMEN END VOYAGE

Three Belleville college students circled the Statue of Liberty in a replica of a Viking ship which ended their 800-mile trip down the east coast in the eighteen-foot craft equipped with oars and sails.

1967   WHEN IT RAINS IT POURS

A state-record 1.2 inches of rain dumped on Detroit in only five minutes.

1964   LEGION SELECTS FIRST WOMAN LEADER

The American Legion's Michigan Department elected its first woman vice-commander, Mrs. David Roselyn Robert (Menominee), a former WAC who served as a physical therapist during World War II.

1949   FORMER GOVERNOR DIES

Frank Murphy, Michigan's thirty-fourth governor, died. Immediately following his single term as governor, Murphy served as the United States attorney general in 1939 and as a member of the U.S. Supreme Court from 1940 until his death. (See also April 13.)

1925   RECORD FALL

Joe Crane (Detroit) dropped from a speeding plane above Seven Mile Road, fell 2,250 feet before pulling the rip cord, and set, at that time, a world record for delayed jump.

20

1977   HUNTERS SEE ORANGE

Governor William G. Milliken signed a law making it mandatory for wild-game or bird hunters to wear fluorescent orange vests, jackets or caps.

1973   MA BELL SETS MARK

Michigan Bell installed its five-millionth Michigan phone at Greenfield Village.

1948   MICHIGAN JETS FIRST ACROSS THE ATLANTIC

Sixteen Lockheed Shooting Stars under the command of Col. David Carl Schilling took off from Mount Clemens and completed the first west-to-east transatlantic jet flight by arriving at Odiham, England, ten hours and forty minutes later.

1947   TIGERS CROWD THEM IN

The Tigers' largest crowd ever, 58,369 fans, jammed into Briggs Stadium to watch a doubleheader between Detroit and the New York Yankees. Detroit won the opener 4-1, rallied to tie in the bottom of the ninth inning of the second game, and won it 12-11 in eleven innings.

1907   DEADLY TRAIN WRECK

An eleven-coach excursion train, carrying eight-hundred employees of the Pere Marquette Railway from Ionia to Detroit for an annual holiday, collided head-on with an oncoming freight train near Salem, killing thirty-three and injuring one hundred.

1838   A MICHIGAN FOLLY

Amid much fanfare at Mt. Clemens, Governor Stevens T. Mason lifted the first shovelful of earth to begin excavation of what was to be a canal that would connect the Clinton and Kalamazoo rivers and make it possible to cross southern Michigan by boat from Lake St. Clair to Lake Michigan. The excavation reached a point near Rochester then stopped in 1843 when money ran out.

Remains of the Clinton-Kalamazoo Canal near Rochester. Work on the proposed artificial waterway across lower Michigan stopped after five years of construction had completed only sixteen miles (see July 20).

1818   MECHANICS UNITE

The Detroit Mechanics Society, Michigan's first union, organized at Detroit for "mutual protection and benefit."

21

1945   TIGERS PLAY NEARLY THREE GAMES IN ONE

The Detroit Tigers and the Philadelphia Athletics were tied 1-1 at Philadelphia when, after twenty-four innings, darkness ended the longest game in Tiger history.

1930   DETROIT OUSTS MAYOR

Detroit Mayor Charles Bowles, whom many residents blamed for the unchecked corruption and loose law enforcement that plagued their city during the Prohibition era, became the nation's first large-city mayor ever to be recalled.

1928   URBAN COACH ROBBERY

In wild-west, stagecoach-holdup style, two masked bandits jumped onto an interurban-railroad car traveling from Flint to Saginaw-Bay City and, at pistol-point, robbed nineteen passengers of $300.

1865   GOVERNOR BORN

Fred M. Warner, Michigan governor 1905-10, was born at Hickling, Nottinghamshire, England. The businessman was one of only four governors who served more than two consecutive terms and was also the first three-term Republican governor.

22

1930   COMMENTATOR MURDERED

At one a.m., three unknown men shot and killed popular radio-commentator Jerry Buckley who had vigorously campaigned against corruption in Detroit and had helped recall the city's mayor. (See July 21.)

1924   SINGER BORN

Margaret Whiting was born at Detroit. Whiting sold more-than-twelve-million records during the 1940s and 1950s including "It Might As Well Be Spring" and "I'm Getting Married In the Morning."

1890   WOMEN JOURNALISTS ASSOCIATE

At Traverse City, the Michigan Women's Press Association organized "for the betterment and extension of good journalism among newspaper-women."

1880   BOAT COLLISION KILLS

Sixteen persons drowned when the Detroit steamship *Garland* collided with the yacht *Mamie* in the Detroit River near Fighting Island.

MICH-AGAIN'S JULY

1817   GOVERNOR BORN

Andrew Parsons, Michigan governor 1853-54, was born at Hoosick, New York. Upon the appointment of Governor McClelland to the position of U.S. secretary of interior (see March 3), Lt. Governor Parsons became governor and finished out the term. In 1854 Parsons was elected to the state legislature and served until his unexpected death, at age thirty-eight, two years later.

23   1967   NATION'S WORST RIOT BEGINS

Shortly after 4:00 a.m. police raided a Detroit bar illegally serving liquor after hours and arrested seventy-three customers and the bartender. Rumors spread through a gathering crowd that police had beaten some of those arrested and someone threw a brick through a window starting a week of rioting, looting and burning that reached a scale unknown in the twentieth century.   The riot left forty-three dead, two thousand injured,   five thousand homeless   and caused $50 million   in damage.

1961   TIGERS FINISH IN MARATHON TIME

The Tigers beat the Athletics 17-14 in a nine-inning game at Kansas City that took a (since-broken) major-league-record three hours, fifty-four minutes to play.

1913   TRAGIC STRIKE

Fifteen-thousand upper-peninsula copper miners, demanding a $3 minimum daily wage, an eight-hour workday, and recognition of the Western Federation of Miners as their bargaining agent, walked off their jobs and picketed the major shafts in the copper country's first strike. Before the strike ended in April 1914, it tore the copper country into two bitterly opposing factions, caused at least four murders, and led to one of the biggest tragedies in Michigan history. (See December 24.)

1829   FIRST TYPEWRITER

William A. Burt (Mount Vernon) received a patent for the nation's first typewriter which he called a "typographer."

24   1951   LANDING COMMEMORATED

The U.S. Post Office issued a three-cent blue stamp at Detroit to commemorate the 250th anniversary of the landing of Cadillac.

1832   GOVERNOR BORN

John J. Bagley, Michigan governor 1869-72, was born at Medina, New York. Under Bagley's leadership, the state militia organized into the National Guard and a state board of health and a fish commission were established.

1788   CANADA COURT MICHIGAN

The Canadian Council, in creating several North American judicial districts, included Detroit in the District of Hesse and sent Judge William Dunmore Powell to conduct the first court proceedings ever held in Michigan.

1701   DETROIT FOUNDED

Antoine de la Mothe Cadillac, a French commander, arrived at the mouth of the Detroit River and began construction of Fort Ponchartrain du Detroit to protect the strategic water route from Lake Erie to Lake Huron from English invasions.

25 1966   GREASING THE SQUEAKY WHEELS

Secretary of State James Hare appointed 26-year-old Gordon Alexander (Lansing) as Michigan's first and the nation's second state ombudsman who took on the task of handling complaints from citizens about their government.

1817   SUCCESSFUL PAPER BEGINS

The first issue of the *Detroit Gazette*, Michigan's first successful, regularly issued newspaper, was published at Detroit. The paper was published weekly for thirteen years at an initial subscription cost of $4 per year.

1817   FIRST BOOKSTORE AD

Michigan's first known bookstore placed an advertisement in the first issue of the *Detroit Gazette*. The owners of the bookstore, who also owned the paper, listed mostly works of fiction with many titles by Sir Walter Scott.

26 1980   BADGER LANDS RECORD MUSKIE

Dr. William H. Pivar (Eagle River, Wisconsin) caught a Michigan-state-record 45-pound northern muskellenge at Thousand Island Lake (Gogebic County).

1951   FOR SALE BY OWNER

The Bay de Noquet Company, which owned nearly all of the physical assets of the upper-peninsula town of Nahma (pop. 450), ended seventy years of continuous lumbering operations and offered the entire town for sale at an asking price of $250,000. Two years later, the American Playground Device Company (Anderson, Indiana), the nation's largest manufacturer of playground equipment, bought Nahma and developed it as a model industrial-recreation community.

1905   EARTHQUAKE SHAKES COPPER COUNTRY

The pressure of an earthquake that moved through a vast network of underground mine caverns created an air blast which exploded through the Calumet-Lake Linden area smashing windows, toppling chimneys, and causing telephone poles to sway violently.

1701   FIRST CATHOLIC CHURCH BUILT

The foundations for St. Anne's Church, Michigan's oldest and the nation's second-oldest continuous Catholic parish, were laid at Detroit. The structure burned to the ground two years later and, because of other fires or expansion programs, the church moved six more times over the next 180 years.

27 **1980   EARTHQUAKE ROCKS LOWER MICHIGAN**

The upper tail of an earthquake centering in Kentucky rumbled through Michigan. Cars in Allegan, Coldwater, Flint, Hastings, and Mt. Pleasant rocked noticeably; dishes and windows broke in Detroit; and, during the fifth inning of a baseball game, the top levels of Tiger Stadium swayed noticeably.

1934   FIRST FINANCIAL HELP FOR SENIORS

The newly created state Old Age Assistance Bureau mailed the first-ever old-age pension checks, ranging from $5 to $12, to one-hundred applicants in nine counties.

28 **1976   BIRD SWITCH NIXED**

Legislators turned down a proposal to replace the robin, Michigan's official bird since 1935, with the Kirtland warbler. A compromise, however, named the Kirtland warbler as Michigan's official bicentennial bird.

1914   WAR IN EUROPE BEGINS

Austria officially declared war on Serbia, an act that eventually would involve the U.S. in a world war, and more-than-five-thousand Serbians held a rally at Detroit to swear loyalty and offer support to their homeland.

1805   COURT FORMS

The Supreme Court of the Territory of Michigan organized and had jurisdiction over land-title claims, financial disputes exceeding $200, capital criminal cases, and divorce proceedings.

1919   The village of Pleasant Ridge (Oakland County) incorporated. On December 5, 1927, Pleasant Ridge incorporated as a city.

29 1974   PISTONS PURCHASED

A limited partnership headed by William M. Davison bought the National Basketball Association Detroit Pistons for a reported $8.1 million from Fred Zollner, who had owned the club since it debuted at Ft. Wayne, Indiana, in 1941.

1974   POWERFUL DISPLAY

Three consecutive first-inning home runs by Al Kaline, Bill Freehan, and Mickey Stanley and a fourth by Eddie Brinkman set a major-league record for home runs hit in the first inning as Detroit went on to beat Cleveland 8-2 at Cleveland.

1971   BLAMELESS DIVORCES

Governor William G. Milliken signed into law a "no-fault"-divorce bill which allowed Michigan couples to divorce simply by stating that their marriage had irretrievably broken down instead of having to claim adultery, drunkenness, cruelty or desertion as a reason.

1901   The village of Hamtramck (Wayne County) incorporated. On October 10, 1921, Hamtramck incorporated as a city.

30 1980   ATHLETES RELUCTANTLY STAY HOME

President Jimmy Carter, who had ordered an Olympic boycott because of Russia's invasion of Afghanistan, honored 435 nonparticipating U.S. athletes, including twelve from Michigan, in a ceremony at the U.S. Capitol.

1975   LABOR LEADER DISAPPEARS

Former Teamsters union president Jimmy Hoffa mysteriously disappeared from the parking lot of a suburban-Detroit restaurant and sparked one-of-the-biggest manhunts in FBI history. Government officials and the FBI theorized that Hoffa was the victim of a contract murder at the hands of onetime-Teamster allies and organized-crime figures, but the investigation failed to find Hoffa or his body, turn up any witnesses, or result in any indictments. On December 9, 1982, a court decreed Hoffa legally dead.

1968   POST OFFICE HONORS FORD
The U.S. Post Office issued a twelve-cent stamp at Dearborn that commemorated Henry Ford's birth date 105 years earlier.

1938   NAZIS HONOR FORD
Henry Ford, on his seventy-fifth birthday, became the first American to receive Adolph Hitler's Supreme Order of the German Eagle. Hitler praised Ford for his anti-Semitism and, at one time, even hung the auto magnate's picture prominently at Nazi headquarters.

1863   AUTO GREAT BORN
Henry Ford was born on a farm near Detroit.

31

1969   ACCIDENTALLY TRAINED
As a driver's-education student drove down a suburban Flint street, an approaching car suddenly veered across the centerline and smashed into the training car. The instructor was seriously injured in the crash, the first major accident involving a driver's-training vehicle since the education program began in 1953.

1925   GOVERNOR BORN
John B. Swainson, Michigan governor 1961-62, was born at Windsor, Ontario. During his single term as governor, the former state senator and lieutenant governor successfully expanded the state's community-college program. Following his loss to George Romney in a reelection bid, Swainson served as a circuit-court judge 1965-70, and as a state supreme-court justice 1970-75. (See also January 26.)

1923   PUBLIC CROSSINGS BEGIN
State-owned automobile-ferry service began at the Straits of Mackinac with one ferry capable of carrying twenty autos. The ferry service expanded and, when it ceased operations in 1958, had carried twelve-million vehicles and thirty-million passengers.

1911   GM ARRIVES ON WALL STREET
The New York Stock Exchange listed General Motors securities, the first automobile stock to be approved for listing in that body.

1830   FIRST RAILROAD CHARTERED
At a time when not a single mile of track was yet in use anywhere in the

United States, the Pontiac and Detroit Railway Company received Michigan's first railway charter. Eight years later, after re-incorporating as the Detroit and Pontiac Railway, the railroad finally began to run trains.

The Detroit Zoological Park was one of the first zoos in the nation to separate viewers from animals by moats instead of bars (see August 1).

AUGUST

1 1928   ZOO OPENS

The Detroit Zoological Park, one of the first in the nation to feature barless exhibits, opened for the first time. (Photo preceding page.)

1926   PASSENGER FLIGHTS BEGIN

Ford Airport (Dearborn) opened a passenger depot, and Stout Air Services began the nation's first regularly scheduled passenger runs with one daily Detroit-Grand Rapids round-trip flight.

1919   FREIGHT FLIGHTS BEGIN

The Thompson Airline Company began Michigan's first inter-city commercial airfreight service by carrying two-hundred pounds of auto parts from Detroit to Saginaw via Lansing.

1878   INSTITUTION OPENS

The State of Michigan opened the Eastern Michigan Asylum in Pontiac. The asylum, built to supplement the state's first institution at Kalamazoo (see April 23), housed 330 patients and served twenty southeast Michigan counties.

1861   WOMEN CRIMINALS GET FACILITY

A women's wing in the new Detroit House of Correction opened, and female prisoners incarcerated at Michigan State Prison (Jackson), which had been designed exclusively for male inmates, transferred to the new facility. In 1977 Michigan built its first separate state prison for women. (See November 14.)

2 1965   MICHIGAN GETS FIRST TRIMLINES

The nation's first trimline telephones became commercially available to Detroit Michigan Bell customers. Two months later, the company installed the nation's first trimline, a phone with the dial mounted in the receiver, at a Jackson home.

MICH-AGAIN'S AUGUST

1964   STUNT MAN KILLED

As 22,000 watched at floodlighted Tiger Stadium, "Captain Eddie" Knipschild placed his foot into a strap eighty-five feet up a thin pole and began slowly swaying. Suddenly the leather strap broke and the 55-year-old performer fell to his death.

1807   GOVERNOR BORN

Robert McClelland, Michigan governor 1851-53, was born at Greencastle, Pennsylvania. The Monroe lawyer had a long public-service career, serving as state representative, U.S. congressman, and University of Michigan regent before being elected governor. After winning reelection, McClelland resigned from the governorship in 1853 to serve four years as President Franklin Pierce's secretary of the interior. (See also August 30.)

3   1980   FAMILIES CITED

Michigan celebrated its first official American Family Day, a day set aside on the first Sunday in August by law to honor the family. The Michigan lawmaker who introduced the bill to establish the special day has ten children.

1962   FIRST LEFT-FIELD BLAST

Minnesota slugger Harmon Killebrew became the first player to hit a home run over the left-field roof of Tiger Stadium. Killebrew's shot came in the fourth inning of a game won by Minnesota 7-4.

1960   MANAGING A TRADE

In one of the most unusual trades in baseball history, the Cleveland Indians sent their manager, Joe Gordon, to the Tigers in return for their manager, Jimmy Dykes, the first and only time in major-league history two managers were traded for each other.

1881   SPECIAL JUVENILE FACILITY OPENS

The Michigan Reform School at Adrian, headed and fully staffed by women, accepted its first inmate. The institution, the first of its kind in Michigan and the twelfth in the U.S., provided care exclusively for minor female offenders.

1863   HORSING AROUND

Horse-drawn streetcars began their first Detroit routes, running first on Jefferson and Woodward avenues and, two months later, also on Gratiot and Michigan Avenue.

1795   INDIANS SELL MICHIGAN LAND

The United States received its first Michigan land from the Indians. In signing the Treaty of Greenville, the Indians ceded a six-mile-wide strip along the Detroit River between the River Raisin and Lake St. Clair, all of Mackinac Island, and land bordering the Straits of Mackinac.

4 1929   A ROYALE FIRST

A twenty-passenger ferry, the *Water Lily*, began service from Copper Harbor to Isle Royale, and Michigan residents could, for the first time, travel to their great wilderness island in upper Lake Superior by boat directly from Michigan. Prior to the Michigan runs, all Isle Royale visitors traveled by boat from either Duluth, Minnesota, or Port Arthur, Ontario.

1701   INDIANS SAY "YES" TO FRENCH

The French signed a peace treaty with several North American Indian tribes which removed the last obstacle to French expansion of Michigan settlement begun two weeks earlier at Detroit.

5 1965   MYSTERIOUS SPACECRAFT SPOTTED

U.S. Air Force personnel reported solid-radar contact with seven-to-ten unidentified flying objects (UFOs) moving in a "v" formation over Lake Superior. Jet interceptors gave chase over Duluth, Minnesota, but could not maintain the speed of the UFOs and were quickly outdistanced.

1917   GUARD TURNED INTO DOUGHBOYS

The United States Army drafted the entire Michigan National Guard into World War I service.

1899   DETROIT BECOMES THE MOTOR CITY

Detroit's first automobile manufacturer, the Detroit Automobile Company, organized but, after building approximately twenty autos, went out of business.

1958   The city of Swartz Creek (Genesee County) incorporated.

6 1942   DETROIT SPY ESCAPES DEATH

Max Stephan, a Detroit-restaurant owner, was convicted of being a Nazi spy and was sentenced to death for treason, but President Franklin D. Roosevelt commuted the sentence to life imprisonment.

1903   A TRAIN WRECK KILLS ENTERTAINERS

The first sixteen cars of a circus train traveling in two sections from Charlotte to Lapeer stopped at Durand at 4:00 a.m. When the air brakes of the closely following 22-car second section failed, it plowed into the rear of the first train killing twenty-three members of the Wallace Brothers circus and injuring forty others.

1894   FORMER GOVERNOR DIES

Austin Blair, Michigan's twelfth governor, died at Jackson at the age of seventy-six. When Blair took office in 1861, the governorship was considered a part-time position that paid an annual salary of $1,000. After serving two terms as governor, Blair was elected to the U.S. Congress for three terms before he finally retired to his Jackson law practice.

1845   FIRST ALUMNI CREATED

At Ann Arbor's Presbyterian Church, eleven graduates received bachelor-of-arts degrees in the first known University of Michigan commencement.

7 **1976   CHAMP SMOKES COMPETITORS**

William Vargo (Clayton Township) beat eighty other contestants to win his third consecutive world pipe-smoking championship. In winning the previous year's contest, Vargo set a world record by smoking his regulation .1 ounce of tobacco for two hours, six minutes, and thirty-nine seconds.

1973   HEART ATOMICALLY REGULATED

Doctors at William Beaumont Hospital (Royal Oak) implanted Michigan's first nuclear-powered heart pacemaker, which lasts five times longer than battery-operated models, in a 59-year-old Hazel Park auto worker.

1970   GOOSE LAKE ROCKS MICHIGAN

Two-hundred-thousand young people flocked to a rock festival held at Goose Lake, a private park near Jackson. The open sale and use of drugs at the three-day gathering prompted a statewide, anti-drug television address by Governor William G. Milliken, and legislators, outraged by several instances of nude bathing, passed a law regulating such events.

1904   MAN OF PEACE BORN

Ralph Bunche, a statesman who won the 1950 Nobel peace prize for his work in the United Nations, was born at Detroit.

8

1978   FORD DEDICATES THE FORD

Former president Gerald Ford dedicated Interstate 196, a seventy-nine-mile freeway from Grand Rapids to St. Joseph that carries his name.

1942   GOVERNOR BORN

James J. Blanchard, Michigan's forty-fifth governor, was born at Detroit. The former U.S. congressman took office at a time when the state was close to bankruptcy but restored the state to solvency by engineering the passage of a controversial thirty-eight-percent temporary income-tax increase.

1930   SEE WATER BY AIR

Three seaplanes took off from Lake St. Clair and began the nation's first air-water tour. The members of the Detroit Flying Club, organizers of the nine-day trip, visited twenty-six Great Lakes towns and cities in six states and Ontario.

1920   SHORT BUT SWEET

The Detroit Tigers shut out the New York Yankees 1-0 in one hour and thirteen minutes of playing time, the quickest nine-inning game in American League history.

9

1982   SENIOR SKY DIVER

Seventy-year-old Alice Eckardt (Mt. Morris Township), by jumping three-thousand feet from a single-prop plane near Clio, became the oldest sky diver in Michigan history. (*Flint Journal* photo.)

1975   TIGERS BREAK UNWANTED RECORD

The Minnesota Twins shut out Detroit 1-0 and the Tigers suffered their fourteenth consecutive defeat, a club record. The losing streak finally stopped at nineteen games, one short of the American League record.

1974   MICHIGAN'S FIRST PRESIDENT

Richard M. Nixon resigned as president of the United States, and Vice-President Gerald R. Ford took the office as the first president to serve without being chosen in a national election.

10 1950   RUSSIANS SCORE U OF M FOOTBALL

"Wall Street encourages bloodthirsty football games . . . to work up a warlike mood in the U.S.," charged Moscow radio in a broadcast that also said that players in Michigan football games, "are often carried from the field to the hospital . . . or cemetery." The next day the Voice of America offered a season pass to University of Michigan games to any Soviet correspondent who wanted to see whether "flowers and wreaths (really) are in order there."

1946   MICHIGAN ENTERS THE JET AGE

The first jet airplane to fly in Michigan skies, a P-80, took off from Selfridge Field (Mount Clemens) during a Civil Air Patrol show.

11 1971   HELP FOR DAMAGED HEART

Doctors at Detroit's Sinai Hospital implanted the nation's first permanent mechanical heart pump in Haskell Shanks, a 63-year-old Warren plant guard who had suffered congestive heart failure. Shanks survived with the implanted silicone-and-dacron chamber longer than any other recipient of such a device before dying three months later of infection.

1901   ELECTRICITY FOR ALL

A Michigan newspaperman reported that "many electrical appliances are so cheap that their use is well-nigh universal," and that it was "possible for the owner of a house or boat to introduce into it a great many of the latest applications of electrical machinery without going bankrupt in the process, even if he is not a rich man to start with."

12 1912   ALL IN A DAY'S PLAY

Three men attacked and stabbed Detroit Tiger-star Ty Cobb as he stepped out of his car at the Detroit train station to join his team for a trip to Syracuse, New York. Cobb fought off the three would-be robbers, said nothing to his teammates or manager about his wound, and played in the next day's exhibition game.

1912 POWER PRICE-FIXING BEGINS

The state established, through the railroad commission, the first uniform statewide system of filing, reviewing, and regulating light and power rates.

1948 The village of Kaleva (Manistee County) incorporated.

13
1969 LICENSE LANDMARK

In ceremonies at Lansing, Secretary of State James Hare presented Michigan's eight-millionth color-photo driver's license to Unafern Wentworth (Ionia).

1817 FIRST PRESIDENT VISITS

President James Monroe arrived at Detroit, and the city's residents hosted a five-day celebration for the first president ever to visit Michigan while in office.

14
1945 WAR ENDS

The Japanese formally surrendered to the United States, and World War II, in which 673,000 Michigan men served and 10,265 died, ended.

1919 FIRST DRIVERS LICENSED

A state law requiring all drivers of motor vehicles to carry licenses while driving went into effect. About 250,000 who were not required to pass either a written or road test, applied for the licenses.

1906 TEST DRIVER ALL WET

As a test driver for a Lansing automobile company drove on a road around a shallow artificial lake, a tire on his machine suddenly exploded and the auto plunged into the water. The driver, though trapped in the vehicle, managed to keep his head above water until rescuers responded to his screams.

1957 The village of Wixom (Oakland County) incorporated. On November 26, 1957, Wixom incorporated as a city.

15 1976 GANGS ATTACK ROCK FANS

Two-hundred youth-gang members forced their way into a rock concert at Cobo Hall and beat, terrorized, and robbed members of the audience. The violence then spread outside where at least one woman was raped on a sidewalk and several other persons were assaulted and robbed.

1960 MAMMOTH ARENA OPENS DOORS

Though construction was not complete and the facility had no major bookings until October, Detroit's $54-million Cobo Hall and collossal convention center officially opened.

1847 STAMP OF APPROVAL

Postage stamps, issued in five-cent and ten-cent denominations, were used for the first time in Michigan prompting the *Detroit Free Press* to approvingly report that "all that has to be done is to prefix one of the little appendages and the letter goes direct."

1796 OLDEST COUNTY ESTABLISHED

Wayne County, which included within its boundaries practically all of (present-day) Michigan as well as portions of northern Ohio and Indiana and parts of Illinois and Wisconsin bordering on Lake Michigan, was established.

16 1965 FIRST BLACK TOP COP

The Dowagiac city council named George Grady as the head of their city's police department which made him Michigan's first black chief of police. Grady directed the nineteen-member force until 1974 when a heart condition forced him to resign.

1914 WOMEN SERVE MICHIGAN

The federal government reported that the most prevalent occupations for women employed in Michigan were: stenographers — 7,900, teachers — 17,690, and servants — 33,000.

1858 MICHIGAN'S FIRST PLANNED — AND UNPLANNED — BALLOON FLIGHT

Ira Thurston, a well-known and experienced balloonist, lifted off from Adrian and completed Michigan's first hot-air balloon flight by landing seventeen miles away in Riga Township (Lenawee County). While releasing gas after landing, Thurston accidentally let go of one of the hold-down ropes, and the bag shot into the air with the hapless aeronaut desperately clinging to the top. Four hours later the deflated bag came to earth without

Thurston, and his bones were found years later only a few miles from the point of the unplanned ascent.

1812   DETROIT SURRENDERED

During the War of 1812, General William Hull, fearing he was vastly outnumbered, surrendered Detroit to the British without firing a shot in resistance. Hull was later court-martialed for the act but President Madison set aside the resulting death sentence because of Hull's Revolutionary War heroism.

17 1982   COURT DEALS WITH HOCKEY VIOLENCE

In the first civil case of its kind involving National Hockey League players, a Detroit federal jury awarded Detroit Red Wing Dennis Polonich $850,000 in damages for facial injuries he suffered during a 1978 game when, according to the suit and several witnesses, Wilf Paiement of the Colorado Rockies hit him with his stick in a baseball-bat-type swing.

1967   SPECIAL I.D. ISSUED

The state presented its first identification cards for the legally blind to Rep. Robert D. Mahoney (Detroit) and his wife Jennie. The cards were designed for use by blind persons as official identification in situations in which sighted persons would use driver's licenses.

1920   PLANE LETTERS

A seaplane, arriving from Cleveland, landed at Detroit with the first batch of mail ever delivered to Michigan by air. Regular airmail service, however, did not begin for nearly six more years. (See February 15.)

1954   The village of Birch Run (Saginaw County) incorporated.

18 1978   McCOURT COURTS WINGS

Under National Hockey League free-agency rules, an arbitrator awarded Detroit Red Wing center Dale McCourt to Los Angeles as compensation for the Wings' signing of former LA goalie Rogie Vachon. McCourt, however, refused to report to his new team and appealed his case through the judicial system to the U.S. Supreme Court. But before the Supreme Court heard the case, the Kings and Wings negotiated a settlement and McCourt stayed with Detroit until 1981 when he was traded to Buffalo.

1976   FORD RUNS FOR REELECTION

Almost exactly two years after he became the nation's first nonelected president (see August 9), Gerald R. Ford received the Republican party's nomination for president, beating his closest competitor, Ronald Reagan, 1,187 to 1,070. Ford and his running-mate Sen. Robert Dole (Kansas) won Michigan's electoral votes but lost the November election to former Georgia-governor Jimmy Carter.

1967   FIRST BLACK STATE TROOPER

Jack Hall, former Benton Township police officer, was sworn in as Michigan's first black state policeman.

1926   PRESIDENT GETS EXTRAORDINARY PIE

The Hawkins Bakery (Traverse City) baked a three-foot-diameter, 42-pound cherry pie then hand-delivered the special dessert to President and Mrs. Calvin Coolidge and several guests who were attending a distinguished dinner party at the president's summer white house in the Adirondack Mountains of New York.

1922   LEARN WHILE LISTENING

Michigan State University radio-station WKAR (East Lansing) went on the air as Michigan's first educational radio station.

19 1959   WALK AND SHOP

The nation's first permanent pedestrian mall, a shopping area created by closing several city blocks to traffic, opened at downtown Kalamazoo.

1951   TIGERS ON THE SHORT END

St. Louis-owner and showman Bill Veeck sent 3'7'' midget Eddie Gaedell in as a pinch hitter for the Browns' leadoff batter in the second game of a doubleheader against the Tigers. Gaedell, wearing number 1/8, walked on four straight pitches, but the Tigers retired the rest of the side and went on to win 6-2. Following the game, major-league rules were hastily rewritten to prevent the situation from recurring.

1929   METAL AIRSHIP FLOWN
The ZMC2, the nation's first all-metal dirigible, rose into the air from Grosse Isle Airport. After the successful test flight, the navy purchased the ship from the manufacturer, the Detroit Aircraft Corporation.

20
1981   NEW PRISON OPENS
The Huron Valley Men's Facility, the state's third maximum-security prison, opened near Ypsilanti. Twenty maximum-security inmates from the Marquette prison were the first of 411 of the toughest prisoners in the state to move to the $20-million facility.

1971   A LEGENDARY FESTIVAL STARTS
Oscoda's first annual Paul Bunyan Festival began. Oscoda residents decided to hold the celebration after learning that the *Encyclopedia Brittanica* had credited an Oscoda native, *Detroit News-Tribune*-reporter James MacGillivary, with being the first to write about the legendary lumberman.

1916   OAKLAND COUNTY FIRST TO CELEBRATE
Oakland County began a week-long centennial celebration, the first staged by any Michigan county.

1780   GOVERNOR BORN
William Woodbridge, Michigan governor 1840-41, was born at Norwich, Connecticut. Before being elected in 1839 as Michigan's second governor, Woodbridge had served as Michigan's first territorial congressional delegate, state supreme-court justice, and state senator. (See also October 20.)

1923   The village of Flat Rock (Wayne County) incorporated. On April 5, 1965, Flat Rock incorporated as a city.

21
1973   FIRST METRIC MILEAGE
The Highway Department installed a metric highway sign, Michigan's first, beside northbound U.S. 27 near Dewitt that put the distance to St. Johns at nineteen kilometers or twelve miles.

1917 AHEAD OF HIS TIME

Robert E. Frederick (Rogers City) received a patent for "new-and-useful improvements in Flying Machines" which turned out to be a forerunner of helicopters.

22

1971 PROS PLAY AT COLLEGE

The University of Michigan football stadium hosted its first professional-football game as the Detroit Lions beat the Baltimore Colts 23-20 before a crowd of 91,475. A share of the exhibition game's gate receipts went to the university's scholarship-and-building fund.

1942 CARRIER CHRISTENED

The *U.S.S. Wolverine*, the Great Lakes' first and only aircraft carrier, was commissioned at Chicago. The *Wolverine* was used on Lake Michigan to train student aviators in carrier landings and takeoffs.

1937 PRIEST'S CAREER DECLINES

The Rev. Fr. Charles E. Coughlin collapsed while conducting services at the Shrine of the Little Flower (Royal Oak) and was ordered to take a complete rest by his physician. Five years before, Father Coughlin had, through radio talks in which he supported Franklin D. Roosevelt and attacked big business and bankers, become widely known and respected as the "radio priest of Royal Oak." But by 1937, his broadcasts had become little more than anti-Semitic, anti-Roosevelt diatribes, and when he was ordered by the church hierarchy to cancel his radio program, he futilely battled the decision to the point of exhaustion.

23

1975 LIONS MOVE INDOORS

A crowd of 62,094 watched the Detroit Lions beat the Kansas City Chiefs 27-24 in the first game played on their new-home field at the Pontiac Silverdome.

1973 WONDER WOMAN WINS DUAL TITLES

Sheila Young (Detroit) became the first woman from the United States ever to win a world cycling championship. With her victory at San Sebastian, Spain, Young, who six months earlier had captured the world speed-skating title at Sweden, also became the only person to ever win a world championship in both sports.

1873 DETROIT GETS THE NEWS

The first issues of the *Detroit News*, founded by James E. Scripps, were sold on Detroit streets.

1679   THE VOYAGE OF THE *GRIFFIN*

Robert Cavalier de la Salle, a French explorer on an expedition from Niagara Falls to the mouth of the Mississippi River, sailed into the Detroit River in the *Griffin*. The ship, whose prow featured a carved figure representing the mythological half-lion, half-eagle, continued up Lake Huron to St. Ignace then on to Green Bay. There, LaSalle went ashore and ordered the *Griffin* back to Niagara, but it and the entire crew mysteriously disappeared, presumably sunk, on the return voyage. (See also March 20 and November 1.)

24   1969   FANTASTIC VOYAGE

Victor Jackson (East Lansing) landed near Manitowoc, Wisconsin, after completing a 14½-hour trip across Lake Michigan — in a bathtub. The 32-year-old father of six made the 65-mile journey in a household-type tub welded to a frame supported by four thirty-gallon oil drums and powered by a twenty-horsepower outboard motor.

1915   STATE BUYS DEAD RODENTS

A statewide bounty of five cents per rat began.

25   1892   WOMAN AERONAUT DIES

Gertrude Carmo, the first Michigan woman to go aloft in a balloon, died in a balloon accident at the Detroit Exposition grounds.

1872   OFF SICK

A disease that spread through Detroit's horse population temporarily halted streetcar runs and forced express companies to deliver and collect goods in handcarts.

1840   PRACTICALLY PLANTED

Joseph Gibbons (Adrian) patented the nation's first practical seeding machine, a grain drill with cavities to deliver seed at a regulated volume.

26   1976   DEFLATED DOME

During a heavy rain-and-hail storm, winds gusting up to fifty miles per hour tore off two forty-foot-square panels of the Pontiac Silverdome's fabric ceiling, and the world's largest air-supported roof collapsed.

1935   UNION BORN

As a part of a strong post-depression unionization movement, the United Auto Workers officially organized. A little more-than-a-year later, after joining the Congress of Industrial Organizations (C.I.O.), the U.A.W. staged an historic sit-down strike to win recognition at the industry's largest firm, General Motors.

1889   MAN STAGES FINAL HOLDUP

Reimund Holzhey, while robbing a stagecoach traveling between Gogebic Station and Lake Gogebic, shot and killed one of the four passengers. Holzhey was sentenced to life imprisonment for the murder during, what turned out to be, the last stagecoach robbery in Michigan.

1817   UNIVERSITY CREATED

The Michigan territorial legislature enacted that "there shall be a Catholepistemiad or University of Michigania" at Detroit. The governor and judges, who composed the legislature, also appropriated $300 towards the erection of a university building and set the salary of the president at $25 per year, the vice-president at $18.75 per year, and professors at $12.50 per year. (See also September 8.)

1817   FIRST BOOKSHELVES STOCKED

Michigan's first library, the City Library of Detroit, incorporated and was initially financed by selling ninety shares of stock at $5 each to members of the organizing library society.

1902   The village of Daggett (Menominee County) incorporated.

27 1982   JAPANESE SINK THEN BAIL OUT STATE

A consortium of Japanese banks agreed to help Michigan's borrowing problems by providing the state with a $500-million line of credit. At the time, Michigan had the lowest credit rating of any state in the nation which made it both difficult and expensive to borrow money in America. Many Michigan residents and officials, however, viewed the Japanese aid with irony since the state's economic problems, high unemployment and sagging auto industry had been blamed on domestic inroads made by Japanese automakers.

1946   MICHIGAN GETS PARK

Isle Royale, a lush wooded Michigan island in northern Lake Superior, was officially dedicated as a national park.

1913   ASHES TO ASHES

Representatives of crematories from all over the nation assembled at the Detroit Crematorium's chapel and founded the Cremation Association of America.

1856   LINCOLN'S MICHIGAN ADDRESS

An obscure lawyer named Abraham Lincoln spoke at a rally held in Kalamazoo's Bronson Park for the newly formed Republican party. Lincoln's speech, in support of the party's presidential candidate, was his first and only Michigan appearance.

1818   FIRST STEAMBOAT ARRIVES

Stores and shops closed, and residents flocked to the wharf as the boom of a cannon announced the first arrival at Detroit of the *Walk-In-The-Water*, the first steamboat to sail on the Great Lakes. The vessel carried passengers at a fare of $18.00 each on biweekly Detroit-Buffalo round trips until October when she was wrecked in a storm near Buffalo.

28 1976   MICHIGAN BEAUTY WINS

Kimberlee Marre Foley (Southfield) won the Miss World-USA beauty crown and represented America in a November Miss World Pageant held at London.

1964   MOTORIZED VEHICLES ONLY

A state law went into effect that banned hitchhikers and bicycles from freeways.

1923   The village of Kingsford (Dickinson County) incorporated. On March 10, 1947, Kingsford incorporated as a city.

29 1891   STUNT MAN KILLED

John Hogan (Jackson) died when he fell one-hundred feet while performing on a trapeze suspended from a hot-air balloon flying over the Detroit Exposition.

1805   IN DEED

The first act requiring the registering of deeds in the Michigan territory was passed.

30 1937   FUELISH RECORD

Two Jackson aviators landed after a 29-hour flight in a low-powered airplane during which they refueled forty-three times by raising a two-gallon gasoline can by rope from a speeding auto. The pair then claimed a sustained-flight record but found that the American

Aeronautical Association did not recognize flights in which refueling is done by automobile.

1905   STAR STARTS
A tall eighteen-year-old who threw with his right hand and batted with his left stepped onto the field at Detroit, and Tiger fans got their first glimpse of Ty Cobb who would, during his legendary career, help Detroit win pennants in 1907, 1908 and 1909, set more than twenty-five major-league records, and become the first player inducted into baseball's Hall of Fame.

1880   FORMER GOVERNOR DIES
Robert McClelland, Michigan's eighth governor, died at his home in Detroit at the age of seventy-three. After serving as U.S. secretary of interior for four years, McClelland set up a Detroit law office in 1857 and practiced there until his death. (See also August 2.)

1840   GOVERNOR BORN
Hazen S. Pingree, Michigan governor 1897-1900, was born at Denmark, Maine. Governor Pingree, a former shoe manufacturer and four-time Detroit mayor, enacted a scientific system, the nation's first, of appraising railroad and corporation property for tax purposes.

31

1973   PLAYING BILLY BALL
American League President Joe Cronin suspended Billy Martin for three days after the Detroit Tiger manager had ordered his pitchers to throw illegal "spitballs" then told newsmen about it. Two days later the Tigers fired Martin.

1972   HOW SWEDE IT IS
The Detroit Red Wings signed their first European hockey player, Thommie Bergman of the Swedish National Team. Bergman, a 24-year-old defenseman, played 246 games for the Wings over five seasons.

1942   BELL MILESTONE
Michigan Bell installed its one-millionth Michigan phone.

1920   FIRST ON THE AIR
The Detroit News radio station (later WWJ), with a broadcasting range of about one-hundred miles, began the nation's first regularly scheduled radio programming. The station, during their first broadcast, sent primary results over the airwaves to an audience of approximately three-hundred set owners and, during the first week, expanded programming to include

baseball news, foreign-affairs bulletins, and campaign proceedings.

1909   FIRST ACCIDENT POSTED

A motorized fire engine, claimed to be the first in the nation (see December 17), skidded on wet pavement at Lansing and, in the nation's first known accident involving an automobile fire engine, crashed into a hitching post.

1809   MICHIGAN'S FOURTH ESTATE BEGINS

Michigan's first newspaper, the *Michigan Essay or Impartial Observer*, was published at Detroit by James M. Miller who printed the four-page sheet on a press brought to Michigan by Father Gabriel Richard. The first issue, which contained news, essays, advertisements, and a column-and-a-half of French abstracts of the important articles, is the only one known to have been published.

SEPTEMBER

1 1972   FROM STAR TO DEADLY STATISTIC
Thirty-year-old Reggie Harding (Detroit), the only player ever to go straight from high school into the National Basketball Association, was shot twice in the head during an argument at an east-side Detroit residence and died the next day. The Detroit Pistons signed Harding in 1964 immediately after his graduation from Detroit Eastern High School, but Harding's pro career and his life steadily declined. In 1965 the NBA suspended him for a conviction of assault and battery on a policeman; in 1966 the Pistons traded him to Chicago; and in September 1969 he was sent to Southern Michigan Prison (Jackson) for parole violations.

1969   HISTORIC TRANSPLANT
Michigan's first lung transplant took place at the University of Michigan when a Bloomfield Hills man received the lung of a seventeen-year-old Jackson High School traffic-accident victim. The recipient died four days after the transplant.

1969   HEADGEAR MANDATORY
A law requiring Michigan motorcyclists to wear helmets or face a $100 fine and a ninety-day jail sentence went into effect. The state had enacted a helmet law in 1967, but it was ruled unconstitutional, so the second, constitutionally correct law was written and has been in effect since.

1945   THIRD FORD TAKES OVER FORD
After an unusual two-year series of events that began in 1943 with the death of Ford Motor Company President Edsel Ford and included the return of eighty-year-old Henry I to the presidency, a bitter intra-company fight for control, and a special presidential release of Henry Ford II from naval duty, Henry II became president of the Ford Motor Company.

1939   COMEDIENNE BORN

Lily Tomlin was born at Detroit as Mary Jean Tomlin. Tomlin joined NBC television's "Laugh In" in 1969, and her characters Ernestine, Edith Ann, and Suzie Sorority transformed the unknown comic to a national phenomenon who has collected several Emmys for her TV specials.

1914   RECORD STORM

9.78 inches of rain fell on Bloomingdale in the greatest 24-hour rainfall in Michigan history.

1912   WORKERS PROTECTED

Michigan passed a workmen's compensation law which obligated industry, for the first time, to pay money for personal injuries arising out of industrial accidents.

1891   BOOKED UP

Members of the Michigan Library Association gathered at Detroit and held their first formal meeting.

1884   COLLEGE ESTABLISHED

Woodbridge N. Ferris, who later became governor of Michigan and U.S. senator (see January 6), founded the Big Rapids Industrial School at Big Rapids. The school later changed its name to the Ferris Industrial School, then Ferris Institute, and finally, Ferris State College.

2

1977   JOINING THE JET SET

In ceremonies held at Williams Air Force Base (Arizona), Mary Livingston (Manistique) received her silver wings as Michigan's first woman air-force jet pilot.

1922   FORD ENFORCES TEMPERANCE

Henry Ford posted a notice at his Detroit factory warning each employee that he would lose his job if he had "the odor of beer, wine, or liquor on his breath" or was found to "possess any intoxicants on his person or in his home." The poster also added, "The Eighteenth Amendment (Prohibition) is a part of the fundamental laws of this country. It was meant to be enforced."

1902   FIRST CAR CASUALTY

Michigan recorded its first traffic fatality when George W. Bissell, a well-to-do lumberman, was killed when a car struck his carriage on a Detroit street.

1857   The village of St. Johns (Clinton County) incorporated. On March 14, 1904, St. Johns incorporated as a city.

155

3 1911   GRAND RAPIDS TAKES OFF

The Wright brothers brought a biplane to the West Michigan Fair at Grand Rapids and gave that area's residents their first chance to fly.

1783   MICHIGAN JOINS AMERICA

Great Britain and America signed the Treaty of Paris ending the Revolutionary War, and Michigan officially became a part of the United States of America. But to retain control of Michigan's lucrative fur trade, Britain did not abandon military or political position in Michigan for another thirteen years.

1917   The village of Copper City (Houghton County) incorporated.

4 1982   TINY TRANSPLANT

Doctors at the University of Michigan's Holden Perinatal Hospital (Ann Arbor) placed a new kidney into a seventeen-day-old, four-pound, fourteen-ounce Ypsilanti baby girl and, a month later, discharged her as the smallest infant in the nation to successfully undergo a kidney transplant.

1969   BLACK BEAUTY WINS

Shirley Washington, a nineteen-year-old Detroit model, was crowned the nation's first Miss Black America in a pageant held at Asbury Park, New Jersey.

1900   HARE-RAISING SCHEME

The *Michigan Farmer* advised its readers not to get swept up in a Belgian-hare craze that had taken hold in some sections of Michigan. The large rabbits could, according to promoters who sold breeding stock, bring as much as $500 each to those who raised them, but, warned the *Farmer*, only promoters were making money and, since the unsalable rabbits multiplied so fast, people were turning them loose and they were quickly becoming pests.

5 1918   PRISONERS PROFIT

The Board of Control for Michigan State Prison (Jackson) issued an annual report that showed their facility had ended its fiscal year with a $330,813.53 profit which, according to the report, was "unequaled in any other penal institution in the United States."

1881   DISASTROUS FIRE SWEEPS THUMB

Strong southwesterly winds fanned several small fires, set by farmers to clear their lands of loggers' slashings and stumps, into a devastating inferno that raged through Michigan's Thumb area for three days. A heavy rain finally doused the blaze but not until it had killed 282 people, burned over a million acres of land, destroyed 3,400 buildings and left 15,000 destitute survivors, who became the first in the nation to be helped by a new organization called the American Red Cross.

6 1969   MICHIGAN MISS AMERICA

Pamela Anne Eldred, a 21-year-old ballet dancer from Birmingham, was named Miss America at the beauty pageant held in Atlantic City, New Jersey.

1901   PRESIDENT ASSASSINATED

Leon F. Czolgosz, a former Michigan farmer and factory worker, assassinated President William McKinley at the Pan American Exposition in Buffalo, New York. Following an 8½-hour trial held four days after McKinley's funeral, (Auburn) New York Penitentiary officials electrocuted Czolgosz then dumped acid on his body to disintegrate it.

1837   METHODISTS MEET

The first session of the Michigan Methodist Conference was held at Detroit.

1932   The city of Birmingham (Oakland County) incorporated.

7 1959   FIRST BRIDGE HIKE

The first annual Labor Day Mackinac Bridge walk was held, and more than 15,000 hikers joined Governor G. Mennen Williams as he set the first time-record for governors, crossing the 4½-mile distance in sixty-five minutes.

1956   FLYING HIGH

Captain Iven Kincheloe (Cassopolis) set a world's altitude record of 156,000 feet in a Bell X-2 rocket plane.

1950   LAST CYCLE BATTER

During a ten-inning tie game against Cleveland at Detroit, Tiger outfielder Hoot Evers hit for the cycle — a single, double, triple and home run — the last Tiger to do so.

8 1919   HELP WANTED

Michigan's Employment Bureau reported that "in every line of (Michigan) industry there was a shortage of labor . . . and . . . more jobs than workmen."

1896 FIRST FINNISHING SCHOOL

Suomi College, the first Finnish college in the country, opened in rented quarters at Hancock with twenty-seven students.

1817 COLLEGE GETS PROFESSORS BUT NO STUDENTS

All thirteen professorships for the newly created University of Michigania (see August 26) were conferred upon two clergymen, Reverend John Monteith who was made president of the school and held seven professorships, and Father Gabriel Richard who became vice-president and held six professorships. The university at Detroit did not become a reality, but Monteith and Richard established a primary school and academy that operated in the building built for the college until 1827.

1873   The village of Hancock (Houghton County) incorporated. On March 9, 1903, Hancock incorporated as a city.

9

1947 POLICE PILOT PLANE

The Michigan State Police purchased their first airplane for use in their law-enforcement work. (See also June 28.)

1925 OPEN HOUSING STARTS VIOLENTLY

A mob of seven-hundred screaming, rock-throwing whites, angry that a black family had moved into a home in a white neighborhood, charged the house as the owner, Dr. Ossian Sweet, his family, and several armed friends huddled inside. Suddenly a shot rang out from an upstairs window. The crowd scattered as ten more shots quickly cracked and popped then abruptly stopped. Across the street, a man who had watched the mob from a friend's porch lay dead with a bullet in his back, and the Sweet family was charged with his murder. Famous attorney Clarence Darrow, however, defended the family, and in a open-housing and civil-rights milestone, all were found innocent when Darrow successfully argued that Sweet was ". . . justified in defending himself when he apprehended that his life was in danger."

VILLAGES INCORPORATED THIS DAY
1924   Halfway (Macomb County), which changed its name and, on September 17, 1928, incorporated as the city of East Detroit.
1946   Martin (Allegan County).

10

1972 POACHER KILLS WARDEN

Shortly after midnight, conservation-officer Gerald Welling and his partner spotted a man in a pickup truck illegally "shining" and shooting at bears on a dump near Hermansville (Menominee County). They left their patrol car and, as they approached the truck, the driver suddenly drove over Welling, killing him. The driver served a 9½-month prison sentence for the death of the fourth and last Michigan conservation officer killed while on duty.

1942   PLANE FACTS

The Ford Motor Company's Willow Run plant completed assembly of the first World War II B-24 Liberator Bomber. The plant produced, at its peak, eighteen of the huge planes each day and, over the course of the war, assembled a total of 8,500 B-24s.

1896   EYE TO EYE

The Michigan Optical Society organized at Grand Rapids. In 1904, the professional society changed its name to the Michigan Society of Optometrists.

1805   HEAD TAX

A Michigan territorial law directed that ". . . every male inhabitant in the territory over the age of sixteen years should pay annually the sum of one dollar as a capitation tax." The total number of taxpayers in the territory at the time was 525, and all paid.

1822   Lapeer, Lenawee, Sanilac, Shiawassee and Washtenaw counties were established.

11 1982   AN UNDERWATER MICHIGAN

The second of the nation's new Trident missile-carrying submarines, the *U.S.S. Michigan*, was formally commissioned in brief ceremonies at Groton, Connecticut.

The Trident submarine *U.S.S. Michigan* under construction at Groton, Connecticut.

1978   BRIDGE CRASH KILLS THREE

During a pea-soup fog, a small plane carrying three U.S. Marine Corps reserve officers smashed into the Mackinac Bridge and plunged two-hundred feet into the water, killing all occupants.

1971   UNIQUE NAME SWITCH

After a Lansing wedding ceremony, the groom, Richard T. Smith, took his wife's, Karen Sommers, last name because of the many problems he had experienced with his own extremely common name.

1971   TEEN WINS TITLE

Sharon Sexton (Detroit), 17, was crowned Miss Black Teenage America in competition at Baltimore.

1800   CHURCH WORKER REACHES MICHIGAN

Sent by the Congregational Missionary Society of Connecticut, David Bacon, Michigan's first Protestant missionary, arrived at Detroit.

12   1942   FIRST FREEWAY OPENS

Michigan's first expressway, constructed along U.S.-12 from Detroit to the Ford Motor Company's Willow Run bomber plant, formally opened.

1887   COLLEGE BEGINS

Alma College, established by the Presbyterian Synod of Michigan, opened with ninety-five students and nine faculty members.

13   1980   THE LAST THRILL OF VICTORY

The Eastern Michigan Football team beat Bowling Green then began a college-football record-breaking 27-game losing streak that lasted until November 6, 1982, when they beat Kent State 9-7.

1832   "PATRON SAINT" OF DETROIT DIES

Father Gabriel Richard, priest, educator, and civic leader, died of weakness and exhaustion after heroically caring for the victims of a cholera epidemic that swept Detroit and lower Michigan. (See July 4.)

14   1976   HIGH POINT REACHED

The 73-story Plaza Hotel, the world's tallest and the center-piece in downtown Detroit's Renaissance Center, was officially topped with a gold beam decorated with U.S. and Canadian flags and a tree. (See also April 15.)

1974   U OF M FIELDS WOMEN

The University of Michigan used pom-pom girls at a football game for the first time in the school's history. Only two years before, when women were allowed to join the band, had the school broken the 94-year monopoly held by men on all on-the-field activities.

1946   JUST PLANE FOLKS

Sixty-two charter members met at Capitol City Airport (Lansing) and organized the Michigan Flying Farmers.

VILLAGES INCORPORATED THIS DAY
1926   Inkster (Wayne County) which incorporated as a city October 21, 1963; Lochmoor (Wayne County), which on March 13, 1939, changed its name to Grosse Pointe Woods and became a city; and Bloomfield Hills (Oakland County) which incorporated as a city May 16, 1932.

15 1957   CALLS AIRED

The first air-to-ground public telephone service in the country began in the Detroit-Chicago area when about twenty airplanes were equipped for the two-way service. Rates varied from $1.50 to $4.25 for a three-minute call depending on the location of the airplane and the telephone on the ground.

1913   WATERGATE PARTICIPANT BORN

John Mitchell, U.S. attorney general during the administration of President Richard M. Nixon, was born at Detroit. Because of his role in the Watergate conspiracy, break-in, and attempted cover-up, Mitchell became, in 1977, the first U.S. attorney general in history to serve a prison sentence.

1886   ENGINEERING SCHOOL OPENS

The first classes of the Michigan Mining School were held, because no building was provided, at the Houghton town hall. The school, which was created to train engineers, later changed its name to the Michigan College of Mines, then Michigan College of Mining and Technology, and finally Michigan Technological University.

1878   FIRST PHONE BOOK PUBLISHED

Michigan's first telephone directory was issued at Detroit.

1806   DON'T BANK ON IT.

The territory granted a charter to Michigan's first bank, the Bank of Detroit. The bank printed $1,665,000 in notes which were sold at discount in the East. But when the notes found their way back to Detroit for payment in gold or silver and the bank couldn't pay, Congress quickly voted the bank out of existence.

16
1972   MICHIGAN'S FIRST BLACK QUARTERBACK
Dennis Franklin started at quarterback for the University of Michigan football team in their season-opening 7-0 victory over Northwestern. Franklin, the first black quarterback in University of Michigan history, started regularly for the next three seasons then played one year for the Detroit Lions.

1931   THE COLLINGWOOD MASSACRE
Four members of the Purple Gang, one of Detroit's most vicious and notorious Prohibition-era underworld groups, executed three rival racketeers and bootleggers at a residential Collingwood apartment house.

1908   AUTO GIANT CREATED
William C. Durant, head of the Buick Motor Company (Flint), purchased more-than-thirty other existing automobile companies, including Oldsmobile, Pontiac (then called "Oakland"), and Cadillac, and chartered the General Motors Company.

1957   The village of Westwood (Oakland County) incorporated. On March 9, 1959, Westwood changed its name to Beverly Hills.
1957   The city of Southfield (Oakland County) incorporated.

17
1944   GM WORKERS SUPPORT WAR EFFORT
General Motors' Series E Victory war bond number two million, representing the sixty-millionth dollar (maturity value) in the World War II victory certificates sold by GM through a payroll deduction plan, was presented to a Flint AC worker.

1923   WORKMEN'S COMP COVERS SUICIDE
The state department of labor and industry ruled that a janitor's suicide was a compensable injury under the state's workmen's compensation law. The janitor, who had injured his inner ear while working at an Alpena school, had cut his throat while he was in a delirium brought on, according to doctors, by his injury. The department ruled that, since the suicide resulted from his on-the-job injury, the janitor's family was entitled to compensation.

18
1981   GRAND RAPIDS GETS SPECIAL MUSEUM
President Ronald Reagan, former president Gerald Ford, House Speaker "Tip" O'Neill, and entertainers Bob Hope,

Danny Thomas, and Sammy Davis Jr. all helped dedicate the (Gerald R.) Ford presidential museum at Grand Rapids.

1918   FIRST DOUGHGIRL

Hazel Stimson (Flint) responded to a pamphlet that invited her to "work side by side with the men of the Marine Corps" and became the first Michigan woman to enlist in the Marines during World War I. Stimson served fourteen months before being honorably discharged with the rank of corporal.

1891   UNIQUE DIG FINISHED

The St. Clair railway tunnel, the world's first underwater tunnel to join two countries, officially opened beneath the St. Clair River between Port Huron and Sarnia. Prior to the tunnel's construction, railway cars had to be slowly ferried across the busy waterway.

19 1968   MAN GETS PRISONER'S HEART

Michigan's first heart transplant took place at the University of Michigan when a Kalamazoo man received the heart of a Southern Michigan Prison inmate who had died during surgery. The recipient lived for a year then died of infection and rejection of his new heart.

1876   A CLEAN SWEEP

Melville R. Bissell (Grand Rapids) received a patent for the nation's first carpet sweeper. The dusty packing straw Bissell had used in his china shop had aggravated his allergic headaches so he invented a sweeper which scooped up the dust rather than scattered it, patented the device, then formed the Bissell Carpet Sweeper Company.

1864   PIRACY ON THE DETROIT RIVER

The passenger steamer *Philo Parsons*, which had just left Detroit, was boarded by Confederate pirates who, in a bizarre plot, planned to use the ship to seize the warship *U.S.S. Michigan* and free Confederate prisoners held at Ohio. But the plan failed and most of the Confederates were captured and sent to join the men they had hoped to rescue.

1848   JEWELS EXPOSED

George Doty installed five-foot-by-seven-foot imported French plate-glass windows in his Detroit jewelry store then advertised his window display as being the largest west of New York City.

1844   ORE ACCIDENTALLY DISCOVERED

While establishing township lines and making geological observations for the federal government near Negaunee, William Austin Burt noticed peculiar fluctuations in his magnetic compass. Burt asked his men to find the cause and they soon returned with pieces of iron ore. Three years later the Jackson Mining Company began digging at the spot, and by 1890, Michigan led the nation in iron-ore production.

20 1968 MARQUETTE HONORED

Three-hundred years after Father Jacques Marquette founded Michigan's first white settlement near the rapids of the St. Mary's River, the U.S. Post Office issued, at Sault Ste. Marie, a six-cent black, apple-green and orange-brown stamp that honored the explorer and missionary.

1932 WATER SPEED RECORD SET

Gar Wood (Detroit), one of the greatest speedboat racers of all time, piloted his *Miss America X* to a world-record 124.86 miles per hour on the St. Clair River.

1860 ROYAL VISIT

Britain's Albert Edward, the first Prince of Wales ever to visit the United States, arrived at Detroit, his first stop.

21 1920 POST OFFICE WATERMARKED

The Detroit Marine Post Office, the only one in the world at the time, delivered its 1,250,000th piece of mail. The post office, located aboard a boat in the Detroit River, began delivering mail in 1894 to Great Lakes' seamen who had no other communication with relatives during the week to ten-day trip from Duluth, Minnesota, to Lake Erie ports.

1877 SHORT-DISTANCE SERVICE

Michigan's first commercial telephone line was strung at Detroit and ran between Stearn's Drugstore and their laboratory.

22 1959 WORST SMALL-CRAFT ACCIDENT

Michigan's worst small-boat tragedy occurred when twelve members of a Skandia family all drowned when their overloaded, twelve-foot motorboat swamped in Lake McKeever near Munising.

1850 FIRST JEWISH CHURCH FORMED

Twenty-five German Jewish families, who had arrived at Detroit from the New York area, formally organized the Beth El Society and became

Michigan's first Jewish congregation. The members met initially in a private house, then a room over a downtown store before purchasing an old French Methodist church in downtown Detroit.

1773   NO SPRAWLING METROPOLIS YET

A census taken at Detroit showed a total population of 1,367.

23   1978   MICHIGAN BULLFIGHT STAGED

At Detroit's Cobo Hall, four-thousand spectators watched what was billed as the Midwest's first bloodless bullfight. Bulls were not tormented with lances or darts, and instead of killing the animals, matadors placed a single red rose between their horns as a sign of victory.

1968   COUGARS FOLD

The Detroit Cougars of the North American Soccer League, disbanded after only six months in operation because of financial losses.

1934   FIRST LION GAME

The Detroit Lions played their first National Football League game, beating the New York Giants 9-0 at the University of Detroit stadium before a crowd of 12,000.

1905   CURES FOR WHAT AILS YOU

Most state newspapers routinely featured daily advertisements for scores of "wonder" cures including:
Pe-Ru-Na for Pelvic Catarrah and Female Weakness
Sa-mu-lah Blood Purifying Tablets
Cascarets for Dyspepsia
Wine of Cardui for Women's Relief
Dr. Kennedy's Remedy for Kidney and Liver Cure
Hostetter's Stomach Bitters for Ailments Peculiar to Women

1963   The village of Chatham (Alger County) incorporated.

24   1974   MEMORABLE HIT

Al Kaline doubled in the fourth inning in a game between Baltimore and Detroit at Baltimore and became only the twelfth player in major-league history to get three-thousand hits. Kaline finished the season and his career with 3,007 hits.

1965 TIGER GAMES NUMBERED

The Tigers celebrated their 10,000th American League game by losing in ten innings to Cleveland 3-2 at Detroit.

1928 FANS STAY HOME IN DROVES

In their final game of the season, the Detroit Tigers beat the Boston Red Sox 8-0 before 404 fans, the smallest crowd ever to watch a game at Detroit.

1830 GRUESOME ENTERTAINMENT

Stephen G. Simmons, who had murdered his wife in a drunken fury, was hanged at Detroit. Officials had erected bleachers for the nearly 1,200 spectators who attended, and a military band provided music. As a result of the carnival-like atmosphere, public opinion began turning against executions, and in 1846, Michigan became the first state to abolish capital punishment for murder. (See May 4.)

25 1926 DETROIT GETS PRO HOCKEY

A group of Detroit businessmen purchased a National Hockey League franchise and imported the Victoria Cougars of the Western Canada League to represent the motor city. The team was renamed the Falcons in 1930 and the Red Wings in 1933.

1879 UNIQUE PARK CREATED

The city of Detroit paid $200,000 to several private owners and purchased Belle Isle to, as the *Free Press* reported, "insure a magnificent park to Detroit for all time to come."

1849 A FAIR BEGINNING

The nation's first state fair, then called the Fair Michigan State Agricultural Society, began at Detroit and has been held annually since.

26 1963 NEWEST COLLEGE OPENS

Registrations for the first freshman class were taken at Grand Valley State College (Allendale), Michigan's first separate, four-year, state-supported liberal-arts college to open in sixty years.

1963 WILD ELEPHANT ON RAMPAGE IN LANSING

A 3000-pound elephant broke loose from a parking-lot act at a Lansing shopping center and, while being chased by a crowd of thousands, bulled through the front window of a department store, crashed up and down the aisles, then cut a two-mile swath of destruction and confusion through nearby residential neighborhoods. After two futile hours of trying to capture the animal, police finally killed "Little Rajjee" with rifles.

1948   TIGERS CROWD THEM IN

The largest Tiger Stadium single-game crowd in history, 57,888, watched Cleveland-pitcher Bob Feller hurl a five-hit 4-1 victory over Detroit.

1896   MSU PLAYS FIRST GAME

The Michigan Agricultural College football team, in its first scheduled game, beat nearby Lansing High School 10-0.

27 1962   MICHIGAN ENTERS THE NUCLEAR AGE

At Big Rock Point on the shores of Lake Michigan near Charlevoix, a button was pressed that started a controlled chain reaction in the world's first high-power density boiling-water nuclear reactor for generating electricity. A month later, the facility, Michigan's first nuclear power plant and only the fifth in the country, began producing commercial electricity for Consumers Power customers.

1950   LOUIS ATTEMPTS COMEBACK

A year and a half after announcing his retirement as the world's longest-reigning heavyweight champion, Joe Louis attempted to regain his title but lost a fifteen-round decision to Ezzard Charles at New York City. (See also March 1, May 23, June 22 and June 25.)

MICH-AGAIN'S SEPTEMBER

1913 CURE FOR CRIME

The warden of Jackson prison, in commenting about new medical equipment received at his facility, said that he would soon, "by the use of surgery and proper remedies for diseases which are known to make men criminals," be able to cure his inmates of their criminal tendencies.

28 **1973 BREWING ERA ENDS**

The Bosch Brewing Company (Houghton), the last of the Upper Peninsula's twenty-two breweries, closed and ended a 99-year industry that was interrupted only by Prohibition.

1971 PAVING THE WAY

Brooks Products, Incorporated (Holland), resurfaced its 50,000-square-foot parking area with "glassphalt" which made the area the nation's first to be paved with the new mixture of recycled crushed glass and asphalt.

1970 LAWYERS' DRESS APPROVED

Chief Justice of the Michigan Supreme Court Thomas E. Brennan ruled that it was acceptable for female lawyers to wear pantsuits in court.

1887 INTERNATIONAL-SPORTS ADMINISTRATOR BORN

Avery Brundage, U.S. Olympic Committee chairman from 1929 to 1953, was born at Detroit.

1806 GOVERNOR BORN

Alpheus Felch, Michigan's fifth governor, was born at Limerick, Maine. Felch served for a little more than a year, January 1846 to March 1847, then resigned after being elected to the U.S. Senate.

29 **1975 FIRST BLACK BROADCASTERS**

Michigan's first black-owned-and-operated television station, WGPR-TV, channel 62 (Detroit), went on the air for the first time.

1926 MISDEMEANOR LEADS TO MURDER

A deer hunter shot and killed two game wardens who had caught him hunting out of season near Gwinn. Roy Nunn, 46, was convicted of the murders of the first two Michigan game wardens ever killed in the line of duty and spent the remaining twenty-two years of his life in prison.

1844   MICHIGAN COMMISSIONED.

The *U.S.S. Michigan*, the first iron warship built for the U.S. Navy, was commissioned. The sixteen-gun steamer patroled the Great Lakes until 1911 when she was decommissioned, then during World War I went back into service as a training ship.

30 1981   DELUGE WASHES LOWER MICHIGAN

A thick band of storms swept across lower Michigan from Grand Rapids to Detroit dropping as-much-as-nine inches of water on some parts of the state. The storm wiped out more-than-$5 million in crops, drowned $1 million worth of cars at a Farmington Hills dealership, knocked out power to 100,000 residents, and submerged homes and businesses.

1977   MILITARY BASE CLOSES

Brief ceremonies ended nearly twenty-five years of air force presence at Kincheloe Air Force Base near Sault Ste. Marie. Three months later, the state converted part of the base, built in 1941 to defend the Soo locks, to a medium-security state prison.

OCTOBER

1 1973   BLAMELESS ACCIDENTS

A "no-fault" insurance law went into effect that required insurance companies to immediately pay their insured drivers' medical claims without waiting to determine accident blame.

1971   30-AND-OUT BEGINS

A retirement plan that allowed auto workers with thirty years of service to retire at age fifty-eight with $500-per-month pension went into effect. Only about five thousand of the 35,000 UAW members eligible at Ford, General Motors, and Chrysler left at the first opportunity.

1967   TITHING TO THE STATE

Michigan's first state income tax, 2.6 percent on individual incomes, 5.67 percent on corporate profits, and seven percent on banks and other financial institutions, went into effect.

1934   GRADES ELIMINATED

Olivet College became the nation's first college to dispense with the normal system of credits, hours, points and grades. Instead, the college required candidates for bachelor's degrees to pass a preliminary and a final exam and have at least three years of instruction.

1928   ACTOR BORN

George Peppard was born at Detroit. Peppard had several lead roles in films such as *Breakfast At Tiffany's* (1961), *The Carpetbaggers* (1964), and *The Blue Max* (1966), but was then shifted into routine thrillers and westerns before finding his way to televisions' popular "The A-Team" series.

1859   LEGALLY EDUCATED

The University of Michigan started a law school, the first in Michigan.

1839 FIRST FAIR FAILS

Michigan's first agricultural fair was scheduled to take place at Ann Arbor. But the man in charge made no preparations and forgot to show up, only two exhibitors arrived, and Ann Arbor residents totally ignored the event.

1836 RAILROAD OPENS WITH HORSE POWER

The Erie and Kalamazoo Railroad, Michigan's first functioning railroad and the first in the country to be built west of the Allegheny Mountains, began operating. The train, whose cars were drawn by horses at a top speed of ten miles per hour, ran thirty-three miles between Adrian and Toledo.

2 1975 RAISING THE ROOF

Nine blowers running for nearly three hours inflated, for the first time, the teflon-coated, fiberglass-fabric roof over the Pontiac Silverdome. The air-supported roof, which covers ten acres and weighs two-hundred tons, is the world's largest.

1971 COLLEGE RUSHING RECORD SET

Central Michigan University running-back Jesse Lakes (Flint), by gaining 185 yards in twenty-eight carries in his team's 21-6 victory over Indiana State, became the first Michigan college-football player to ever gain over three-thousand career rushing yards. Lakes ended his college career later that season with a total of 3,639 rushing yards.

1961 BREAK A LEG

The Fisher Theatre (Detroit), one of the very few new legitimate playhouses built in the country since the depression, held its opening night by staging a $400,000 world-premier musical, "The Gay Life."

1853   BREAKING TRADITION
    The *Detroit Free Press* became the first Michigan newspaper to regularly issue Sunday-morning editions.

3 1939   SPECIAL SALT PUSHED
    The state health department, in a renewed campaign to reduce goiter, distributed leaflets to all schoolchildren advising their parents to use iodized salt. Health-department officials felt that the state's first campaign, begun fifteen years before when a survey showed that as many as 64% of Michigan schoolchildren suffered from goiter, needed reviving because a new generation of parents were unaware of the dangers of goiter and the advantages of iodized salt.

1913   FATAL FALL
    A 27-year-old Laingsburg stunt man rose in a balloon over the Alpena County Fairgrounds, parachuted out, but became entangled in the chute's ropes and drowned after landing in the Thunder Bay River.

4 1818   RELIGIOUS INSTRUCTION BEGINS
    Michigan's first Protestant Sunday School, founded by members of various Protestant denominations, began at Detroit.

1641   CHRISTIANITY REACHES MICHIGAN
    Only twenty-one years after the landing of the Mayflower at Plymouth, Massachusetts, Fathers Isaac Jogues and Charles Raymbault, French missionaries from the Christian Island Mission on Georgian Bay, made contact with Chippewa Indians at the rapids that connect Lake Superior to Lake Huron. After conducting the first Christian religious services ever held in Michigan, the missionaries named the spot Sault de Sainte Marie (Saint Mary's Rapids), then returned to Canada.

5 1979   SCORELESS SCORING RECORD
    The Big Bay de Noc high school football team lost to Bark River Harris 46-0, their last in a string of fourteen consecutive shutout losses during which opponents had outscored Big Bay a national record 774-0.

1861 FORMER GOVERNOR DIES

Kingsley S. Bingham, Michigan governor 1855-58, died of apoplexy at Green Oak (Livingston County). At the conclusion of his second term as the nation's first Republican governor, Bingham served in the U.S. Senate until his sudden death. (See also December 16.)

1852 NORMAL CEREMONY HELD

The Michigan State Normal School at Ypsilanti was dedicated as the state's first college established to train teachers. Later the school changed its name to Eastern Michigan University.

1835 MICHIGAN GETS FIRST CONSTITUTION

Voters, by an overwhelming majority of 6,752 to 1,374, approved Michigan's first state constitution. The constitution created a bicameral legislature (House and Senate), and specified that state officials, with the exception of governor, lieutenant governor, representatives and senators, be appointed.

6 1975 LIONS CROWD THEM IN

The largest crowd in Detroit Lion history, 80-642, watched their team lose to Dallas 36-10 in the regular-season home-opener at the Pontiac Silverdome.

1972 PICTURE-PERFECT PARK

Pictured Rocks National Lakeshore, 73,653 acres of massive, multicolored-rock formations, sand dunes, beaches, and forests near Munising, was officially dedicated.

1833 DETROIT BECOMES A CATHEDRAL CITY

Frederick Rese was consecrated at Cincinnati as the first bishop of the Diocese of Detroit, Michigan's first Roman Catholic diocese.

7 1935 TIGERS WIN FIRST SERIES

The Detroit Tigers won their first-ever world championship with a 4-3 seventh-game victory over the Chicago Cubs at Briggs Stadium. (See also October 10.)

1934 RECORD BOOT

Glenn Presnell kicked the Detroit Lions' longest field goal, 54 yards, in a game at Green Bay.

8 1938   BRIDGING THE ST. CLAIR
The Blue Water Bridge, crossing the St. Clair River between Port Huron and Sarnia, was formally dedicated. (See also June 24.)

1871   FIRE RAZES LOWER MICHIGAN
On the same day the famous Chicago fire began, fires started along Michigan's western shoreline and, fanned by high winds, quickly swept across the state to Lake Huron. Holland and most of Manistee were destroyed, students at the Michigan Agricultural College struggled heroically to save Lansing, and in the Thumb District ninety percent of the homes were destroyed.

1846   GRAVE BUSINESS BEGINS
Elmwood Cemetery (Detroit), Michigan's oldest active graveyard, opened.

1805   FIRST WELFARE LAW ENACTED
A new Michigan-territorial law directed that, on notice to three justices of the peace that a person was poor and incapable of self-support, the justices were authorized to arrange for the support of such person at a cost not exceeding twenty-five cents per day.

9 1971   THE STRANGE TRAIL
A 31-year-old Pontiac ex-convict, by holding a cocked gun to a flight-attendant's head, hijacked a plane at Detroit's Metro Airport

and forced it to fly to Cuba. The Eastern Airlines flight, with thirty-three passengers, six crew members and five attendants, landed in Cuba, uniformed men escorted the skyjacker away, and the plane and all passengers then flew to safety in Miami.

Four years later, South Haven police arrested a man suspected of killing one of their officers and, during a routine FBI-identification check, were shocked to discover that their suspect was the hijacker. The man was convicted of both the police-officer's murder and the hijacking but never revealed how he got out of Cuba or what he was doing in South Haven.

1935 CAPTIVE AUDIENCE

The Ionia Reformatory became the only prison in the world, at the time, to make radio service available to every inmate. Convict-laborers had run wires to each cell in the prison, and inmates who paid twenty-five cents a month for the privilege could plug headphone jacks into one of the three outlets, each of which was connected to one of the three major broadcasting networks.

1782 MICHIGAN STATESMAN BORN

Lewis Cass, Michigan-territorial governor, U.S. secretary of war, ambassador to France, U.S. senator, presidential candidate, and U.S. secretary of state, was born at Exeter, New Hampshire. (See also March 6, May 29 and June 17.)

10 1976 KING RUNS AGAINST PATRIOTS

Detroit Lion running-back Horace King carried the football a club-record thirty-two times and rushed for one-hundred yards in a 30-10 win over New England at the Pontiac Silverdome.

1968 TIGERS WIN THIRD SERIES

Mickey Lolich became the first left-hander to pitch three complete-game World Series wins, and the Tigers won their third world championship, beating the St. Louis Cardinals 4-1 in game seven at St. Louis.

1945 TIGERS WIN SECOND CHAMPIONSHIP

The Detroit Tigers won their second World Series, beating Chicago 9-3 in game seven at Chicago.

1967   Norton Township (Muskegon County) incorporated as the city of Norton Shores.
VILLAGES INCORPORATED THIS DAY
1870   Morley (Mecosta County).
1892   Lake Ann (Benzie County)
1898   Stephenson (Menominee County) which incorporated as a city August 27, 1968.

11
1974 WHEELS GO FLAT
The infant World Football League cut the Detroit Wheels from the remainder of its 1974 schedule when the Detroit franchise, with $2 million in debts, declared bankruptcy. (See also January 22.)

1973 PERSONALIZED PLATES PRODUCED
The first batch of "vanity" license plates emerged from the drying oven in the license-plate plant at Southern Michigan Prison (Jackson). More-than-3,500 car owners, including "Big Ed" and "Big Erv," ordered the special plates at an additional $25 cost.

1966 MAJOR BANK GOES BROKE
In a secret late-night court session, a Detroit judge declared the Detroit Public Bank insolvent, and Michigan experienced the largest bank failure since the days of the great depression. Within a few hours, however, the Federal Deposit Insurance Corporation sold all assets and liabilities to the larger Bank of the Commonwealth which opened the bank the next day without officially losing a day of business or a customer's dollar.

1910 NO NUMBER — NO GLORY
A *Michigan Daily* editorial strongly requested that University of Michigan football players be identified during future games by sewing numbers on their jerseys. But Coach Fielding H. Yost vetoed the idea, saying he feared it would interfere with teamwork by singling out the efforts of individuals, and University of Michigan players were not assigned numbers until the 1916 season.

VILLAGES INCORPORATED THIS DAY
1858   Corunna (Shiawassee County) which incorporated as a city March 12, 1869.
1898   Suttons Bay (Leelanau County).

12
1973 NIXON NAMES FORD
President Richard M. Nixon, after the resignation of Spiro T. Agnew who had pleaded guilty to income-tax evasion, nominated Michigan's Gerald R. Ford to replace the vice-president.

1908 TIGERS WIN FIRST SERIES GAME
The Detroit Tigers beat the Chicago Cubs 8-3 at Chicago to win their first World Series game since joining the American League but lost the series four games to one.

1852 TEACHERS ORGANIZE
The Michigan State Teacher's Association, forerunner of the Michigan Education Association, organized.

VILLAGES INCORPORATED THIS DAY
1863   Charlotte (Eaton County) which incorporated as a city March 29, 1871.

1869   Ithaca (Gratiot County) which incorporated as a city January 12, 1960.
1893   Bear Lake (Manistee County).

13 1972   THE UDDER LAW PREVAILS

A Federal Appeals Court ruled that a lenient federal law preempted Michigan's strict standards governing the contents of hot dogs and luncheon meats. The U.S. Supreme Court rejected Michigan's appeal of the ruling, and for the first time, hot dogs and lunch meat sold in Michigan could contain ears, lips, eyes, lungs, udders, snouts, spleens and bladders.

1921   LICENSED TO BROADCAST

WWJ (Detroit) became Michigan's first licensed radio station.

1853   BLOOMER SPEAKS

Mrs. Amelia Bloomer, originator of Bloomer undergarments, lectured at Detroit's Firemen's Hall on the subject of "Women's Rights."

VILLAGES INCORPORATED THIS DAY
1863   Cassopolis (Cass County) and Dowagiac (Cass County) which incorporated as a city March 26, 1877.
1885   Perry (Shiawassee County) which incorporated as a city March 9, 1964.

14 1969   TOP BLACK EDUCATOR

Dr. John W. Porter was unanimously selected by the state board of education as state superintendent of public instruction and became the nation's first black to hold such a post.

1922   AIRSPEED RECORD SET

At a national airplane meet at Selfridge Field (Mount Clemens), Lt. Lester James Maitland flew an airplane faster-than-two-hundred miles per hour for the first time in aviation history.

1919   VETERANS CONVENE

At Grand Rapids, the Michigan American Legion held its first state convention. (See also May 10.)

1845   SCIENTIST DIES

State geologist Douglass Houghton, who extensively surveyed and mapped much of Michigan, drowned in a Lake Superior storm while working near Eagle River.

1954   The city of Keego Harbor (Oakland County) incorporated.
VILLAGES INCORPORATED THIS DAY
1868   Wayland (Allegan County) which incorporated as a city May 18, 1965.
1870   Douglas (Allegan County).
1872   Evart (Osceola County) which incorporated as a city March 14, 1938.
1884   Morrice (Shiawassee County).
1890   Kingsley (Grand Traverse County).
1901   Fairgrove (Tuscola County).
1903   Northport (Leelanau County).

15

1966   PARK CREATED

President Lyndon B. Johnson signed a bill that established the Pictured Rocks National Lakeshore along thirty-five miles of Lake Superior shoreline from Munising to Grand Marais. (See also October 6.)

1951   TV STATION BROADCASTS INTERNATIONALLY

WWJ-TV (Detroit) sent its mobile unit and announcer Bud Lynch to Government Dock (Windsor, Ontario) and, in the world's first international-television broadcast, featured live coverage of an informal reception given Philip, Duke of Edinburgh, and Princess Elizabeth of Great Britain. Four months later, Elizabeth became Queen of England.

1730   DETROIT FOUNDER DIES

Antoine de la Mothe Cadillac, founder of Detroit, died at Castelsarrasin, France.

VILLAGES INCORPORATED THIS DAY
1895   Central Lake (Antrim County) and Custer (Mason County).
1897   Elkton (Huron County).
1898   Caseville (Huron County).
1902   Pigeon (Huron County).

16

1981   SCHOOL'S OUT

After three back-to-back millage defeats, the Alpena School District ran out of cash, declared itself broke, and closed. The first-and-only school-district closing in Michigan history shut down fourteen schools and sent 6,800 students home for two weeks when a renewal millage finally passed.

1970   BORDER-TO-BORDER WALK

Eric Ryback (Belleville) at age eighteen set foot on the Mexican border and became the first man to hike the entire Pacific Crest trail, 2,313 mountainous miles from Washington through Oregon and California to Mexico.

1966   LONGEST BOMB

During the fourth quarter of a Lion 45-14 loss at Baltimore, Detroit quarterback Karl Sweetan took the snap at his own one-yard line, dropped back into his end zone, and threw a pass to Pat Studstill. Studstill gathered in the throw on the dead run at the Lion forty-five and completed the National Football League's longest passing play (ninety-nine yards) by running for a touchdown.

1954   LIONS FINISH STREAK

The Detroit Lions beat the Baltimore Colts 35-0 at Detroit, their last win in a club-record ten-consecutive-game-winning streak. The streak began November 7, 1953, and included six regular-season games in 1953, the 1953 world-championship game, and three regular-season games in 1954. On October 24, 1954, San Francisco ended the streak, beating the Lions 37-31 at San Francisco.

1946   HOWE DO YOU DO

In his first National Hockey League appearance, an eighteen-year-old rookie named Gordie Howe scored Detroit's second goal as the Wings tied Toronto 3-3 in their Olympia season-opening game. Howe continued to play professional hockey for an unbelievable thirty-two seasons in two leagues and set more than a dozen unbroken NHL records. (See also March 12, November 10 and November 27.)

VILLAGES INCORPORATED THIS DAY
1867   Bellevue (Eaton County).
1879   Webberville (Ingham County).
1895   Empire (Leelanau County).
1906   Montgomery (Hillsdale County).

17

1980   CRASHING STANDS END CHEERS

With a sound like popping firecrackers, bleachers in the East Lansing High School gym leaned forward from the wall and collapsed, injuring, none seriously, thirty-three students and three teachers who were standing on them during a pep rally.

1909   MADE IN MICHIGAN

Edwin Elton Smith (Traverse City) soared six-hundred feet at an altitude of fifty feet and completed the first successful flight of the first glider ever built in Michigan. Smith flew the craft, built by Charles Augustine (Traverse City), at a farm near Arburtus Lake a few miles out of Traverse City.

1899   THREE OAKS GETS A CANNON

At the village of Three Oaks, President William McKinley dedicated a cannon captured by Admiral George Dewey during the Spanish-American War's battle of Manila. Three Oaks had won the war trophy by raising the largest per-capita contribution of any U.S. community for a memorial to the men of the *Maine* sunk in Havana Harbor in 1898. (See February 15.)

1900   The village of Elk Rapids (Antrim County) incorporated.

18

1979   UNIQUE BASKETBALL GAME PLAYED

When the Detroit Pistons beat the New York Nicks 129-115 at the Pontiac Silverdome, it marked the first time in NBA history that teams composed entirely of black players competed against each other in a regular season game.

1978   HOLLY GETS A FIRST-DAY ISSUE

The nation's 1978 Christmas stamp, featuring a child on a hobby-horse, was issued at Holly, Michigan.

1971   DEATH RACE

Bill Muncey (Royal Oak), popular hydroplane-racing figure with Detroit fans and the sport's all-time leader in victories, died when his boat flipped backwards at about 170 miles per hour during a championship race at Acapulco, Mexico.

VILLAGES INCORPORATED THIS DAY
1866   Saline (Washtenaw County) which incorporated as a city January 15, 1931.
1870   Clayton (Lenawee County).
1895   Forestville (Sanilac County) and Woodland (Barry County).

19 1979   COFFIN BOTTOMS OUT

As the widow, friends and relatives accompanied the casket of a Brighton man to its grave, the bottom of the casket suddenly came loose and, according to a subsequent lawsuit, the body "surrounded by rags, newspapers, shredded paper, and what appeared to be panty hose, rolled onto the ground."

1918   MICHIGAN'S FIRST CHURCHLESS SUNDAY

At 12:01 a.m., following a conference of mayors and health officers of fifty Michigan cities, Governor Albert Sleeper issued a statewide order closing theatres, movie halls, churches, and all other public places for the remainder of the weekend in an effort to contain a severe Spanish flu epidemic.

1875   FORMER SENATOR PICKED FOR INTERIOR

Zachariah Chandler, former U.S. senator and major force in Michigan Republican politics, became secretary of the interior in the Cabinet of President Ulysses S. Grant. Chandler, who the year before had been defeated in an attempt at reelection to a fourth consecutive term to the U.S. Senate, used the Cabinet position to retain his political base, came back to regain his senate seat by appointment in 1879, but died of a stroke a few months later.

VILLAGES INCORPORATED THIS DAY
1871   Vicksburg (Kalamazoo County).
1899   Maybee (Monroe County) and Montrose (Genesee County).
1901   Mesick (Wexford County).

20 1983   MICHIGAN WOMAN HONORED

Sojourner Truth, a former slave and advocate of women's rights and human freedom, was the first of seventeen women to be inducted into a new Michigan Women's Hall of Fame located at the

Michigan Women's Historical Center (Lansing).

1921   DOWN THE DRAIN — NOT THE HATCH

Under court order, federal officers poured the contents of 1,500 confiscated bottles of liquor into the sewers at the Detroit federal building.

1872   GOVERNOR BORN

Fred W. Green, Michigan governor 1927-30, was born at Manistee, Michigan. The former Ionia mayor showed little interest for any reforms and, with the exception of expanding the state highway program, little was done during his two terms. (See also November 30.)

1861   FORMER GOVERNOR DIES

William Woodbridge, Michigan's second governor, died at Detroit. Woodbridge had served only half of his two-year term as governor when, in 1841, he resigned to become a U.S. senator. The Whig served six years as senator then retired to his Detroit farm where he resided until his death. (See also August 20.)

VILLAGES INCORPORATED THIS DAY
1903   Grayling (Crawford County) which incorporated as a city March 11, 1935.
1908   Walkerville (Oceana County).

21 1970   MICHIGAN GETS THIRD NATIONAL PARK

President Richard M. Nixon placed his signature on a bill authorizing establishment of the Sleeping Bear Dunes National Lakeshore (Leelanau County), and the beautiful beach of shifting sands joined Isle Royale and Pictured Rocks National Lakeshore in the national-park system.

1929   UNIQUE MUSEUM OPENS

The Edison Institute (Dearborn), composed of Greenfield Village (an outdoor exhibit of more-than-a-hundred historic buildings), the Ford Museum (a vast collection of automobile-industry artifacts), and a school (a learn-by-doing education center), was officially dedicated. President Herbert Hoover attended the daylong ceremonies, and Thomas A. Edison reenacted his successful lighting of the incandescent lamp fifty years earlier.

1842   STATE POET BORN

Will Carleton, author of "Over the Hill to the Poorhouse," was born on a sixty-acre farm two miles east of Hudson (Lenawee County). *Harper's Weekly* once said Carleton was one of America's "most-popular . . . poets and the one whose writings have been more widely read and appreciated than those of any poet since the days of Whittier and Longfellow." Carleton was so popular that the state decreed his birthday as an official holiday.

22 1979 MAN DIES — UNIQUE TREATMENT APPROVED

A Beaverton man who was the first in Michigan to admit to illegally smoking marijuana to ease the pain of his cancer treatments died. Only hours later, Lt. Governor James Brickley, in Governor Milliken's absence, signed a bill legalizing the drug for medical purposes.

1955 MARKING TIME

The first official marker in the Michigan Historical Commission's program to register and mark state and local historic sites was dedicated at Michigan State University (East Lansing). The Registered Historic Site No. 1 commemorates the founding of MSU, the first agricultural college in the nation. (See May 13.)

1907 CONSTITUTION COMPOSED

Ninety-six delegates assembled at Lansing to write Michigan's third constitution. A year later voters approved their work, basically a rewrite of the 1850 constitution (see November 5), nearly two-to-one.

1898 FIRST TO FLY?

Augustus Moore Herring (Benton Harbor) may have flown the world's first airplane five years before the Wright brothers' famous flight. A reporter for the *Benton Harbor Evening News* reported the brief flight from Silver Beach (St. Joseph) but did not take an in-flight picture of the motorized chanute glider. In the absence of any conclusive proof that Herring's plane left the ground under its own power, Orville and Wilbur Wright were given credit for the first manned flight in 1903.

1864   The village of Chelsea (Washtenaw County) incorporated.

23 1977 GETTING HIS KICKS

Detroit Lion punter Ray Williams kicked a club-record eight times in a 28-7 loss at San Francisco.

1965 LOCOMOTIVE RETIRES

The last steam-operating locomotive in Michigan, owned by the Canadian National Railroad, traveled from Durand to Detroit on its final run.

1949 RECORD FOOTBALL THEFTS

Detroit Lion defensive-back Don Dole intercepted a club-record four passes against the Chicago Cardinals during a game at Chicago won by Detroit 24-17.

VILLAGES INCORPORATED THIS DAY
1896   Britton (Lenawee County).
1908   Kent City (Kent County).

24

1941   UNSNARLING TRAFFIC PROBLEMS

Michigan became the first state in the union to employ a full-time traffic expert who, at an annual salary of $7,800, centralized surveys, education, safety and other traffic-related functions previously performed by at least four other state agencies.

1901   OVER A BARREL

Annie Edson Taylor, a Bay City schoolteacher, became the first person to survive a barrel ride over Niagara Falls. She took the plunge in a self-designed, wooden barrel made by a Bay City cooperage.

25

1977   DETROIT GETS SOCCED AGAIN

Nine years after the Detroit Cougars folded (see September 23), the North American Soccer League granted another franchise to Detroit, and the team, called the Detroit Express, began play the following spring. (See April 1.)

1971   TRAGIC PLAY

With a minute left in a game against the Chicago Bears, 28-year-old Detroit Lions wide-receiver Chuck Hughes collapsed on the field and died less than an hour later of a heart attack brought on by hardening of the arteries.

1924   FIRST TY GAME

WWJ radio (Detroit) with Ty Tyson at the microphone, broadcast the first radio play-by-play of a University of Michigan football game. The broadcast generated so many ticket requests for Michigan's next game that Coach Fielding H. Yost gave WWJ permission to broadcast all home games.

1889   PENINSULAS CONNECTED

Michigan's Upper and Lower Peninsulas were joined at the Straits of Mackinac by a submarine telephone cable.

1825   WATER ROUTE COMPLETED

New York state's 360-mile Erie Canal, connecting Lake Erie to New York's Hudson River, officially opened, and for the first time, eastern settlers had easy access to Michigan and Michigan products could be cheaply transported to the East.

26

1981   MEEECHIGAN ANNOUNCER DIES

The radio voice of University of Michigan football, 61-year-old Bob Ufer, who enthusiastically and with no hint of impartiality broadcast 364 University of Michigan football games, died of cancer.

1972   MICHIGAN'S WORST DRIVER PUNISHED

A 34-year-old Detroit phonograph salesman had his driver's license revoked — for twenty-one years — and was sentenced to ninety days in the Detroit House of Corrections for amassing more-than-one-hundred driving points, the most in state history according to the Michigan secretary of state. Under Michigan law, drivers automatically lose their licenses if they accumulate only twelve points, assessed for serious moving violations, in two years.

1887   ARCHITECTS ORGANIZE

The Michigan State Association of Architects, Michigan's first architectural society and forerunner of the Michigan Chapter, American Institute of Architects, was founded.

1818   Mackinac County was created.

27

1974   EXECUTIONER DIES

Ira M. Smith, Michigan's last hangman and Michigan's only hangman since it achieved statehood, died at Midland. The former Midland County sheriff had pulled the lever at the 1938 hanging of Anthony Chebatoris. (See July 8.)

1975   FIRST BIG-MONEY BOWLER

Earl Anthony (Tacoma, Washington) won $8,000 at the Buzz Fazio Open at Battle Creek and became the first bowler to earn more than $100,000 in one year from tournaments. The Battle Creek win was Anthony's seventh PBA victory and brought his earnings to $100,890.

1972   GET THE LEAD OUT

Pontiac became the first Michigan city to ban lead-based paint which can cause brain damage if eaten by children. The Pontiac ordinance forbid use or sale of lead-based paint and required corrective action on existing homes.

1857   LADIES ONLY

The cornerstone for the Female Seminary, Michigan's first and the Midwest's third school for women, was laid at Kalamazoo. The high school or "finishing" school, sponsored by the Presbyterian church, didn't open until 1867 but then ran for forty years until the church withdrew support in favor of coeducational Alma College.

1811   FIRST GOVERNOR BORN

The State of Michigan's first governor, Stevens T. Mason, was born at Loudon County, Virginia. Mason came to Michigan in 1830 when President Andrew Jackson appointed his father, John Mason, as the secretary of the Michigan territory. Within a year, Stevens T. Mason, at the age of nineteen became acting territorial governor and, five years later, was elected as the State of Michigan's first governor. (See also January 4.)

28 1970   LAST STREAK WIN

The Detroit Pistons won the last game in a club-record nine-straight-game-winning streak beating Baltimore 109-103 at Baltimore. Three days later, the New York Knicks ended the streak, which had begun October 14, by beating the Pistons 107-89 at New York.

1942   DEADLY CRASH

A train crashed into a bus that had stalled at a Detroit crossing killing sixteen children and factory workers and injuring twenty more.

1912   PLANE ELOPED

Art Smith and Aimee Cour left Fort Wayne, Indiana, in a biplane, flew seventy-five miles with only one stop for gasoline, then crash-landed on the campus of Hillsdale College. Despite their injuries, the couple made their way to a Presbyterian church where the pastor completed the nation's first aerial elopement.

VILLAGES INCORPORATED THIS DAY
1902   River Rouge (Wayne County) which incorporated as a city March 14, 1921, and Ecorse (Wayne County) which incorporated as a city September 15, 1941.
1919   Marysville (St. Clair County) which incorporated as a city March 3, 1924.

29 1982   FRANKLY A HOAX

Hygrade Food Products Corporation (Southfield) halted production of frankfurters at its Livonia plant and ordered its products removed from store shelves after razor blades were reportedly found in two of the company's hot dogs. Several days later, the two victims admitted they had planted the blades themselves.

1950   MANY HAPPY RETURNS

Wally Triplett of the Detroit Lions returned four kickoffs for a NFL-record 294 yards, but in spite of his feat, the Lions were trounced by Los Angeles 65-24 at Los Angeles.

1920 MONEY HUNGRY

In preparing the state budget for 1921, the Michigan budget director announced that he had found "none of (our) institutions backward in asking for needs," and that only the game, fish and forest department had not asked for an increase in funding.

1829 Barry, Berrien, Branch, Calhoun, Cass, Eaton, Hillsdale, Ingham, and Van Buren counties were created.
1885 The village of Lake Linden (Houghton County) incorporated.

30 1971 ON PINS AND NEEDLES

A new state law went into effect making it a felony to place pins, needles, razor blades, or other harmful objects inside food with the intent to harm the consumer.

1969 RUSSIAN SPACEMEN TOUR DETROIT

Two Soviet cosmonauts, Maj. Gen. Georgy Beregovoy and Konstantin Feoktistov, as part of a national tour, arrived in Detroit for a whirlwind tour of social events and sight-seeing.

31 1962 SPANNING THE SOO

The $20-million International Bridge, connecting Sault Ste. Marie, Michigan, and Sault Ste. Marie, Ontario, over the St. Mary's River and Soo locks and canal, officially opened.

1926 GREAT PERFORMER DIES

After an October-23rd performance in Montreal, a college student, thinking that Harry Houdini had flexed his muscles, hit the great escape artist full force in the stomach. Though his appendix had ruptured, Houdini traveled to Detroit, performed, collapsed offstage, and died of infection on Halloween night in room No. 401, Grace Hospital (Detroit).

1825 GOVERNOR BORN

Charles Croswell, Michigan governor 1877-80, was born at Newberg, New York. During his two terms, the state House of Correction at Ionia and Eastern Asylum at Pontiac opened. (See also December 13.)

NOVEMBER

1 1979   BIRTHDAYS LICENSED
    A new automobile license-plate law took effect that changed the deadline for purchasing plates to car owners' birthdays. Previously, all Michigan license plates had expired on the same date.

1974   DON'T CHEW
              ADVERTISE
    Barn advertising in Michigan became illegal and forty-seven barns, which displayed the illegal signs, mostly for chewing tobacco, were painted over at a cost to the taxpayers of $7,534.

1973   LONGEST EXPRESSWAY DONE
    Near West Branch, Governor William G. Milliken formally opened the final link of Michigan's longest freeway, 395-mile I-75, calling it the "crowning achievement of our highway network."

1966   CHRISTMAS STAMPS
    The U.S. Post Office issued a five-cent multicolored Christmas stamp featuring a Madonna and child at Christmas, Michigan.

1963   BORDER-TO-BORDER EXPRESSWAY
    A 22-mile segment of I-75 opened in the Upper Peninsula which per-

mitted driving from the Ohio border to Sault Ste. Marie on, what was then, the nation's longest toll-free four-lane expressway. Though I-75 itself was not completed for another ten years, drivers could use a nonstop 380-mile route composed of I-75, U.S. 23, U.S. 10, and U.S. 27.

1957   FIRST CROSSING

At 2:00 p.m., the Mackinac Bridge officially opened, and Chicago jazz-drummer Al Carter, driving a 1951 station wagon, made the first trip across the span.

1937   ONLY UNENCUMBERED CITY

The city of Kalamazoo paid a final bond installment and became the only city in the nation, 50,000-or-more population, at that time, to be free of debt.

1935   FIRST CENTURY COMMEMORATED

The U.S. Post Office released Michigan's centennial postage stamp, a three-cent purple stamp featuring the Michigan state seal, from Lansing as a first-day issue. A total of 176,962 "First-Day Covers" were mailed from Lansing, breaking all previous records.

1907   COLORED CANS REQUIRED

A state law went into effect mandating that all gasoline be sold and kept only in red cans.

1835   FIRST LAWMAKERS MAKE IT BRIEF

The first legislature of Michigan under state constitution convened at Detroit, met only one day, passed only seven laws, then adjourned until February 1, 1836.

1679   MIAMI BUILT AT ST. JOSEPH

French explorer Robert Cavalier de la Salle, after traveling by canoe from Green Bay, erected a fort at the mouth of the St. Joseph River at (present-day) St. Joseph. The wooden stockade, the first non-Indian post in the Lower Peninsula, was named Fort Miami. (See also March 20 and August 23.)

2

1977   RECORD FISH CATCH

Vernon Bauer caught a world-record three-pound, four-ounce round whitefish at Leland Harbor.

1976   VOTERS BAN THROWAWAYS

Unswayed by a million-dollar advertising blitz by beverage and bottling industries, Michigan voters overwhelmingly approved a ban on the sale of nonreturnable bottles and flip-top cans. The ban, which took effect November 3, 1978, was enacted to reduce litter and save energy and materials by recycling.

1954   YES TO VETS — NO TO BETS

Michigan voters approved an $80-million bonus to Korean War veterans but rejected legalization of bingo for charitable purposes.

1954   MICHIGAN SENDS FIRST BLACK TO CONGRESS

Charles Diggs, a licensed mortician and former state senator, was elected to the U.S. Congress as representative from the 13th district (Detroit). Diggs, Michigan's first black U.S. congressman, served for twenty-six years then resigned after being convicted on twenty-nine counts of payroll padding and mail fraud. (See also June 3.)

1920   FIRST LADY LAWMAKER

Eva M. Hamilton (Grand Rapids) was elected by a 8,872-vote majority to the state senate and became the first woman state legislator in Michigan history.

3

1972   MOTOR BAN LIFTED

Mackinac Island residents passed a law allowing snowmobiles to be driven in areas outside the state-park boundaries, and the machines became the first motor-driven vehicles on the island since 1949.

1970   RELATIVELY REPRESENTED

Rep. Lucille McCollough (Dearborn) won reelection to the Michigan House of Representatives, and her son, Patrick (Dearborn), won election to the state senate making them the first mother-son legislative team in the state's history.

1930   TUNNELING TO CANADA

The Detroit-Windsor tunnel, the world's first underwater vehicular tunnel to a foreign country, opened to traffic. From portal-to-portal, the tunnel measures nearly a mile with 2,200 feet of the roadway lying fifty feet below the Detroit River.

1926   MINE DISASTER

Fifty-one miners, working eight-hundred feet below the surface of the Barnes-Hecker iron mine near Ishpeming, died when a swamp bottom sank suddenly into the shaft and washed away the workers in a wall of mud and quicksand.

1913 UNINTENTIONAL FIRST NIGHT FLIGHT

Toward evening, William E. Scripps (Detroit) took off in a pontoon plane from the Detroit Motorboat Club for a brief flight over Detroit. But, while circling over Grand Circus Park, Scripps developed engine trouble, landed on the Detroit River, completed repairs at dusk, and set out to taxi the plane down the river and Lake St. Clair to the club. As it got darker, however, Scripps feared he might strike a boat so he took off and completed the nation's first night airplane flight by successfully landing back at the club.

1911 NEW AUTO DIVISION CREATED

William C. Durant organized the Chevrolet Motor Company. While still in control of General Motors (see September 16), Durant had personally financed Buick racing-car driver Louis Chevrolet, and when Chevrolet developed a six-cylinder car for production, Durant formed the new company.

VILLAGES INCORPORATED THIS DAY
1858   Lawton (Van Buren County).
1953   Franklin (Oakland County).

4 1979 MICHIGANIANS TAKEN HOSTAGE

Iranian militants overran the U.S.-embassy compound in Teheran and took fifty-two Americans, including four from Michigan, prisoner. The hostages endured a total of 444 days of despair, trauma, uncertainty, torture, and extreme mental stress before being released January 20, 1981.

1976 WING PUNISHED

Detroit Red Wings' defenseman Bryan "Bugsy" Watson, who had fractured the jaw of Chicago's Keith Magnuson in a hockey brawl during a late-October game, was suspended by NHL President Clarence Campbell for ten games, the longest suspension ever incurred by a Red Wing. Less than a month later the Wings traded Watson to Washington.

1952 MICHIGAN LADY NATION'S FIRST

Cora Brown (Detroit) was overwhelmingly elected to the Michigan senate and became the first black woman in any state senate.

1862 POLISH FIRST

Ludwik Wesolowski was elected as the Macomb County surveyor which made him, according to author Harry Milostan in *Enduring Poles*, the first person of Slavic extraction to become an elected official anywhere in the U.S.

1816   SPREADING THE WORD

Territorial Governor Lewis Cass, future congressman and governor William Woodbridge, and Protestant missionary John Monteith organized, at Detroit, Michigan's first Bible Society. During its first year the society, which sold Bibles and used the proceeds to distribute Bibles to those who couldn't afford them, received $146 but ceased to exist after 1820.

5 1974   GROCERIES AND MEDICINE TAX-FREE

Voters repealed the state's sales tax on food and drugs.

1968   OUTDOOR RECREATION EXPANDS

Increasingly congested conditions at Michigan's popular state parks led voters to approve a unique $100,000,000 bond issue to be used to provide more parks and other recreational facilities, especially in the inner-core areas of Detroit and other large cities.

1950   PASSING LAYNE

Detroit Lion quarterback Bobby Layne passed for a club-record 374 yards against the Chicago Bears at Detroit. Layne completed twenty-three of forty-five tosses but for only one touchdown in the Lions' 35-21 win.

1850   SECOND CONSTITUTION APPROVED

Michigan's second constitution was adopted by a vote of the people. The new constitution established the governor's salary at $1,000 and changed the secretary of state, state treasurer, supreme-court justice and other principal state officials from appointed to elected positions.

1968   The city of Romulus (Wayne County) incorporated.

6 1867   LADY PIPES UP

Mary Ann Seadorf (Byron Center) became Michigan's first licensed female plumber.

1965   WILD GOBBLER HUNT BEGINS

The first modern-day Michigan wild-turkey hunt began with some four-hundred hunters stalking about six hundred of the birds scattered throughout Allegan County. Eighty-two turkeys were killed during the nine-day season.

1861   MICHIGAN LADIES FIRST TO ASSIST

The nation's first Ladies Soldiers Aid Society organized at Detroit to supply comfort to Civil War soldiers at hospitals, camps and battlefields.

191

7 1972 SPRING FORWARD — FALL BACK

Michigan voters approved daylight saving time for the state which added an extra hour of daylight from the last Sunday in April to the last Sunday in October.

1873 GOVERNOR BORN

Alexander J. Groesbeck, Michigan governor 1921-26, was born at Warren Township, Michigan. During the former state attorney general's three consecutive two-year terms, he centralized the planning, financing, and construction of the state's highway system. (See also March 10.)

1707 FIRST CAUCASIAN EXECUTED

Detroit soldiers, under the order of their commandant, Cadillac, carried out the first legal execution of a white man in Michigan by bludgeoning a deserter to death.

8 1970 SPECIAL BOOT BEATS LIONS

Tom Dempsey of the New Orleans Saints kicked a NFL-record 63-yard field goal with two seconds left in the game to beat the Detroit Lions 19-17 at New Orleans. What made Dempsey's accomplishment even more remarkable was the fact that he was born without part of his right foot and kicked while wearing a special shoe.

1870 BLACKS GRANTED SUFFRAGE

Negroes voted for the first time in a Michigan state election.

1836 MICHIGAN SELECTS FIRST PRESIDENT

Michigan citizens voted, for the first time, in a U.S.-presidential election and helped place Martin Van Buren in the oval office.

1966   A portion of Taylor Township (Wayne County) incorporated as the city of Taylor.

9 1973 NINE-GAME SHUTOUT

The Saginaw Arthur Hill Lumberjacks high-school football team won their season's final game 64-0 and became the first Class A team in sixty years not to allow a single point during the season. Arthur Hill had out-scored their opponents 443-0 in rolling to a 9-0 record.

1913 LAKES STORM TAKES GREATEST TOLL

The most-devastating storm in Great Lakes history began with winds blowing at hurricane-force for sixteen straight hours. When the storm finally rolled eastward after three long days, it had sunk forty ships and killed 235 seamen.

1938   The village of Ellsworth (Antrim County) incorporated.

10

1975   RARE CLOSING

For only the third time in its eighteen-year history, the Mackinac Bridge closed when ninety-mile-per-hour winds whipped across the span. That same day, about one-hundred miles away on Lake Superior, the 587-foot-long *Edmund Fitzgerald* sank, and all twenty-nine crew members were lost.

1963   HOWE GREAT HE IS

During a 3-0 Red Wing victory over Montreal, Gordie Howe scored his 545th regular-season goal which made him the greatest goal-scorer in the history of the NHL. When Howe retired in 1980, he had scored 801 goals in the National Hockey League and another 270 in the World Hockey League. (See also March 12, October 16 and November 27.)

1929   AMBASSADOR DEDICATED

The Ambassador Bridge, linking Detroit and Windsor, Ontario, across the Detroit River, was dedicated. Four days later, the world's longest and grandest automobile bridge of its time, opened to traffic.

1923   FLAG DAY

The J. L. Hudson Company, as a beginning to their annual Thanksgiving Day parade, displayed, for the first time, the world's largest flag on the front of their Detroit headquarters. The company unfurled the ninety-by-123-foot American flag annually for twenty-six years, then replaced it with an even-bigger stars-and-stripes. (See June 14.)

1918   WAR TO END ALL WARS ENDS

Cities, towns and villages across Michigan held mass peace rallies to celebrate the end of World War I. Michigan had sent more-than-133,000 men into the armed forces during the war, nearly five thousand of whom didn't return.

12 1963   FIRST BLACK "BIG-THREE" DEALER

Edward Davis, 49, received a Detroit Chrysler-Plymouth franchise and became the first black in Michigan to become a big-three (General Motors, Ford, and Chrysler) new-car dealer.

1941   DESIGNER GENES

The nation's first heredity clinic, designed to research and counsel families on the effects of inherited characteristics, opened at the University of Michigan (Ann Arbor).

1922   ACTRESS BORN

Actress Kim Hunter was born at Detroit as Janet Cole. Hunter won a Best Supporting Actress Oscar in 1951 for her performance in *A Streetcar Named Desire*. During the late sixties and early seventies she also appeared in several "Planet of the Apes" films.

13 1972   STATE-SPONSORED GAMBLING BEGINS

In public ceremonies held at the state Capitol to mark the official beginning of the Michigan state lottery, Governor William G. Milliken bought the first ticket then donated it to the Michigan Historical Commission. (See also November 24.)

1966   GOT HIS KICKS

Field-goal kicker Garo Yepremian kicked a Detroit Lion club-record six field goals as his team beat the Minnesota Vikings 32-31 at Minnesota.

1907   VETS ISOLATED

The city of East Lansing furnished beds and food to one-hundred Michigan State University veterinary students who were quarantined in their classrooms for two weeks when three of their fellow students were diagnosed as having smallpox.

14 1977   FOR SPECIAL LADIES ONLY

The $10.5-million Huron Valley Women's Facility (Ypsilanti), the state's first prison built exclusively for women felons, was formally dedicated.

1914   FIRST DODGE MANUFACTURED

John and Horace Dodge, Niles natives, turned out the first Dodge brothers' automobile at a twenty-acre plant at Hamtramck. (See also May 30.)

1878   The village of Sand Lake (Kent County) incorporated.

15 1975   HUDSON SETS RECORD

The Hudson Tigers high-school football team won their seventy-second consecutive game, a national record, by beating Kalamazoo Hackett 24-14 in the MHSAA Class C state play-offs. Hudson's streak ended the next week when they lost to Ishpeming in the Class C finals 38-22.

1971   MAIL-ORDER LICENSES

Michigan drivers could, for the first time, order automobile license-plate tabs by mail.

1944   OFFENSIVE OUTBURST

In the third period of an NHL game at Toronto, the Detroit Red Wings scored three times and the Maple Leafs twice in only one minute, thirty-nine seconds to set a National Hockey League record for the fastest five goals by two teams. Detroit won the game 8-4.

16 1933   HITTING A HUNDRED

The general manager of the Pontiac Motor Division predicted that, in less than ten years, production automobiles would be able to go one-hundred miles per hour.

1922   CREATIVE SENTENCING

Judge Charles L. Bartlett (Detroit), exasperated with an epidemic of wild driving that plagued his city, took thirty convicted reckless drivers to a nearby hospital, forced them to visit with maimed children and other auto-accident victims, then sent them to jail for two to thirty days. The judge later expanded his unique rehabilitative program by forcing convicted speeders to visit the morgue and ordering public mental tests to determine their sanity.

17 1902   GRISLY FIND
A deer hunter discovered a human skeleton dangling by a rope from a tree limb in the woods twenty miles north of Marquette. Police speculated it was the remains of a Big Bay lighthouse keeper who had disappeared and was thought to have committed suicide 1½ years earlier.

1829   GOVERNOR BORN
David H. Jerome, Michigan governor 1881-82, was born at Detroit. Jerome, a businessman, state senator, and Michigan's seventeenth governor, was the first Michigan governor to be born in the state of Michigan.

1818   MICHIGAN BAPTIZED
The first Baptist family known to migrate to Michigan arrived at L'Anse Creux then traveled to Pontiac where they settled in a crude log hut.

18 1982   WAS ANYONE STILL LISTENING?
Rev. M. Gregory Gentry (Canton Township), pastor of the Canton Calvary Assembly of God church, preached a 97-hour sermon, breaking a Guinness Book world record by four hours.

1926   PRO HOCKEY HITS DETROIT
The Detroit Cougars played their first National Hockey League game, losing to the Boston Bruins 2-0. Construction of Olympia Stadium had just begun, so the team, later re-named the Red Wings, played all home games of their first season at Border Cities Arena, Windsor.

19 1966   PRESSED IN
An historic showdown at Spartan stadium for the nation's number-one ranking between the undefeated Michigan State University and Notre Dame football teams attracted what is believed to be a record media turnout—745. The teams tied 10-10 but Notre Dame was ranked national champion at the season's end.

1940   SHORT-TERM FIRST
Governor Luren Dickinson, who had become governor when Frank D. Fitzgerald died in office (see March 4), appointed Matilda Dodge Wilson

(Rochester) as his successor. But Michigan's first woman lieutenant governor served only the forty-five days remaining in the unexpired term.

20
1982 PORTAGE MARCHES FOR DOLLARS

According to the *World Almanac and Book of Facts, 1984*, Portage Northern High School raised $6,212 for the March of Dimes Breadlift, the largest amount raised by any high school in the U.S. for this program.

1953 REACH OUT AND TOUCH SOMEONE

Birmingham became Michigan's first and the nation's second community to have direct-distance dialing which enabled customers to dial their own long-distance calls without operator assistance.

1887   The village of Wakefield (Gogebic County) incorporated. On October 14, 1919, Wakefield incorporated as a city.

21
1983 BAD PLANNING

A Detroit man, claiming he had a bomb, hijacked an airplane at Kalamazoo and demanded to be taken to Chicago to talk to presidential-candidate Jesse Jackson. Ironically, the flight's scheduled destination *was* Chicago, and as the plane approached O'Hare International Airport, crew members and passengers overpowered the hard-luck hijacker.

1977 FINAL CONNECTION

The final link in the 193 miles of I-96 from Muskegon to downtown Detroit, a twelve-mile segment at Livonia, opened.

1945 MARATHON LABOR DISPUTE BEGINS

Two-hundred-thousand members of the UAW went on strike at all General Motors plants and, 119 days later, after the longest walkout in the union's history, won an 18.5-cent hourly raise.

1938 ACTRESS BORN

Actress Marlo Thomas was born at Detroit. Thomas, who as a child sat on her father Danny's lap during his script conferences (see January 6), conceived and starred in her own television hit show, "That Girl," from 1966 to 1970. In 1980 Thomas married popular talk-show host Phil Donahue.

22
1983 FIRST SOLON OUSTED

Sen. Philip O. Mastin, a Democratic state senator from Pontiac, became the first legislator in Michigan history to be re-

called. The recall stemmed from Mastin's support of a controversial 38%
temporary income-tax increase. A week later Senator David M. Serotkin
(D-Mount Clemens), was similarly recalled.

1976 FIRST REPAIRMEN CERTIFIED
Secretary of State Richard Austin issued Michigan's first three
automobile-mechanic's certifications to Charles Gaines (Pontiac), Julian
Wilson (Detroit), and Juan Ramanauskas (Warren). Under a new state law,
repair facilities had until December 1977 to employ at least one certified
mechanic in each repair category (engine, transmission, brakes, etc.) performed at their facility.

1975 FIRST OFFICIAL FOOTBALL CHAMPS
Livonia Franklin (Class A), Dearborn Divine Child (Class B), Ishpeming (Class C), and Crystal Falls (Class D) won the first MHSAA state high-
school football championship games ever played.

1927 COUGARS GET A HOME
The Detroit Cougars (later re-named Red Wings) lost to the Ottawa
Senators 2-1 in the first National Hockey League game played at their new
rink, Olympia Stadium. (See also November 18.)

1824 MICHIGAN EPISCOPALS GATHER
Michigan's first Episcopal church organized at Detroit. For three
years, the group held services at the Detroit Council House and Fort, then
purchased a lot on Woodward Avenue, moved a wooden church owned by
the Presbyterians from it at a cost of $150, and began construction of St.
Paul's.

23 1899 FIRST UNOFFICIAL GRID CHAMP
Pontiac beat Plainwell 6-5 at Ann Arbor in the first high-
school championship football game ever played. No formal play-
off setup had been developed or established, so both teams, as the only
unbeaten teams in the state, had simply agreed to meet to determine the
unofficial state championship.

1893 DETROIT GOES AMERICAN
The Detroit Baseball Co., which from 1881 to 1888 had played in the
National League, joined the Western Baseball League. The league later
changed its name to the American League, and the team changed its name
to the Detroit Tigers.

24
1972   FIRST LUCK OF THE DRAW

In an elaborate stage setting at Detroit's Cobo Hall, Michigan's first lottery numbers, 130 and 544, were drawn creating the first 24,000 weekly winners.

1966   BEAR FACTS

Robert Haatja (Ahmeek) shot a state-record bear, 570 pounds dressed weight, near Hoar Lake (Keweenaw County).

1949   LONGEST INTERCEPTION

During the fourth quarter of a game against the Chicago Bears at Detroit, Detroit defensive-back Bob Smith ran back an interception a NFL-record 102 yards for the Lions' only touchdown in the 28-7 loss.

1924   LADY OF THE HOUSE IS IN

Cora A. Anderson (L'Anse) was elected without opposition as Michigan's first woman state representative.

1945   The village of Michiana (Berrien County) incorporated.

25
1983   WINGS CROWD THEM IN

The largest crowd in Red Wing history, 21,019, watched their NHL club beat the Pittsburgh Penguins 5-2 at Joe Louis Arena.

1981   MSU SMASHES ATOMS

At Michigan State University (East Lansing), the world's first super-conducting cyclotron smashed its first atom showing it was ready to help scientists probe the makeup of atomic nuclei.

1824   MICHIGAN GIVES THANKS

By decree of territorial Governor Lewis Cass, who was influenced by the steady influx of New Englanders, Michigan celebrated its first official Thanksgiving.

26
1867   TRAINED ICE

J. B. Sutherland (Detroit) patented the nation's first refrigerator car.

27 1960   HOWE REACHES MILESTONE

Detroit Red Wing Gordie Howe scored two goals in a game against Toronto at Detroit and became the first professional-hockey player ever to score one-thousand points. Twenty years later Howe finished his legendary NHL career with 801 goals and 1,049 assists for a total of 1,850 points. (See also March 12, October 16 and November 10.)

1935   SUBSTANTIAL PENALTY FOR EARLY WITHDRAWAL

An assistant cashier at the Lennon State Bank embezzled $14,000 which so depleted the bank's assets that it was forced to close for good.

28 1963   PAPER ROUTE

Bob Berger (Lincoln Park) won the very first *Detroit Free Press* Marathon in 2:32:50. Twenty-four runners started on the route which took them five times around Belle Isle, but only twelve finished. In 1983 more-than-four-thousand runners entered the popular annual event.

1909   CAUGHT DEAD TO RIGHTS

As a game warden and his keen-nosed bird dog stepped onto the loading platform at the Fleetwood (Dickinson County) train station, the dog suddenly dashed to a coffin being loaded onto the train and began barking. The dog made such a fuss that the officer removed the coffin lid and, instead of finding a man who had supposedly died in a hunting accident, discovered five-hundred dead partridges illegal-market hunters had planned to smuggle to Milwaukee.

29 1906   DARING DIVE

With snow falling, famous escape artist Harry Houdini, naked to the waist and hands cuffed behind his back, jumped from the center span of the Belle Isle Bridge into the 30°F. water twenty-five feet below and disappeared. Less than a minute later, Houdini broke the surface, waved the still-locked handcuffs to the applauding crowd, then swam to a waiting boat.

1880   PRO BALL COMES TO DETROIT

The Detroit Baseball Company, forerunner of the Detroit Tigers, organized and played in the National League until 1888.

1847   MODERN COMMUNICATION CONNECTED

Michigan's first telegraph line was completed along the Michigan Central railroad tracks between Detroit and Ypsilanti. The first messages sent were long and ranged from the price of wheat and putty to the Mexican War and military reputation.

1835   MR. LYON GOES TO WASHINGTON

Lucious Lyon (Kalamazoo), one of Michigan's first two U.S. senators, arrived at Washington, D.C., and called on President Andrew Jackson.

1760   FRENCH OUT — BRITAIN IN

Captain Francoise de Bellestre formally surrendered Fort Ponchartrain (Detroit) to the British, and French rule in Michigan ended forever.

1683   FIRST CAPITAL PUNISHMENT

Daniel de Gresolon Sieur du L'Hut (Duluth), commandant of Fort DeBaude (St. Ignace), ordered a firing squad to execute two Indians who had murdered two French traders, and, under the laws of France, the forty-two soliders carried out Michigan's first legal execution.

30 1979   TEACHERS WALK — THEN SIT

Seventy-three striking teachers marched into the Armada (Macomb County) Elementary School, vowed not to leave voluntarily without a new contract, and became the first teachers in Michigan history to use a sit-in as a bargaining lever. Seventy-two hours after the sit-in began, a contract was negotiated and the strike ended.

1936   FORMER GOVERNOR DIES

Six years after leaving office, Michigan's thirtieth governor, Fred W. Green, died. (See also October 20.)

1885   MENTAL HOSPITAL OPENS

The Traverse City State Hospital for the Insane opened as the state's third such institution.

VILLAGES INCORPORATED THIS DAY
1914   Honor (Benzie County).
1926   Hudsonville (Ottawa County) which incorporated as a city June 18, 1957.

DECEMBER

1 1973   WOMEN DISCUSS WOMEN

More than 550 Michigan women, from conservatives to radicals, and a scattering of men met at Michigan State University (East Lansing) for the first statewide Women's Conference, sponsored by the Michigan Women's Commission to share ideas and concerns of importance to all women.

1953   FIRST FLYING GOVERNOR CRASHES

Former Governor Kim Sigler and three companions were killed when his personal airplane crashed into a radio tower near Battle Creek. Six-and-a-half years earlier Sigler had received his private-pilot's license and had become Michigan's first flying governor. (See also May 2.)

1910   The village of Akron (Tuscola County) incorporated.

2 1933   LONG-DISTANCE NUPTIALS

Judge John Watts (Detroit) married Bertil Hjalmer Clason (Detroit) and Sigrid Sophia Margaret Carlson (Stockholm, Sweden) in the world's first transatlantic-telephone wedding ceremony.

1925   ACTRESS BORN

Actress Julie Harris was born at Grosse Pointe Park. Though Harris won several Tony and Emmy awards for her subtle and sensitive portrayal of complex roles, she never became a box-offfice star. Harris' films include: *East of Eden* (1954), *Requiem For a Heavyweight* (1962), and *Voyage of the Damned* (1976).

1921   DRYING UP MICHIGAN

The state public safety department issued a report that said that, from July through October 1921, its Prohibition division had made 500 arrests for liquor violations, had seized 2,106 gallons of beer, 957 gallons of wine, 106 gallons of cider, 75 gallons of gin, 14,110 gallons of mash, and had eliminated 128 moonshine stills.

3 1950 BOX UPS RECORDS

Cloyce Box, Detroit Lion end, set several club records in a 45-21 win over Baltimore at Baltimore including: most passes received (twelve), most yards gained receiving (302), most points scored (twenty-four) and most touchdowns receiving (four).

1929 WALL STREET DOWN — FORD WAGES UP

Despite the collapse of the stock market, Edsel Ford announced at Detroit that Ford Motor Car Company employees would get an increase in the daily minimum wage from $6 to $7.

1896 FARMERS GET MAIL

Two carriers started out with horses and road carts from the Climax post office on the nation's first rural free-delivery route.

4 1915 THE FORD PEACE SHIP

Henry Ford set out with a group of peace advocates on a chartered Danish vessel, the *Oscar II*, in an effort to settle the war in Europe (see July 28) so that the U.S. would not become involved. As a result of the voyage, a peace conference was arranged, but with intensified German-submarine warfare, the conference disbanded and a year and four months later the U.S. declared war on Germany. (See April 6.)

1844 COLLEGE FOUNDED

Michigan Central College, the first college in Michigan and only the second in the nation to confer degrees upon women, was founded by Baptists at Spring Arbor. In 1853 the college moved and reopened as Hillsdale College.

1843 FIRST LODGE FORMED

Michigan Lodge No. I of the Order of Odd Fellows organized at Detroit.

VILLAGES INCORPORATED THIS DAY
1910   Carleton (Monroe County).
1928   Dewitt (Clinton County) which incorporated as a city December 15, 1964.
1948   Gastra (Iron County) incorporated as a city.

5 1975 OLD-FASHIONED HUNTING BEGINS

Michigan's first muzzle-loader deer season opened. More-than-a-thousand hunters, using black powder and a round ball in a single-shot gun or rifle like America's forefathers used, stalked bucks only during the ten-day season.

1964   HUNTERS THIN ELK HERD

Three-hundred hunters pursued 3,500 elk over 577 square miles in four counties on the first day of Michigan's first elk-hunting season since the pioneer era. The eight-day experimental season was held again the next year to control elk overpopulation, then discontinued until 1984.

61960   SAFETY FIRST

Michigan became the first state to receive an outstanding-achievement award from the National Insurance Institute for Highway Safety. Michigan was selected for the honor because 99% of the state's 543 high schools had conducted approved driver's-training programs and 100% of Michigan's eligible students had taken the course during the preceding year.

1928   ICY BEGINNING

At Ann Arbor, workmen started up special refrigeration equipment, and a few hours later, the University of Michigan became the first Big Ten school to have its own indoor hockey rink.

71953   SEE-THROUGH CAR MANUFACTURED

The Ford Motor Company introduced the nation's first transparent-top, production-model automobile, the Mercury Sun Valley whose roof was partially composed of transparent green-tinted Plexiglass.

1950   MARGARINE NO LONGER PALES BY COMPARISON

For the first time in nearly fifty years, yellow oleomargarine could legally be sold in Michigan, but public institutions (schools, hospitals, etc.) were still banned from serving the artificial spread.

1932   ACTRESS BORN

Ellen Burstyn was born at Detroit as Edna Rae Gillooley. In 1974 Burstyn won an Oscar for her performance in *Alice Doesn't Live Here Anymore* and, in 1975, received both an Oscar and a Tony for the play and film, *Same Time Next Year*.

1914   SERVICE CLUB BEGINS

The Supreme Lodge of the Benevolent Order Brothers organized at Detroit but, dissatisfied with the name of their fraternity, changed their name and, on January 21, 1915, were chartered as the world's first Kiwanis.

8 1919   MICHIGAN SHUTS DOWN

More-than-250,000 Michigan workers were idled when the United States fuel administrator ordered all nonessential industries to close because of a coal shortage caused by a national month-long coal miners' strike. The strike, which also halted passenger-train runs and display lighting, was settled December 10, but Michigan and the rest of the nation did not return to normal for another month.

1823   CLERIC CONGRESSMAN

Father Gabriel Richard, representative from the Michigan territory, took his seat in the U.S. Congress as the first Catholic priest (and the only one for nearly 150 years) to serve in that body.

1947   The city of Auburn (Bay County) incorporated.

9 1978   RECORD PASSING ATTACK

Detroit Lion quarterback Gary Danielson passed for 352 yards and a club-record five touchdowns in a 45-14 Lion victory over the Vikings at Minnesota.

1972   BLACK SANTA LEADS PARADE

Grand Rapids became the first Michigan city to climax its traditional Christmas parade with the arrival of a black Santa Claus.

1935   LIONS WIN FIRST CROWN

The Detroit Lions defeated the New York Giants 26-7 for their first NFL championship. The Lions repeated as champions in 1952, 1953 and 1957.

10

1905   CAPTIVE LABOR NIXED

The state attorney general ruled that private industries could no longer contract with prisons to have inmates manufacture cigars (Marquette), brooms (Jackson), cut granite (Jackson) or other products for them.

1887   ASHES TO ASHES

The first cremation of a dead body in Michigan took place at the Detroit Crematorium, the first such facility in Michigan and only the fifth in the United States.

1917   The village of Ferndale (Oakland County) incorporated. On April 4, 1927, Ferndale incorporated as a city.

11

1977   FLAMES OF DEATH

A short-circuited light fixture started a fire that demolished a four-story, 69-year-old Bay City apartment building and killed ten residents, including two who jumped from ledges, and injured sixty more.

1971   FATAL BLAST

Unaware that deadly methane gas was filling their confined work space, construction workers poured concrete inside a six-mile-long tunnel being constructed under Lake Huron from Port Huron. Suddenly the gas ignited, exploded like a bomb, and killed twenty-one of the workmen.

1955   FILLING THE AIR WITH FOOTBALLS

Detroit Lion quarterback Harry Gilmer attempted a club-record forty-nine passes but completed only twenty-four for 254 yards as Detroit lost to New York 24-19 at Detroit.

1929   FIRST AIRLINE REACHES FIRST MILESTONE

Stout Airlines (see August 1) became the nation's first airline to carry 100,000 passengers and, in doing so, traveled 900,000 miles over three years with a perfect safety record. The airline was later absorbed by United Air Lines.

12

1981   TRIPLE BIRTHDAY PRESENT

Mrs. Tom Bogus (Grand Rapids) gave birth to triplets, three boys, on her husband's birthday. Doctors calculated the odds of such a birth at 3,285,000 to one.

1919   WALKOUT ENDS — DANCING RESUMES

University of Michigan coeds ended a dance strike, begun a week earlier because females were not permitted to use the Michigan Union taproom, when the men announced they would continue the dances with outside girls as their guests.

VILLAGES INCORPORATED THIS DAY
1922   Riverview (Wayne County) which incorporated as a city April 22, 1958.
1927   Orchard Lake (Oakland County) which changed its name and incorporated as the City of Orchard Lake Village March 3, 1964.

13 1983 OFFENSIVE GAME
The Detroit Pistons and the Denver Nuggets played the highest-scoring game in National Basketball Association history at Denver with Detroit winning in triple overtime 186-184.

1982 WOMAN SHUTS UP MEN
Pamela Withrow, assistant deputy warden at Southern Michigan Prison (Jackson), was selected as the new superintendent of the Michigan Dunes Correctional Facility (Holland) making her the first woman to take charge of a Michigan men's prison.

1886 FORMER GOVERNOR DIES
Six years after leaving office, Charles M. Croswell, Michigan's sixteenth governor, died at Adrian. (See also October 31.)

1819 FIRST PLANNED ROAD
Michigan's first surveyed road, the Pontiac Road (now known as Woodward Avenue within Detroit), was laid out by commissioners at Detroit.

14 1964 CROSSED UP
An eleven-mile stretch of I-196 officially opened and made Grand Rapids the first city in the nation to have two freeways (I-196 and U.S. 131) intersect in its downtown district.

1932 AUTO EXEC HEADS COMMERCE DEPARTMENT
Roy D. Chapin (Lansing), a University of Michigan graduate and executive with several automobile companies including Oldsmobile, E. R. Thomas, Chalmers, and Hudson, became secretary of commerce in the Cabinet of President Herbert Hoover.

1918   The village of Mineral Hills (Iron County) incorporated.

15 1983 MARATHON PADDLE
Verlen Kruger and Steven Landick returned home (Lansing) after completing the world's longest canoe trip. The trip, which

had begun three-and-a-half years before at Red Rock, Montana, covered 28,043 miles and took the pair through forty-four states, Canada, part of Mexico, all five Great Lakes, and three oceans.

1919   AIRPORT WEATHER REPORT

The United States Weather Bureau equipped and established three air-mail bases — Bay City, Kalamazoo, and Pontiac — as Michigan's first divisional stations in a national weather-forecasting system.

1921   SPECIAL HOSPITAL OPENS

The first patient entered a new hospital at Camp Custer (Battle Creek), the only tuberculosis hospital in the country, at the time, operated by the American Legion for the treatment of servicemen.

16   1981   MICHIGAN SPRUCES UP THE NATION'S CAPITOL

A 65-year-old 52-foot white spruce, cut in Michigan's Hiawatha National Forest and decorated with 2,500 lights, five-thousand plastic ornaments, and six-hundred stained-glass discs, was lit at the White House as the nation's official Christmas tree.

1979   END OF AN ERA

The Detroit Red Wings tied Quebec 4-4 in their final National Hockey League game at Olympia Stadium before moving to the new downtown Joe Louis Arena. The Wings had treated fans to eleven regular-season championships and seven Stanley Cups during their fifty-three seasons on Olympia's ice.

1909   PLANE ASSOCIATION

Forty-four prominent Detroiters met at the Ponchartrain Hotel (Detroit) and, with the help of guests Orville and Wilbur Wright, organized Michigan's first aero club. The following day the members conducted Detroit's first airport survey — by car.

1808   GOVERNOR BORN

Kingsley S. Bingham, Michigan's tenth governor, was born at Camillus, New York. In 1854 the farmer and former state representative was elected as Michigan's and the nation's first Republican governor. During his two terms, Michigan State University was founded and the Soo canal and locks were completed. (See also October 5.)

VILLAGES INCORPORATED THIS DAY
1912   Fountain (Mason County).
1925   Estral Beach (Monroe County).

17
1908   LANSING GETS SPECIAL EQUIPMENT
The nation's first factory-built motorized fire engine officially went into service at Lansing.

1798   FIRST SORE LOSER
Michigan's first participation in an American election began at Detroit with each voter verbally announcing his choice for a delegate to a Northwest Territorial Assembly. At the conclusion of the three-day election, the loser accused the winner of buying votes with whiskey and threatening voters.

18
1976   SPECIAL SCHOLAR
Denise Thal (Huntington Woods), a Harvard University senior, became one of the world's first thirteen women to receive a Rhodes Scholarship for study at prestigious Oxford University in England.

1927   NO-PASSING ZONES SET
The state highway department began painting the first "no-passing" solid yellow lines on curves and hills of Michigan highways and also posted, for the first time, speed limits at dangerous curves. The following summer the highway commissioner also had to post signs on highways entering Michigan that informed out-of-state visitors what the yellow lines meant.

1908   STATE BROKE
The state treasury was out of money and could not meet its employees' next payroll. Several railroad companies volunteered to pay $750,000 in advance on their taxes to help out.

19
1953   PRISON BREAK
Thirteen convicts broke through a drain tunnel and escaped from Southern Michigan State Prison (Jackson) by running under the prison wall. All escapees, including five who had held two women as hostages for ten hours, were captured within four days.

1919   HOLLAND IS FIRST-RATE
The newly created public utilities commission established its first utility rate by setting the price for natural gas produced by the Holland Gas Works at $1.45-per-thousand-cubic-feet.

VILLAGES INCORPORATED THIS DAY
1883   Otter Lake (Lapeer-Genesee counties).
1925   Roseville (Macomb County) which incorporated as a city April 26, 1957.

20
1971   FIRST HUNDRED-GRAND MAN

After playing with the team for nineteen years and compiling a career .300-batting average, Al Kaline signed a contract with the Detroit Tigers that made him the first Tiger to earn a $100,000-per-year salary.

1948   BEERTENDRESSES BANNED

The U.S. Supreme Court, in a 6-3 decision, upheld a Michigan law banning women bartenders.

1923   COLLEGE GIVES INDIVIDUAL ATTENTION

University of Michigan officials announced that the school would, henceforth, publicize the names of students who were expelled and the reason for the expulsion. The university had to take the added step, the spokesman added, because the student body had grown so large that expulsion alone was no longer an effective deterrent since expelled students left without attracting much notice.

21
1981   HIGH ROLLERS

Michigan residents spent $1.6 million on lottery tickets, the highest single day of wagering in Michigan lottery history.

1966   BRIDGING THE 10,000TH GAP

Michigan's 10,000th highway bridge, a $3.5-million project with thirteen separate spans, opened and began carying Eight Mile Road traffic over the Lodge Expressway at the Detroit-Oak Park city limits.

1912   ROAD REPORT

A Nebraska man, who had personally picked up a Buick in Flint then driven it 823 miles to his home, reported that he had used 44¾ gallons of gas, seven pints of oil, ten pints of water, and five cents worth of hand grease on the trip. The man also added that he traveled twenty-two miles per hour on Iowa's good dirt roads, but was lucky to do sixteen miles per hour "plowing through the sands of Michigan."

1926   The village of Oak Park (Oakland County) incorporated. On June 11, 1945, Oak Park incorporated as a city.

22 1972   ON THE REBOUND

Bob Lanier set a single-game Detroit Piston rebounding record by snagging thirty-three in a 109-97 win over Seattle at Cobo Arena.

1913   BUSINESSMEN FINGERED

Two Lansing businessmen opened envelopes they thought contained Christmas cards and discovered, instead, decomposed human fingers. Police speculated that the fingers were either a gruesome practical joke or perhaps a forerunner of contacts by organized crime.

1820   Chippewa County was created.

23 1978   RAISE A DRINK

A law took effect that, after nearly seven years at eighteen (see January 1), returned Michigan's drinking age to twenty-one. Voters had approved the November constitutional amendment because of increased teenaged alcohol-related automobile accidents and use of alcohol in high schools.

1974   LADY DOCTORS INMATES

Dr. Virginia Lauzun (East Lansing) became the first female physician to work in the department of corrections when she was assigned to supervise twenty-five physicians and three dentists who worked part-time at Southern Michigan Prison (Jackson).

1873   I HEAR MUSIC

Adrian College granted the nation's first bachelor of music degree to Mattie Pease Lowrie who had completed a four-year course in vocal and instrumental music.

24 1978   MIRACULOUS SURVIVAL

In the predawn hours a car driven by George Sinadino (Lansing) left the road and crashed into a cyclone fence sending a two-inch-wide pipe through the cafe owner's windshield. The pipe pierced

Sinadino's midsection, passed within an inch of his heart and spine, skewered him to the car seat, and finally lodged against the rear fender of his car. Police, fire fighters, and paramedics worked for two hours to cut the pipe in front and in back of him to remove him from the car. Sinadino survived and earned a place in *Ripley's Believe It or Not*.

1913 TRAGEDY AT CALUMET

Five-hundred youngsters, mostly children of impoverished striking miners, packed into a second-story ballroom at Calumet's Italian Hall for a Christmas party. Suddenly, an unidentified man — said to be wearing the badge of a group bitterly opposed to the strikers — burst into the crowded hall and yelled, "Fire!" Panic-stricken adults and children rushed toward the single fire escape, pressed through the narrow exit and tumbled over each other down a steep staircase.

Firemen, who rushed to the hall, found no fire but a gruesome pile of seventy-two dead bodies, mostly children.

25 1944 REMARKABLE BIRTH

A 37-year-old Battle Creek victim of infantile paralysis, who had spent the previous fifteen weeks inside an iron lung, gave birth to a 2½-pound daughter. During the hour-long delivery at Community Hospital, the woman alternated five-minute periods inside the lung with two-minute periods outside during which the attending doctor and four nurses administered artificial respiration.

1847 CAPITOL UNCEREMONIOUSLY MOVED

The state Capitol was officially moved from Detroit to temporary buildings that had been erected at a wilderness site on the banks of the Grand River near (present-day) Lansing.

1660 MICHIGAN'S FIRST CHRISTMAS

Father Rene' Menard, who had established a mission near Keweenaw Bay, held Michigan's first known Christmas celebration with, as he wrote, "all the fervor possible under the trying conditions of a primitive wilderness with a few French *coureurs-de-bois* (woods rangers) and a small group of Huron converts as companions."

26 1944 THE FIRST RIGHT VET

Floyd M. Edwards (Kalamazoo), a World War II navy veteran, purchased a home with the help of a loan guaranteed by the Veterans Administration and became the first Michigan veteran to take advantage of the "G.I. bill of rights."

1903 DEADLY TRAIN WRECK

High winds extinguished a kerosene warning light, and two Pere Marquette passenger trains collided near Grand Rapids killing twenty-two persons and injuring thirty.

27 1981 BRITISHER TAGS GRAND RAPIDS FAMILY

A lonely British soldier stationed in Ireland, who wanted to talk to someone in America, dialed a number by matching the digits on his military identification tag. The number belonged to the Tom Troyer family (Grand Rapids) who talked to the soldier for ninety minutes.

1918 CARS CLOSING IN

The *Flint Journal* reported that "the time is not far distant when enclosed motorcars will be the standard form of passenger automobiles, and the (open) touring car will be built only for those who can afford to have this type for summer-use only."

1821 DUBIOUS DISTINCTION

Ketaukah and Kewaubis, two Indians, were hanged in Detroit after being convicted of killing two white men. Their executions were the first in Michigan after it had become a part of the United States.

28 1977 CRIME PAYS

In a ceremony held on the Capitol steps, Governor William G. Milliken presented checks to the first recipients covered under a new crime-victim compensation law. A Flint man, who had been assaulted by a gang, received $377 for medical expenses, and a Lansing couple, whose daughter was murdered, received $1,500 for burial expenses.

1931 ACTOR BORN

Martin Milner was born at Detroit. Milner, who started in films during the 1940s, became a popular television actor by starring in the shows "Route 66" and "Adam 12."

1915 FELLOWS RULES IN FAVOR OF GALS

State Attorney General Grant Fellows ruled that the state board of education had no power to regulate private boardinghouses in Ypsilanti where young women who attended the State Normal College resided, and that rules governing, for example, gentlemen callers were up to each landlady.

29

1981   OFF THE CHARTS

A Rives Junction (Jackson County) woman shocked the medical world when she gave birth to twins — at age fifty-one. Childbearing by women over age fifty happens so rarely that the American College of Obstetricians and Gynecologists doesn't even keep records of such births.

1957   KICKING THEM WHEN THEY'RE DOWN

Detroit placekicker Jim Martin kicked a club-record eight extra points as Detroit routed Cleveland 59-14 at Detroit to win their third world title in six years.

1912   TAKING HIS LOSS HARD

W. W. Wedemery, an Ann Arbor U.S. congressman who was despondent over losing a reelection bid, suffered a complete mental breakdown and attempted to jump off a boat into the sea while en route from New York to Panama as part of a committee to study the Panama Canal.

30

1983   INVITATION DRAWS LARGEST CROWD

The largest crowd ever to watch a hockey game on the North American continent, 21,402, watched Michigan State beat Michigan Tech 6-2 in the finals of the Great Lakes Invitational Hockey Tournament played at Joe Louis Arena, Detroit.

1976   TAXES FUND CANDIDATES

Governor William G. Milliken signed a law which allowed Michigan residents to contribute $2 to a gubernatorial-campaign fund through a checkoff provision on their state personal income-tax forms, and Michigan became the first state in the nation to provide partial public funding of governor's elections.

1974   BOARD STRIKES TEACHERS

The Crestwood School District Board of Education (Dearborn Heights) fired 184 striking teachers after ordering them to either report to work or resign. The union appealed the action all the way to the U.S. Supreme Court which upheld the firings.

1964   TWO-MILLIONTH AUTO REGISTERED

Secretary of State James Hare issued Michigan's two-millionth vehicle title to Mr. and Mrs. William Schmitz (Lansing).

1936 WORKERS SIT — UAW RISES

Workers at Flint Fisher Body plants began a sit-down strike that eventually lasted forty-four days, affected 150,000 workers and closed more-than-sixty plants in fourteen states. The strike resulted in a one-page nine-paragraph document in which General Motors guaranteed, for the first time, that it would recognize the UAW as its employees' bargaining agent. (See also February 11.) (*Flint Journal* photo.)

1939 SINGER BORN

Del Shannon was born at Grand Rapids. Shannon, who sang in a distinctive falsetto voice, had several 1960's hits including, "Runaway," "Hats Off to Larry," and "Handy Man."

1872   The village of Reed City (Osceola County) incorporated. On March 14, 1932, Reed City incorporated as a city.

31 1971 MICHIGAN NUKED A SECOND TIME

The Consumers Power Company generated its first commercial electric power from its second nuclear plant, Palisades, near South Haven.

1918   DETROIT SIGNALED

Michigan's first three-way traffic-light signal at Detroit's Michigan and Monroe streets.

1892   FORMER GOVERNOR DIES

Henry P. Baldwin, Michigan's fourteenth governor, died. Following the Republican's two terms as governor, he served as a U.S. senator and later as a trustee of the Eastern Asylum at Pontiac which he had helped establish.

1862   GOVERNOR BORN

Albert E. Sleeper, Michigan's twenty-eighth governor, was born at Bradford, Vermont. (See also May 13.)

MICH-AGAIN'S YEAR

1641
> October 4 - Catholic missionaries arrive at Sault Ste. Marie.

1660
> December 25 - Michigan celebrates first Christmas.

1663
> February 5 - First recorded earthquake.

1671
> June 14 - France claims Michigan.

1675
> May 18 - Father Marquette dies.

1679
> August 23 - First ship enters Lake Huron.
> November 1 - Fort built at St. Joseph.

1680
> March 20 - First white man crosses Lower Peninsula.

1683
> November 29 - First legal execution.

1701
> July 24 - Cadillac founds Detroit.
> July 26 - First Catholic church built.
> August 4 - France signs treaty with Indians.

1704
> February 2 - First white child born.

1707
> November 7 - First Caucasian executed.

1710

    May 5 - First marriage ceremony.

1730

    October 15 - Cadillac dies.

1749

    May 24 - Incentives offered to settle in Michigan.

1760

    November 29 - French rule ends; British rule begins.

1763

    May 6 - Englishmen cannibalized near Port Huron.
    May 7 - Chief Pontiac tries to capture Detroit.
    June 2 - French massacred at Ft. Michilimackinac.

1764

    April 27 - First Masonic lodge formed.

1770

    March 19 - Severe food shortage at Detroit.

1773

    September 22 - Detroit's population is 1,367.

1774

    Detroit merchants limit liquor sales.

1781

    February 12 - Spanish capture Niles.
    May 12 - Chippewas sell Mackinac Island to British.

1783

    September 3 - Michigan becomes part of America.

1788

    July 24 - First courts established.

1792

    July 16 - First elections held.

1795

    August 3 - Indians cede first land to U.S.

1796

    July 10 - First American flag raised over Michigan.
    August 15 - Wayne County established.

1798

    December 17 - First American election held.

MICH-AGAIN'S YEAR

1799
> March 2 - Detroit becomes a port of entry.

1800
> September 11 - First Protestant missionary arrives.

1801
> March 3 - First post road established.

1802
> January 18 - Town of Detroit incorporates.

1803
> May 10 - First future president visits.

1804
> March 26 - First U.S. land office established.

1805
> January 11 - Territory of Michigan created.
> June 11 - Fire destroys Detroit.
> July 9 - Territorial legislature passes first law.
> July 29 - Territorial supreme court organized.
> August 29 - Law requires registering of deeds.
> September 10 - Capitation tax enacted.
> October 8 - First welfare provisions.

1806
> June 16 - Total eclipse of sun occurs.
> September 15 - First bank incorporates.

1809
> August 31 - First newspaper published.

1812
> July 17 - British capture Fort Mackinac.
> August 16 - General Hull surrenders Detroit.

1813
> January 22 - Americans slaughtered at Raisin River.

1816
> November 4 - First Bible society organized.

1817
> July 25 - First successful newspaper published.
> July 25 - First bookstore ad featured.
> August 13 - First presidential visit.
> August 26 - First library formed.
> August 26 - University of Michigan created.
> September 8 - First University of Michigan professors appointed.

1818

March 31 - First Protestant church built.
May 1 - First public auction sale of Michigan lands authorized.
July 20 - First union organizes.
August 27 - First steamboat arrives.
October 4 - First Sunday School meets.
November 17 - First Baptists arrive.

1819

February 16 - U.S. Congress authorizes election of Michigan delegate.
July 3 - Territorial legislature authorizes formation of medical society.
December 13 - First road surveyed.

1820

May 3 - Second post road established.
May 8 - First personal-property tax enacted.
June 16 - Last British flag to fly over Michigan and U.S. removed.

1821

December 27 - First execution since joining America.

1822

May 25 - Second steamer arrives.
June 6 - Dr. Beaumont studies digestive process by using man with a "window in his stomach."
July 6 - American troops reconfirm U.S. authority over Sault region.

1823

December 8 - Father Gabriel Richard becomes first priest in U.S. Congress.

1824

March 2 - Father Richard requests money for Detroit-Chicago road.
May 5 - First Michigan copyright issued.
June 7 - First legislative council convenes.
June 24 - No Michigan residents in jail or prison.
November 22 - First Episcopal church organizes.
November 25 - First official Thanksgiving celebrated.

1825

April 4 - Detroit elects first mayor.
April 21 - Lands sold for tax nonpayment.
May 24 - Detroit-to-Chicago road surveyed.
October 25 - Erie canal opens.

1826

January 28 - First road map published.

1828

May 5 - First capitol building occupied at Detroit.
June 10 - Baptists get land for first church.
June 16 - Territorial library created.
July 3 - Historical Society of Michigan organized.

1829

March 5 - First journalist jailed.
July 23 - William Burt patents nation's first typewriter.

1830

February 19 - First temperance society organized.
July 31 - First railroad chartered.
September 24 - Hanging leads to abolishment of capital punishment.

1831

January 8 - Daily mail begins arriving from the East.
May 5 - Forerunner of *Detroit Free Press* published.

1832

June 21 - First formal concert presented.
July 4 - First cholera epidemic begins.
September 13 - Father Gabriel Richard dies.

1833

April 22 - Forerunner of Kalamazoo College authorized.
April 27 - Luxury steamer *Michigan* launched.
October 6 - First Michigan Catholic diocese created.

1835

March 23 - Forerunner of Albion College chartered.
May 20 - First sewer authorized.
June 22 - Official state seal adopted.
October 5 - First state constitution approved.
November 1 - First state legislature convenes.
November 29 - Michigan's first senator arrives at Washington, D.C.

1836

January 10 - First window-glass factory opens.
March 20 - Michigan borrows first funds.
March 26 - State supreme court established.
July 8 - Regular Detroit-to-Saginaw steamer service begins.
October 1 - First railroad begins operating.
November 8 - Michigan voters participate in their first U.S.-presidential election.

MICH-AGAIN'S YEAR

1837

January 20 - First railroad locomotive arrives.
January 20 - Indians cede last lower-peninsula land to U.S.
January 26 - Michigan becomes America's 26th state.
February 22 - First governor presents first state flag.
March 18 - University of Michigan authorized to move to Ann Arbor.
April 3 - First labor strike begins.
September 6 - First Michigan Methodist Conference held.

1838

April 3 - Construction on first prison begins.
July 20 - Excavation of Clinton-Kalamazoo canal begins.

1839

February 18 - Detroit Boat Club founded.
April 10 - Marshall College chartered.
October 1 - First state fair fails.

1840

August 25 - Joseph Gibbons patents nation's first seeding machine.

1841

January 19 - First farm journal published.

1842

May 16 - First tax-supported schools open.
October 21 - State poet Will Carleton born.

1843

December 4 - Odd Fellows Lodge No. 1 organized.

1844

February 24 - Olivet College founded.
May 2 - First public high school opens.
September 19 - Iron ore discovered.
September 29 - Iron warship *U.S.S. Michigan* commissioned.
December 4 - Forerunner of Hillsdale College founded.

1845

June 9 - First hospital opens.
July 4 - Hog Island re-named Belle Isle.
July 10 - Frankenmuth founders arrive.
August 6 - University of Michigan holds first commencement.
October 14 - State geologist Douglass Houghton drowns.

1846

May 4 - Michigan becomes first state to abolish capital punishment for murder.
October 8 - Michigan's oldest active graveyard opens.

MICH-AGAIN'S YEAR

1847

  February 9 - Holland founded.
  February 13 - Legislature apropriates money for Mexican-American War involvement.
  March 17 - Legislature meets for final time at Detroit.
  August 15 - Postage stamps first used.
  November 29 - First telegraph line completed.
  December 25 - New capital officially established at Lansing.

1848

  January 3 - Epaphroditus Ransom first governor inaugurated at new capital.
  March 1 - Detroit-New York telegraph line completed.
  May 29 - Democrats nominate Michigan's Lewis Cass for U.S. president.

1849

  September 25 - First annual Michigan State Fair begins.

1850

  July 8 - James Jesse Strang crowned king of Beaver Island.
  September 22 - First Jewish congregation formed.
  November 5 - Voters approve second constitution.

1852

  July 7 - First iron ore shipped down the Great Lakes.
  October 5 - Forerunner of Eastern Michigan University dedicated.
  October 12 - Michigan State Teachers' Association organized.

1853

  March 4 - Governor McClelland becomes U.S. secretary of interior.
  June 4 - Excavation of Soo canal and locks begins.
  October 2 - First Sunday newspaper issued.
  October 13 - Amelia Bloomer lectures at Detroit.

1854

  July 6 - National Republican party founded at Jackson.

1855

  February 13 - Legislature prohibits arrest of runaway slaves.
  May 31 - Soo canal and locks officially open.

1856

  June 16 - King Strang assassinated.
  August 27 - Abraham Lincoln speaks at Kalamazoo.

1857

  March 6 - Lewis Cass becomes U.S. secretary of state.
  May 13 - Michigan Agricultural College opens.
  July 16 - Telegraph cable laid under Detroit River.
  October 27 - Cornerstone for Michigan's first women's college laid.

1858

  August 16 - First hot-air balloon flight.

1859

> March 28 - Adrian College chartered.
> April 12 - First international billards championship played.
> April 23 - First mental institution opens.
> October 1 - First law school started.

1860

> September 20 - Prince of Wales arrives.

1861

> March 15 - Legislature authorizes governor to provide men for Civil War.
> May 16 - First Michigan infantry arrives at Washington, D.C.
> July 6 - Detroit House of Correction opens.
> August 1 - Women's wing of Detroit House of Correction opens.
> November 6 - Nation's first ladies aid society organized.

1862

> February 3 - Thomas Edison publishes newspaper for train passengers.

1863

> February 17 - First Michigan colored infantry organized.
> March 6 - Race riot at Detroit.
> June 29 - Michigan Cavalry Brigade organized under the command of Gen. George Armstrong Custer.
> July 1 - Michigan unit opens the Battle of Gettysburg.
> July 30 - Henry Ford born.
> August 3 - Horse-drawn streetcars first used at Detroit.

1864

> September 14 - Confederates pirate *Philo Parsons*.

1865

> April 9 - Civil War ends.
> April 12 - Michigan cavalry captures Jefferson Davis.

1866

> May 14 - Hope College chartered.
> June 5 - Michigan State Medical Society formed.
> June 10 - Last Civil War regiment returns.
> July 4 - First Civil War monument erected.
> July 4 - Civil War flags presented to state.

1867

> March 15 - University of Michigan becomes nation's first property-tax-supported college.
> April 18 - First Eastern Star chapter organizes.
> May 7 - Parke, Davis and Co. organized.
> November 26 - J. B. Sutherland patents nation's first refrigerator car.

1868

> May 18 - Forerunner of Wayne State University organized.

1869

April 3 - First statewide tax-supported school system established.
May 29 - Memorial Day first observed in Michigan.

1870

January 5 - Women allowed to attend University of Michigan.
February 2 - First woman registers at University of Michigan.
February 7 - "Underground railroad" slave-escape routes close.
November 8 - Blacks vote for first time in Michigan election.

1871

March 27 - First women graduate from University of Michigan.
April 3 - Woman votes in a Detroit election.
October 8 - Devastating forest fire sweeps across lower Michigan.

1872

January 10 - First Grange forms.
August 25 - Horse disease stops Detroit streetcar runs.

1873

August 23 - *Detroit News* begins publication.
December 23 - Nation's first bachelor of music degree awarded.

1875

January 26 - Nation's first electric dental drill patented.
March 3 - Mackinac Island becomes national park.
April 13 - State Firemen's Association forms.
July 17 - First balloon flight across Lake Michigan.
October 19 - Zachariah Chandler becomes U.S. secretary of interior.

1876

April 15 - Michigan celebrates its first Arbor Day.
July 4 - Big Delia throws free party for Muskegon lumberjacks.
September 19 - Melville Bissell patents nation's first carpet sweeper.

1877

March 6 - Telephone first demonstrated at Detroit.
September 21 - First commercial phone line installed.

1878

January 12 - First *Free Press* woman's section published.
August 1 - Eastern Michigan Asylum opens.
September 15 - First phone directory published.

1879

January 1 - Present capitol building dedicated.
January 14 - Undertakers Association of Michigan formed.
May 18 - First ad for an electric light.
May 29 - Detroit forbids cattle in public streets.
June 1 - First phone exchange to use women operators established.
September 25 - Detroit purchases Belle Isle.

MICH-AGAIN'S YEAR

1880

January 20 - First international telephone line opens.
March 22 - World's first hydroelectric plant organizes.
July 22 - Boat accident in Detroit River kills sixteen.
November 29 - Detroit Baseball Company organizes.

1881

January 22 - State Telephone System goes into operation.
March 20 - First commercial use of incandescent electric lamps.
April 2 - J. L. Hudson's opens.
May 3 - Leonidas Woolley patents nation's first electric locomotive headlight.
May 17 - Gold discovered.
June 9 - Michigan turns over Soo locks and canal to U.S.
August 3 - Michigan Reform School opens.
September 5 - Disastrous fire sweeps across Thumb.

1884

April 11 - Nation's first planting of brown trout.
September 1 - Forerunner of Ferris State College established.

1885

November 30 - Traverse City State Hospital for the Insane opens.

1886

September 15 - Forerunner of Michigan Technological University opens.

1887

March 15 - Nation's first game warden hired.
July 10 - Grand Hotel opens.
September 12 - Alma College opens.
October 26 - Michigan State Association of Architects founded.
December 10 - First body cremated in Michigan.

1888

January 16 - Don M. Dickinson becomes U.S. postmaster general.
February 25 - First public ski-jumping meet held.

1889

July 10 - Meteorite hits Allegan.
August 26 - Last stagecoach robbery.
October 25 - Submarine telephone cable laid under Straits of Mackinac.

1890

May 1 - House of David established.
July 22 - Michigan Women's Press Association organized.

1891

January 16 - Nation's first major ski association forms.
August 29 - Trapeze stunt man killed.
September 1 - Michigan Library Association forms.
September 18 - First international underwater railway tunnel opens.

228

1892
>   May 21 - First national notice given a Michigan vehicle.
>   August 25 - First woman aeronaut killed.

1893
>   January 27 - First capitol building burns.
>   April 17 - Tidal wave hits St. Joseph.
>   May 23 - Prisoner lynched at Corunna.
>   November 23 - Detroit Baseball Company joins Western Baseball League.

1894
>   January 30 - D. B. King patents nation's first pneumatic hammer.

1896
>   March 6 - First horseless carriage driven in public.
>   June 4 - Henry Ford test-drives his first car.
>   September 8 - Suomi College opens.
>   September 10 - Michigan Optical Society organizes.
>   September 26 - Michigan Agricultural College plays first football game.
>   December 3 - Nation's first rural free mail delivery begins at Climax.

1897
>   April 28 - Apple blossom adopted as state flower.
>   July 13 - Michigan's longest marriage begins.

1898
>   February 15 - Battleship *Maine* blown up.
>   April 24 - Michigan National Guard joins Spanish-American War.
>   May 14 - Bread doubles in price.
>   June 20 - First excursion steamer arrives at Bob-Lo Island.
>   June 21 - Gen. William Rufus Shafter (Galesburg) lands 16,000 men at Cuba without a casualty.
>   October 22 - Michigan man may be first to fly.

1899
>   August 5 - Detroit's first auto company organizes.
>   October 17 - President McKinley presents Three Oaks with Spanish-American War prize.
>   November 23 - First high-school championship football game played.

1900
>   April 6 - World's first heavyweight-championship fight held at Detroit.
>   May 22 - E. S. Votey patents nation's first pneumatic player piano.
>   September 4 - Rabbit-raising scheme sweeps Lower Michigan.

MICH-AGAIN'S YEAR

1901

April 9 - Butter sells for 17 cents a pound.
April 25 - Detroit Tigers play first American League game.
April 26 - Kalamazoo saloon keepers sign cheese-and-crackers agreement.
May 1 - Post office issues Soo locks' stamp.
May 1 - Tigers commit team-record twelve errors.
May 2 - Tigers win first American League forfeit.
September 6 - Michigan native assassinates President McKinley.
October 24 - Bay City teacher goes over Niagara Falls in barrel.

1902

January 2 - University of Michigan wins first Rose Bowl game ever played.
March 11 - Lansing prohibits drug-peddling.
September 2 - First automobile-accident fatality.

1903

January 12 - Tiger manager commits suicide.
March 30 - Phone switchboards installed; bells and batteries removed.
May 6 - Tigers and White Sox commit American League-record eighteen errors.
June 16 - Ford Motor Company incorporates.
August 6 - Circus-train wreck kills twenty-three.
December 26 - Train wreck kills twenty-two.

1904

January 12 - Henry Ford sets speed record.
February 21 - National Ski Association organized at Ishpeming.
February 27 - Michigan Audubon Society forms.

1905

May 8 - Dwight B. Huss sets first transcontinental automobile time record.
June 15 - Michigan Red Cross organizes.
July 1 - State highway department established.
July 26 - Earthquake shakes Upper Peninsula.
August 30 - Ty Cobb plays in his first game with Tigers.

1906

February 26 - Nation's first Shrine Circus held at Detroit.
March 10 - Michigan State Telephone Company begins "weather-report" service.
April 1 - First yellow-page telephone directory issued.
June 4 - Tiger Bill Coughlin steals second, third, and home in one inning.
July 4 - Michigan's first dirigible constructed.
November 29 - Harry Houdini performs on Belle Isle Bridge.

1907

June 28 - Two automobile license plates required.
July 20 - Train collision kills thirty-three.
October 22 - Third constitutional convention begins.
November 1 - Gasoline must be kept in red cans.
November 13 - MSU veterinary students quarantined.

1908

March 9 - Stores fall into Kalamazoo River.
September 16 - General Motors chartered.
October 12 - Tigers win first-ever World Series game.
December 17 - Lansing gets nation's first motorized fire engine.
December 18 - State treasury broke.

1909

April 20 - Work begins on nation's first concrete highway.
July 4 - Nation's first mile of concrete highway opens.
July 8 - Nation's first night baseball game played at Grand Rapids.
July 16 - Tigers play American League's longest tie game.
August 31 - Nation's first accident involving motorized fire engine.
October 17 - First Michigan-built glider flies.
December 16 - First aero club formed.

1910

January 4 - "Battlewagon" *U.S.S. Michigan* commissioned.
April 28 - Flint police order first paddy wagon.
April 29 - Official state flag adopted.
May 1 - Optometrists required to be examined and licensed.
July 4 - First airplane flight at Detroit.
October 11 - Numbered jerseys on U of M football players requested.

1911

May 30 - Sarah Bernhardt performs at Calumet.
June 19 - First Michigan woman flies.
July 31 - First automobile stocks listed on Wall Street.
September 3 - First airplane flights at Grand Rapids.
November 3 - Chevrolet Motor Company organized.

1912

May 1 - Two-hundred upper-peninsula saloons forced to close.
May 15 - Ty Cobb suspended.
June 1 - Michigan aviator dies.
June 17 - First newspaper aerial photographs taken.
August 12 - Ty Cobb stabbed.
August 12 - Utility rate-fixing procedure established.
September 1 - First workman's compensation law passed.
October 28 - Nation's first aerial elopement completed at Hillsdale.
December 29 - Defeated congressman attempts suicide.

1913

April 16 - *Flint Journal* places bounty on flies.
May 26 - Former President Roosevelt testifies at Marquette.
May 28 - Michigan Historical Commission organized.
June 20 - Ford Motor Company hires interpreters.
July 1 - First airplane flight across Lake Michigan.
July 23 - Upper-peninsula copper miners strike.
August 27 - Cremation Association of America founded at Detroit.
October 3 - Laingsburg parachutist dies at Alpena.
November 3 - Nation's first night flight.
November 13 - Great Lakes' worst storm begins.
December 24 - Fifty-six Calumet children die in false alarm.

1914

January 5 - Ford raises wages to $5 per day.
January 14 - Ford begins "assembly-line" technique.
February 16 - Longest-jailed prisoner begins term.
February 26 - Detroit Symphony presents first concert.
July 28 - Austria declares war on Serbia.
August 16 - Predominant occupation for Michigan women is servant.
September 1 - Greatest daily rainfall drenches Bloomingdale.
November 14 - First Dodge produced.
December 7 - World's first Kiwanis organized at Detroit.

1915

August 24 - State places bounty on rats.
December 4 - Henry Ford's "peace ship" leaves New York.

1916

July 7 - Oscoda County has not arrested or prosecuted anyone for six months.
August 20 - Oakland County begins state's first county centennial celebration.

1917

March 23 - Grand Rapids and Detroit part of first transcontinental airways.
March 24 - First high-school basketball championship played.
April 6 - U.S. enters World War I.
July 1 - Selfridge Field (Mt. Clemens) opens.
August 1 - Entire Michigan National Guard drafted into U.S. Army.
August 21 - Robert E. Friedrick patents helicopter forerunner.

1918

February 17 - Michigan war bureaus instructed to arrest German aliens.
March 8 - Ft. Custer draftees issued identification tags.
March 10 - Young women advised to avoid Detroit.
May 1 - Michigan enacts Prohibition.
May 24 - Michigan soldier first to die in Germany.
September 5 - Jackson prison shows profit.
September 18 - First Michigan woman enlists in World War I.
October 19 - Flu epidemic closes all public buildings.
November 11 - World War I ends.
December 31 - First three-way traffic signal installed.

1919

January 15 - First all-woman jury selected.
May 10 - Michigan Department of the American Legion forms.
June 10 - Michigan first to ratify women's suffrage amendment.
August 1 - First commercial-airline freight service begins.
August 14 - Motor-vehicle drivers required to have licenses.
September 8 - Michigan experiences labor shortage.
October 14 - Michigan American Legion holds first state convention.
December 8 - Coal shortage shuts down Michigan.
December 12 - U of M coeds end dance strike.
December 19 - Public Utilities Commission sets first rate.

1920

January 2 - Communist hunters arrest thousands.
April 5 - Ferry passengers stranded on ice floe.
June 15 - Nation's first radio wedding held at Detroit.
August 8 - Tigers play American League's shortest ball game.
August 17 - First airmail arrives.
August 31 - WWJ begins nation's first regular radio programming.
September 21 - World's only marine post office delivers 1,250,000th piece of mail.
November 2 - First woman state legislator elected.

1921

January 21 - Michigan and the U.S. become urban.
March 5 - Edwin Denby becomes U.S. secretary of the navy.
May 10 - "Fixing" professional sporting events becomes illegal.
July 9 - Prison warden becomes traveling salesman.
July 18 - Marquette prisoners design escape-proof prison.
October 13 - WWJ receives Michigan's first radio license.
October 20 - Confiscated liquor poured into Detroit sewers.
December 15 - Michigan American Legion opens nation's first tuberculosis hospital for
    veterans.

1922

February 4 - Ford Motor Company buys Lincoln Motor Company.
February 10 - Nation's first radio symphony concert presented.
February 23 - Greatest daily snowfall lands on Ishpeming.
March 25 - First radio station owned by auto company begins broadcasting.
April 10 - Detroit's horse-drawn fire wagon makes last run.
May 4 - WJR begins broadcasting.
May 28 - Nation's first radio orchestra plays.
August 18 - First educational radio station begins broadcasts.
September 2 - Ford enforces Prohibition.
October 14 - Lt. Lester J. Maitland sets airspeed record.
November 16 - Judge sends speeders to hospital and morgue.

1923

July 11 - First thirteen-member jury hears testimony.
July 31 - State-owned automobile-ferry service begins at Straits of Mackinac.
November 11 - Hudson's displays world's largest flag.
December 20 - U of M begins publicizing names of expelled students.

1924

    January 17 - Michigan State Archeological Society organized.
    February 6 - First highway signs installed.
    June 13 - Tiger fans riot and cause forfeit.
    October 25 - First radio broadcast of a U of M football game.
    November 24 - First female state representative elected.

1925

    January 9 - Bus safety measures enacted.
    February 13 - WWJ joins nation's first radio network.
    March 19 - Fishing licenses required.
    June 17 - Tigers score record-setting thirteen runs in one inning.
    July 19 - Detroit man sets free-fall record.
    September 9 - Black doctor defends home against white mob.

1926

    January 1 - State highway department takes control of all roads.
    February 15 - First contract airmail flight.
    March 25 - Automobile license-numbering system revised.
    May 22 - Millionth automobile registered.
    August 1 - Nation's first regularly scheduled air passenger service begins.
    August 18 - President Coolidge gets giant Traverse City pie.
    September 25 - Detroit gets pro hockey team.
    September 29 - Poacher murders two game wardens.
    October 31 - Harry Houdini dies at Detroit.
    November 3 - Fifty-one miners die in Ishpeming disaster.
    November 18 - Detroit Cougars play first National Hockey League game.

1927

    April 16 - Sale of fireworks banned.
    April 20 - First radio broadcast of Tiger game.
    May 8 - Detroit police install nation's first radio sets in cruisers.
    May 18 - Michigan's worst mass murder occurs.
    May 20 - Charles Lindbergh completes first solo flight across Atlantic.
    May 26 - Model T production ends.
    November 22 - Detroit Cougars play first game at Olympia.
    December 18 - First "no-passing" yellow lines painted.

1928

    February 24 - Detroit outlaws marijuana.
    April 21 - Nation's first aircraft show ends.
    May 21 - First statewide traffic-safety program begins.
    May 30 - Chrysler Corporation purchases Dodge Brothers.
    June 29 - First concerted pollution-control program begins.
    July 10 - First round-trip flight across Lake Michigan.
    August 1 - Detroit Zoo opens.
    September 24 - Tigers draw smallest crowd.
    December 6 - U of M gets Big Ten's first indoor hockey rink.

MICH-AGAIN'S YEAR

1929

January 7 - Detroit pilots complete first non-stop Detroit-to-Miami flight.
February 20 - First aviation junket.
March 29 - Nation's first fireworks legislation passed.
April 7 - Women's National Aeronautic Association organizes at Detroit.
May 18 - Holland opens first Tulip Festival.
May 20 - Michigan Board of Aeronautics created.
June 10 - First Michigan Air Tour begins.
June 14 - Board of Aeronautics dedicates first county airport.
June 27 - First air-travel ticket office opens.
August 4 - Boat service from Michigan to Isle Royale begins.
August 19 - Nation's first metal dirigible tested at Grosse Isle.
October 29 - Greenfield Village dedicated.
November 11 - Ambassador Bridge dedicated.
December 3 - Ford raises wages to $6 per day.
December 11 - Nation's first airline carries 100,000th passenger.
December 14 - First municipal airport licensed.
December 15 - First weather-forecasting stations eatablished.

1930

February 11 - Pontiac Airport nation's first to get highest rating.
May 14 - State police carry first first-aid kits.
June 8 - World's largest fruit market opens at Benton Harbor.
June 10 - Nation's first black Housewives League started at Detroit.
June 25 - Amelia Earhart sets airspeed record at Detroit.
July 21 - Detroit ousts mayor.
July 22 - Detroit radio commentator murdered.
August 8 - Nation's first air-water tour begins at Detroit.
November 3 - Windsor tunnel opens.

1931

February 12 - Nation's first commercially used autogiro delivered to *Detroit News*.
April 8 - Robin designated as official state bird.
April 14 - Ford produces twenty-millionth car.
May 29 - Detroit aviators set non-refueling flight record.
September 16 - Detroit gangsters executed in residential neighborhood.

1932

February 17 - Hale Haven peach developed.
March 7 - Security guards and police kill protesting unemployed auto workers.
June 19 - First flying meet for women held.
September 20 - Gar Wood sets world water-speed record.
December 14 - Roy D. Chapin becomes U.S. secretary of commerce.

MICH-AGAIN'S YEAR

1933

January 30 - "The Lone Ranger" radio program begins at WXYZ.

February 14 - Governor closes Michigan banks.

April 7 - State Liquor Control Commission created.

April 27 - Sale of 3.2 beer allowed.

April 27 - Eighteen-year-olds allowed to drink beer and wine.

June 1 - First sales tax approved.

June 22 - Greenfield Village opens to public.

December 2 - First international-telephone wedding held.

1934

January 21 - Charcoal grills installed in state parks.

February 9 - Coldest temperature in Michigan history recorded.

June 19 - World's first movies of the sun taken at Pontiac.

June 30 - Ohio football team moved to Detroit and re-named Lions.

July 27 - First old-age pension checks mailed.

September 23 - Lions play first National Football League game.

October 1 - Olivet College eliminates grades and credits.

October 7 - Lions' longest field goal kicked.

1935

February 15 - Beer diluted.

August 26 - United Automobile Workers organized.

October 7 - Tigers win first World Series.

October 9 - Ionia Reformatory first in world to provide radios for inmates.

November 1 - Michigan centennial stamp issued.

December 9 - Lions win first NFL championship.

1936

February 2 - Ty Cobb first player inducted into Baseball Hall of Fame.

March 24 - Red Wings play in longest Stanley Cup game.

April 11 - Red Wings win first Stanley Cup.

May 22 - Murder of Detroit man exposes statewide terrorist organization.

July 3 - Henry Ford buys Wright Brothers' cycle shop.

July 13 - Hottest temperature in state history recorded.

July 18 - Nine killed in car-train accident.

December 30 - Auto workers begin sit-down strike.

1937

February 11 - General Motors recognizes UAW; sit-down strike ends.

April 6 - UAW becomes bargaining agent at Chrysler.

April 16 - Milk prices slashed.

May 26 - Ford-factory police attack UAW workers.

June 22 - Joe Louis wins first heavyweight championship.

June 24 - Construction of Blue Water Bridge begins.

August 22 - "Radio priest" collapses.

August 30 - Aviators claim unusual endurance record.

November 1 - Kalamazoo is nation's only debt-free city.

1938

March 13 - Carl Liscombe scores Red Wings' fastest three goals.

July 8 - Last execution in Michigan.

July 30 - Adolph Hitler awards Henry Ford the Supreme Order of the German Eagle.

October 8 - Blue Water Bridge dedicated.

1939

January 17 - Frank Murphy becomes U.S. attorney general.

March 16 - Governor Frank D. Fitzgerald dies in office.

May 4 - Ted Williams first to hit ball over Tiger Stadium's right-field roof.

July 11 - Grand Hotel has only eleven paying guests.

October 3 - Anti-goiter campaign revived.

1940

January 11 - General Motors produces 25-millionth car.

February 29 - Dog quarantine ordered.

November 19 - Matilda Dodge Wilson becomes Michigan's first woman lieutenant governor.

1941

April 24 - Chrysler delivers first M-3 General Grant tank.

May 9 - WWJ becomes state's first FM station.

May 21 - UAW represents Ford workers.

May 23 - Joe Louis defends heavyweight crown for seventeenth time.

July 8 - First all-star baseball game played at Detroit.

October 24 - Traffic expert hired by state.

November 12 - Nation's first heredity clinic opens at Ann Arbor.

1942

January 1 - Michigan Civil Air Patrol activated.

February 10 - Last civilian cars produced; auto plants produce war materials.

May 8 - Ingersoll plant constructs navy's first amphibian cargo carrier.

May 31 - Last civilian truck assembled.

August 6 - Detroit spy sentenced to die.

August 22 - *U.S.S. Wolverine* commissioned.

August 31 - Michigan Bell installs one-millionth phone.

September 10 - Ford assembles first B-24 Liberator bomber.

September 12 - First freeway opens.

October 28 - Train-bus crash kills sixteen.

1943

January 18 - Bakeries quit slicing bread.

May 20 - Greenville students get U.S. Treasury award.

June 20 - Interracial riot at Detroit.

July 16 - Nine campers drown in Lake Huron.

1944

January 23 - Red Wings score NHL-record fifteen consecutive goals.
February 3 - Syd Howe scores six goals in one game.
June 6 - Greenville-built glider first to land on D-Day.
September 17 - Two-millionth GM victory bond sold.
November 15 - Red Wings and Maple Leafs score NHL's fastest five goals.

1945

January 11 - Senator Warren G. Hooper murdered.
January 25 - Grand Rapids becomes nation's first city to fluoridate water.
January 31 - Detroit private executed for desertion.
July 21 - Tigers play 24-inning game.
August 14 - World War II ends.
September 1 - Henry Ford II becomes Ford Motor Company president.
October 10 - Tigers win second World Series.
November 21 - UAW begins longest strike.

1946

March 21 - Nation's first microfilm projector installed at Battle Creek.
June 5 - First synthetic surgical sponge marketed.
August 10 - First jet flies in Michigan skies.
August 27 - Isle Royale dedicated as national park.
September 14 - Michigan "Flying Farmers" organize.
October 16 - Gordie Howe plays first game with Red Wings.

1947

January 18 - Tigers sell Hank Greenberg.
March 4 - First television station begins broadcasts.
March 16 - Red Wings' Billy Taylor assists on NHL-record seven goals.
April 7 - Henry Ford dies.
May 27 - Lobbyists required to register.
June 27 - Auto workers receive first pension provision.
July 20 - Tigers draw largest doubleheader crowd.
September 9 - State police purchase first airplane.

1948

January 8 - First education FM station goes on the air.
February 29 - Police try radar.
April 20 - Tiger rookie George Vico hits home run on first major-league pitch thrown
to him.
April 20 - Walter P. Reuther shot.
June 15 - First night pro baseball game played at Detroit.
June 21 - First Bill Knapps' restaurant opens.
June 25 - Joe Louis wins last heavyweight championship.
June 28 - State police nab "wild city fliers."
July 20 - Planes leave Mount Clemens for first transatlantic jet flight.
September 26 - Tigers draw largest single-game crowd.
December 20 - Female bartenders banned.

1949

March 1 - Joe Louis announces retirement.

October 23 - Detroit Lion Don Dole intercepts club-record four passes.

November 24 - Detroit Lion Bob Smith runs back an NFL-record 102-yard interception.

1950

January 15 - Storm drops record snowfall on Calumet.

March 28 - Gordie Howe severely injured.

July 8 - Marquette prison inmates attempt to take governor hostage.

August 10 - Russians criticize U of M football.

September 7 - Hoot Evers last Tiger to hit for the cycle.

September 27 - Joe Louis attempts comeback.

October 29 - Detroit Lion Wally Triplett returns four kickoffs for NFL-record 294 yards.

November 5 - Detroit Lion Bobby Layne passes a club-record 374 yards.

December 3 - Detroit Lion Cloyce Box sets several club records.

December 7 - Sale of colored margarine legal.

1951

February 9 - Draft-evader burns State Office Building.

July 24 - Stamp issued commemorating Cadillac's landing.

July 26 - Town of Nahma up for sale.

August 19 - Midget pinch-hits against Tigers.

October 15 - First international television broadcast.

1952

March 13 - Nation's first synthetic-antibiotic plant opens.

April 20 - Prisoners riot at Jackson.

July 15 - Michigan Bell installs two-millionth phone.

November 4 - Nation's first black woman state senator elected.

1953

January 21 - Arthur Summerfield becomes U.S. postmaster general.

January 26 - Charles E. Wilson becomes U.S. secretary of defense.

June 8 - State's worst tornado hits Flint.

June 18 - Boston Red Sox score seventeen times in one inning against Tigers.

June 30 - First plastic-body sports car produced.

November 20 - Birmingham nation's second city to get direct-distance dialing.

December 1 - Plane crash kills former governor.

December 7 - First transparent-topped automobile produced.

December 19 - Thirteen inmates escape from Southern Michigan Prison.

1954

March 1 - U.S. representative shot.

March 22 - Nation's first shopping center opens at Southfield.

April 30 - First passenger flight leaves Metro Airport.

May 8 - Mackinac Bridge ground-breaking ceremony held.

October 16 - Lions win club-record tenth consecutive game.

November 2 - Voters approve Korean War veterans' bonus; reject bingo.

November 2 - First black U.S. congressman elected.

1955

February 12 - Stamp commemorating Michigan State University issued.
February 27 - Red Wings begin club-record fifteen-game winning streak.
April 5 - Red Wings' winning streak ends.
April 28 - White pine recognized as official state tree.
June 28 - Stamp commemorating Soo locks issued.
October 22 - First official historical marker dedicated.
December 11 - Detroit Lion Harry Gilmer attempts club-record forty-nine passes.

1965

February 3 - Sixty-five-mile-per-hour speed limit goes into effect.
July 6 - Two ironworkers die in Mackinac Bridge fall.
September 7 - Iven Kincheloe sets world altitude record.

1957

September 15 - First air-to-ground telephone service begins.
November 1 - Mackinac Bridge officially opens.
December 29 - Detroit Lion Jim Martin kicks club-record eight extra points.

1958

January 28 - Tigers sign first black player.
April 6 - Michigan's worst airline crash.
June 25 - Stamp commemorating Mackinac Bridge issued.

1959

April 25 - St. Lawrence Seaway opens.
August 19 - Nation's first pedestrian mall opens at Kalamazoo.
September 7 - First Labor Day Mackinac Bridge walk held.
September 22 - State's worst small-boat tragedy occurs.

1960

August 3 - Tigers and Indians trade managers.
August 15 - Cobo Hall opens.
November 27 - Gordie Howe scores one-thousandth NHL point.

1961

January 1 - Briggs Stadium re-named Tiger Stadium.
January 21 - Robert S. McNamara becomes U.S. secretary of defense.
January 23 - William Clay Ford becomes Detroit Lion president.
June 6 - Heroic pigeon dies at Detroit Zoo.
June 11 - Norm Cash becomes first Tiger to hit ball out of Tiger Stadium.
July 1 - Hoboes of America hold international convention in Kalamazoo.
July 23 - Tiger game lasts major-league record three hours, fifty-four minutes.
October 2 - Detroit's Fisher Theatre opens.

1962

January 30 - Two circus performers die in fall.
February 8 - George Romney begins fast-and-prayer session.
March 1 - Nation's first K mart opens at Garden City.
June 24 - Tigers play seven-hour, 22-inning game.
August 3 - Harmon Killebrew becomes first player to hit ball over Tiger Stadium left-

field roof.

September 27 - Chain reaction started in Michigan's first nuclear power plant.

1963

April 1 - Voters approve fourth constitution.

April 17 - NFL suspends Detroit Lion Alex Karras.

June 23 - Martin Luther King leads "Walk-to-Freedom" march at Detroit.

September 26 - Grand Valley State College opens.

September 26 - Escaped elephant shot at Lansing.

October 31 - International Bridge opens.

November 1 - Nation's longest toll-free expressway opens.

November 10 - Gordie Howe becomes NHL's greatest goal-scorer.

November 12 - First black "big-three" car dealer receives franchise.

November 28 - *Detroit Free Press* sponsors first marathon.

1964

January 10 - William Clay Ford becomes Detroit Lions' sole owner.

February 4 - Terry McDermott wins Olympic speed-skating gold medal.

March 4 - Teamsters' President James Hoffa convicted.

March 30 - First kidney transplanted.

May 6 - Tornado hits Upper Peninsula.

June 3 - Photographs on drivers' licenses required.

June 13 - Seaway Tony Calery begins rowboat trip from Sault Ste. Marie to New York.

July 11 - Kalkaska holds first Blueberry Festival.

July 16 - David Rude crosses Lake Michigan suspended from a kite.

July 19 - Michigan American Legion elects first woman vice-commander.

August 2 - Swaying-pole performer dies in fall.

August 28 - Hitchhikers and bicycles banned from freeways.

December 5 - Experimental elk-hunting season begins.

December 14 - Grand Rapids becomes nation's first city with crossing downtown expressways.

December 30 - Two-millionth vehicle title issued.

1965

March 1 - Lone Ranger actor dies.

March 12 - NCAA holds first indoor-track championships at Cobo Hall.

March 24 - Ku Klux Klan members kill Detroit civil-rights worker.

April 11 - Deadly tornado rips through central and southern Michigan.

April 11 - Red Wing Norm Ullman scores Stanley Cup's two fastest goals.

April 24 - Two children killed in carnival ride.

May 12 - First color-photo drivers' licenses issued.

June 3 - Michigan's first astronaut takes off.

June 18 - Trout designated as official state fish.

June 21 - First landing on state's first heliport.

June 28 - Frankenmuth's mayor taps ten-millionth barrel of beer.

August 2 - Nation's first trimline phones become commercially available in lower Michigan.

August 5 - UFOs spotted over Lake Superior.

August 16 - First black police chief appointed.

September 24 - Tigers celebrate ten-thousandth game.

October 23 - Last steam locomotive makes final run.
November 6 - First modern-day wild-turkey hunt begins.

1966

February 8 - Lions hand out first player suspension.
April 2 - First Coho salmon planted.
June 11 - First cattle brought to Mackinac Island.
June 17 - Al Kaline gets two-thousandth major-league hit.
June 24 - Willow Run airport ends passenger service.
July 2 - Manistee holds first Strawberry Festival.
July 25 - First state ombudsman appointed.
October 11 - Detroit Public Bank fails.
October 15 - Pictured Rocks National Lakeshore established.
October 16 - Detroit Lions Karl Sweetan and Pat Studstill combine for NFL's longest-passing play.
November 1 - Christmas stamp issued at Christmas, Michigan.
November 13 - Detroit Lion Garo Yepremian kicks club-record six field goals.
November 16 - MSU-Notre Dame football game attracts record media turnout.
November 24 - Record bear shot.
December 21 - Ten-thousandth highway bridge opens.

1967

January 27 - Michigan astronaut dies.
February 1 - I-94 completed.
March 11 - State purchases first helicopter.
March 14 - Four MSU football players selected in first round of NFL draft.
May 26 - First women join state police.
June 1 - First Soviet freighter enters Detroit River.
June 17 - Tigers play longest doubleheader.
June 23 - Alewives litter Michigan beaches.
July 19 - Record five-minute rainfall drenches Detroit.
July 23 - Riot begins at Detroit.
August 17 - I.D. cards for the blind issued.
August 18 - First black state policeman sworn in.
October 1 - First state income tax goes into effect.

1968

February 1 - 2,500th Centennial Farm marker presented.
March 18 - First "clean-the-slate" pardon issued.
May 16 - Wilbur J. Cohen becomes U.S. secretary of health, education and welfare.
June 6 - Snowmobile-registration law passed.
June 15 - First underwater wedding held.
June 24 - Detroit Tiger Jim Northrup hits grand-slam home runs in consecutive times at bat.
June 30 - Tidal wave floods Keweenaw.
July 14 - Bars allowed to serve liquor on Sunday.
July 30 - Henry Ford birthday commemorative stamp issued.
September 19 - First heart transplanted.
September 20 - Stamp honoring Father Jacques Marquette issued.
September 23 - Detroit Cougars soccer team folds.
October 10 - Tigers win third World Series.

November 5 - Voters approve bond issue for parks.

1969

January 2 - Judges required to be attorneys.

January 22 - George Romney resigns as governor to become U.S. secretary of housing and urban development.

January 26 - Nude actors and actresses arrested.

August 13 - Eight-millionth color-photo driver's license issued.

August 24 - Victor Jackson sails across Lake Michigan in a bathtub.

September 1 - Motorcyclists required to wear helmets.

September 1 - First lung transplanted.

September 4 - Shirley Washington crowned Miss Black America.

September 6 - Pamela Anne Eldred named Miss America.

July 31 - First driver's-training-car accident.

October 14 - Nation's first black state superintendent of public instruction appointed.

October 30 - Russian cosmonauts visit Detroit.

1970

January 1 - First black Ford dealers named.

January 2 - C. R. Wharton becomes nation's first black president of a predominantly white major college.

February 14 - First snowmobiles cross Mackinac Bridge.

February 19 - Detroit Tiger Denny McLain suspended.

February 27 - Western Hemisphere's first ski-flying tournament held at Ironwood.

March 24 - Detroit symphony performs in Upper Peninsula.

April 3 - First all-volunteer dental clinic opens.

April 29 - Clarence Carter becomes first black General Motors' dealer.

May 9 - Walter Reuther dies in plane crash.

May 12 - Detroit's first train robbery.

May 14 - First black-owned bank opens.

May 23 - Bleachers collapse at track meet.

August 7 - Goose Lake Rock Festival begins.

September 28 - Pantsuits for female lawyers approved.

October 16 - Eric Ryback first to hike Pacific Coast Trail.

October 21 - Sleeping Bear Dunes National Lakeshore established.

October 28 - Detroit Pistons win club-record ninth consecutive game.

November 3 - First mother-son legislative team elected.

November 8 - NFL-record field goal beats Lions.

1971

January 5 - Dave Bing becomes first Detroit Piston to get two-thousand assists.

January 7 - Bomber nearly crashes into nuclear power plant.

January 22 - First skyjacking in Michigan skies.

January 31 - Rockets launched from Upper Peninsula.

February 26 - Kirt Barnes first to skate one-hundred miles in less-than-six hours.

March 8 - First bachelor father adopts second child.

April 6 - Tigers draw largest opening-day crowd.

April 7 - Michigan approves U.S. constitutional amendment lowering voting age to eighteen.

May 18 - Michigan lowers blood-donation age to eighteen.

June 15 - Black briefly heads state government.

June 21 - First plastic drivers' licenses issued.
July 1 - Payment for automobile license plates by check permitted.
July 29 - "No-fault" divorce bill passed.
August 11 - Mechanical heart pump implanted.
August 20 - Oscoda holds first Paul Bunyan Festival.
August 22 - U of M hosts first pro football game.
September 11 - Groom takes bride's last name.
September 11 - Sharon Sexton crowned Miss Black Teenage America.
September 28 - Nation's first use of "glassphalt."
October 1 - "Thirty-and-out" retirement plan begins for auto workers.
October 2 - Jesse Lakes becomes first Michigan college football player to gain three-thousand yards.
October 9 - Ex-convict hijacks plane at Metro Airport.
October 25 - Detroit Lion collapses on field and dies.
October 30 - New law prohibits placement of harmful objects inside food.
November 15 - License-plate orders by mail permitted.
December 11 - Port Huron tunnel explosion kills twenty-one workers.
December 20 - Al Kaline becomes first $100,000 Tiger.
December 31 - Second nuclear power plant generates first electricity.

1972

January 1 - Governor loses Rose Bowl bet.
January 1 - Age of majority lowered to eighteen.
February 21 - Chlorastrolite designated as official state gem.
March 1 - World-record price paid for work by a living sculptor.
March 12 - Gordie Howe's number retired.
March 15 - Fred Bear inducted into Archery Hall of Fame.
March 21 - First eighteen-year-old candidate loses election.
May 9 - First girl competes in boys' high-school track meet.
May 16 - Voters approve lottery.
June 5 - Two-hundredth U of M heart transplant performed.
June 21 - Pinball machines allowed in liquor establishments.
July 2 - Lottery established.
August 31 - Red Wings sign first European player.
September 1 - Basketball-star Reggie Harding shot dead.
September 10 - Conservation officer murdered.
September 16 - U of M football team starts first black quarterback.
October 6 - Pictured Rocks National Lakeshore dedicated.
October 13 - Michigan meat laws overridden.
October 26 - Worst driver sentenced.
October 27 - Pontiac first to ban lead-based paint.
November 3 - Mackinac Island allows snowmobiles.
November 7 - Voters approve daylight saving time.
November 13 - First lottery tickets sold.
November 24 - First winning lottery numbers drawn.
December 9 - First black Santa Claus parade held.
December 22 - Bob Lanier grabs Pistons' team-record thirty-three rebounds.

1973

January 2 - "Vanity" license plates authorized.
January 9 - FAA fines Marquette airport.

January 28 - Red Wing Henry Boucha scores NHL's fastest opening goal.

January 28 - Mount Pleasant man last soldier killed in Vietnam.

February 22 - Ohio-Michigan border dispute resolved.

February 22 - Hermus Millsaps becomes first million-dollar lottery winner.

March 5 - Forty-four-thousand pizzas buried.

April 19 - Mysterious craters cause evacuation of Williamsburg.

May 8 - Ypsilanti girl nation's first to play in Little League game.

May 15 - Longest-living heart-transplant patient dies.

June 30 - Horse and buggy crosses Mackinac Bridge.

July 20 - Michigan Bell installs five-millionth phone.

August 7 - First nuclear-powered pacemaker implanted.

August 21 - First metric highway sign installed.

August 23 - Sheila Young wins world cycling championship and becomes first person ever to win world cycling and speed-skating championships.

August 31 - American League suspends Tiger manager Billy Martin.

September 28 - Last upper-peninsula brewery closes.

October 1 - "No-fault" insurance goes into effect.

October 11 - First "vanity" plates produced.

October 12 - Gerald Ford nominated as vice-president.

November 1 - I-75 completed.

November 9 - Saginaw Arthur Hill high-school football team finishes season unscored upon.

December 1 - First women's conference held.

1974

February 5 - State holiday declared for Martin Luther King.

February 16 - Joe Maka spears largest fish ever caught in Michigan waters.

March 2 - Speed limit lowered to fifty-five miles per hour.

March 12 - Michigan exempts itself from year-round daylight saving time.

April 22 - First suicide jump from Mackinac Bridge.

July 1 - Youngest female state legislator sworn in.

July 12 - National Guard infantry unit accepts first women.

July 29 - Pistons sold.

July 29 - Tigers hit major-league-record four home runs in first inning.

August 9 - Gerald Ford becomes U.S. president.

September 14 - U of M features first pom-pom girls at football game.

September 24 - Al Kaline gets three-thousandth hit.

October 11 - Detroit Wheels dropped from World Football League schedule.

October 27 - Last hangman dies.

November 1 - Barn advertisements become illegal.

November 5 - Sales tax on food and drugs repealed.

December 23 - First female department of corrections' physician assigned to Southern Michigan Prison.

December 30 - Striking teachers fired.

1975

January 20 - Nation's first prison college commencement exercises held.

March 12 - Western Michigan University students begin 41½-day phone call.

March 15 - First high-school hockey championships held.

March 31 - Studded tires become illegal.

April 2 - Soo locks complete first 365-day shipping season.

May 1 - Beer salesmen prohibited from buying "one-for-the-house."

June 6 - Southern Michigan Prison inmate escapes by helicopter.

July 14 - Law passed defining death.

July 30 - Former Teamsters' President Jimmy Hoffa disappears.

August 9 - Tigers lose club-record fourteenth consecutive game.

August 23 - Lions play first game in Silverdome.

September 29 - First black-owned television station begins broadcasting.

October 2 - Pontiac Silverdome's air-supported roof inflated for the first time.

October 6 - Lions draw largest crowd.

November 10 - Great Lakes' storm closes Mackinac Bridge, sinks *Edmund Fitzgerald*.

November 15 - Hudson's high-school football team wins national-record seventy-second consecutive game.

November 22 - First official high-school championship football games held.

December 5 - First muzzle-loader deer season begins.

1976

January 25 - MSU football program placed on three-year probation.

January 26 - Former governor and supreme-court justice sentenced to prison.

February 7 - Sheila Young becomes first American to ever win three medals in one winter Olympics.

February 23 - Stamp featuring Michigan state flag issued.

March 9 - Hot-air balloon flights become legal.

March 31 - Red Wings and Maple Leafs receive NHL-record number of penalties.

March 31 - Right turns on red become legal.

April 21 - City of Detroit holds "world's largest garage sale."

April 22 - Seeds carried to the moon planted.

April 26 - Liquor packaged in metric bottles.

May 2 - Earthquake shakes southern Wayne County.

June 14 - Hudson's retires world's largest flag.

July 19 - Belleville college students end viking voyage.

July 28 - Kirtland warbler rejected as new state bird.

August 7 - William Vargo wins third consecutive world pipe-smoking championship.

August 15 - Youth gangs terrorize Cobo Hall rock fans.

August 18 - Republicans nominate Gerald Ford as presidential candidate.

August 26 - Storm deflates Silverdome roof.

August 28 - Kimberlee Foley wins Miss World-USA contest.

September 14 - World's highest hotel officially topped.

October 10 - Detroit Lion Horace King carries football a club-record thirty-two times.

November 2 - Voters approve ban on nonreturnable bottles and cans.

November 4 - Red Wing receives longest suspension.

November 22 - First automobile mechanics certified.

December 18 - Denise Thal becomes first female Rhodes Scholarship winner.

December 30 - New law provides public funds for gubernatorial candidates.

1977

January 3 - First consolidated school district splits up.

January 13 - Woman becomes nation's first to chair natural resources commission.

January 14 - Michigan tree planted at White House.

January 24 - Thymus gland transplanted.

February 1 - Fire destroys Tiger Stadium press box.

February 18 - Karl Thomas ends cross-country balloon voyage.

February 20 - State police begin permanent Detroit city freeway patrol.
February 28 - First high-school basketball tournament game televised.
March 9 - Abused wife kills husband.
March 16 - First black heads prison.
March 22 - Child killer terrorizes Oakland County.
March 28 - Nation's worst outbreak of botulism occurs at Pontiac.
April 2 - Nonsmoking areas required at restaurants.
April 15 - Renaissance Center dedicated.
April 30 - World-record crowd watches rock concert.
May 7 - Space museum dedicated.
July 20 - Law passed requiring hunters to wear orange clothing.
September 2 - Mary Livingston becomes state's first woman Air Force jet pilot.
September 30 - Kincheloe Air Force Base closes.
October 23 - Detroit Lion Ray Williams punts a club-record eight times.
October 25 - Detroit gets second pro soccer franchise.
November 2 - World-record whitefish caught.
November 14 - First women's prison dedicated.
November 21 - I-96 completed.
December 11 - Bay City fire kills ten.
December 28 - First crime victims compensated.

1978

January 1 - Longest-serving mayor completes final term.
January 26 - Worst twentieth-century blizzard strikes.
February 21 - Cat-hunting banned.
March 15 - Billy Beer appears.
April 1 - Detroit Express plays first game.
May 11 - Margaret Ann Brewer becomes Marine Corps' first female brigadier general.
August 8 - Gerald Ford dedicates I-196.
August 18 - Red Wings' Dale McCourt awarded to Los Angeles as compensation.
September 11 - Plane crashes into Mackinac Bridge.
September 23 - Bloodless bullfight held.
October 18 - Bill Muncey dies in hydroplane accident.
October 18 - Christmas stamp issued at Holly.
November 6 - First female plumber licensed.
December 9 - Detroit Lion Gary Danielson throws club-record five touchdown passes.
December 23 - Drinking-age returned to twenty-one.

1979

January 23 - Republicans select Detroit as national-convention site.
January 25 - Robot kills auto worker.
January 29 - Detroit Pistons shoot NBA-record 69.1% from the field.
February 4 - First NBA all-star game held at Silverdome.
March 9 - Detroit Piston Kevin Porter assists on club-record twenty-five baskets.
March 26 - Michigan State wins NCAA Division I basketball championship.
March 29 - Nation's first adoption of surrogate child completed.
April 17 - Coyote bounty repealed.
May 20 - Inmates drink copy fluid and die.
May 25 - Nation's worst airline crash kills Michigan passengers.
June 30 - Cuba bills Frankfort aviation club.
July 12 - Chicago rock fans cause forfeit to Tigers.

October 5 - Big Bay de Noc high-school football team plays fourteenth consecutive game without scoring.

October 22 - Marijuana legalized for medical purposes.

November 1 - License plates expire on drivers' birthdays.

November 4 - Iranians take four Michiganians hostage.

November 30 - First teacher sit-down strike begins.

December 16 - Red Wings play final Olympia game.

1980

January 12 - Transsexual runs for office.

January 31 - World-record burbot caught.

March 24 - Largest pay-out for legal "numbers" lottery game occurs.

April 30 - State lends Chrysler $150 million.

May 13 - Tornado rips through downtown Kalamazoo.

May 20 - Nation's first athroscopic surgery center opens at Lansing.

June 3 - Michigan U.S. congressman resigns after censure for payroll-kickback scheme.

July 2 - Underwater parks approved.

July 14 - National Republican convention opens at Detroit.

July 27 - Earthquake sways Tiger Stadium.

July 30 - Nonparticipating Olympic athletes honored.

August 3 - First Family Day celebrated.

September 13 - Eastern Michigan University's football team begins record-breaking losing streak.

October 17 - Bleachers collapse during high-school pep rally.

1981

April 2 - Line drive kills baseball coach.

April 25 - First man named to women's commission.

May 1 - Ground-breaking ceremony held for General Motors Poletown plant.

June 16 - Sixteen-year-old boys allowed to marry.

August 20 - Huron Valley Men's Facility opens.

September 18 - Gerald R. Ford museum dedicated.

September 30 - Severe storm floods lower Michigan.

October 16 - Alpena school district goes broke, closes schools.

October 26 - U of M football announcer Bob Ufer dies.

November 25 - MSU cyclotron smashes first atom.

December 12 - Triplets born on father's birthday.

December 16 - Michigan Christmas tree lights nation's capital.

December 21 - Highest single day of lottery-wagering.

December 29 - Fifty-one-year-oldwoman gives birth to twins.

1982

January 1 - U of M plays first indoor football game.

January 24 - Superbowl XVI played at Pontiac Silverdome.

March 26 - Red Wings end club-record fourteen-game losing streak.

March 31 - NBA-record crowd watches Pistons.

April 14 - Stamps featuring state bird and flower issued.

June 4 - Mike Ilitch buys Red Wings from Bruce Norris.

June 9 - Largest bank holdup.

June 26 - Queen of Netherlands visits Grand Rapids and Holland.

August 9 - Alice Eckardt becomes state's oldest sky diver.

MICH-AGAIN'S YEAR

August 17 - Red Wings' Dennis Polonich wins damages for injuries inflicted by opposing player.
August 27 - Japanese banks provide Michigan with $500-million credit.
September 4 - Kidney transplanted into smallest infant.
September 11 - Trident missile-carrying submarine, *U.S.S. Michigan*, commissioned.
October 29 - Razor blades reportedly found in hot dogs.
November 18 - Minister preaches for ninety-seven hours.
December 13 - First woman selected to head men's prison.

1983
January 29 - Detroit Piston Kelly Tripucka scores club-record fifty-six points.
March 7 - Michigan Panthers play first game.
May 2 - Worst property-damage storm in state history strikes.
May 11 - Woman gives birth on Mackinac Bridge.
June 2 - Michigan Youth Corps created.
June 3 - Telephone operator wins $2-million lottery prize.
June 7 - Law degree ruled marital property.
July 4 - "Human flies" scale RenCen tower.
July 17 - Michigan Panthers win United States Football League's first championship.
October 20 - Michigan Women's Hall of Fame opens.
November 22 - First state legislator recalled.
November 25 - Red Wings draw largest crowd.
December 13 - Pistons and Nuggets play NBA's highest-scoring game.
December 15 - Lansing men complete world's longest canoe trip.
December 30 - North America's largest hockey crowd watches college game.

1984
January 7 - State-record three-game series bowled.
January 28 - World snowmobile speed record set.
February 18 - Red Wing Reed Larson becomes NHL's highest-scoring U.S.-born player.
March 7 - Michigan Conservation Corps created.
March 12 - Pistons' Isiah Thomas signed to record contract.
March 23 - First "test-tube" baby born.
April 7 - Tiger Jack Morris pitches no-hitter.
April 8 - Traverse City becomes latest All-American city.
April 9 - Pins reported found in Girl Scout cookies.
April 13 - Tigers win club-record eight games without loss to start season.

INDEX

255

THE AUTHOR

Gary W. Barfknecht, 39, was born and raised in Virginia, Minnesota, the "Queen City" of that state's Mesabi Iron Range. After receiving a bachelor of science degree from the University of Minnesota in 1967 and a master of science degree from the University of Washington in 1969, Barfknecht came to Flint, Michigan, as a paint chemist with the E. I. DuPont & deNemours company.

But after only a year on the job, Barfknecht and the chemical giant reached the mutual conclusion that he was not suited for corporate life, and Barfknecht set out on a freelance-writing career. Barfknecht sold the first magazine article he ever wrote, "Robots Join the Assembly Line" (*Science & Mechanics*, October, 1971), and over the next three years, his articles were featured in *Reader's Digest, Science Digest, Lion, Sign, Lutheran Standard, Modern Maturity* and other magazines. During that time Barfknecht also was the ghost writer for the book, *A Father, A Son, and a Three Mile Run* (Zondervan, 1974) and authored a local guide book, *33 Hikes From Flint* (Friede Publications, 1975).

While freelancing Barfknecht also managed a hockey pro shop at a Flint ice arena. That job led to a position as hockey commissioner and, in 1977 when Barfknecht took over the directorship of all amateur hockey programming (youth, adult and high school) in the Genesee County area, he had to postpone his writing efforts.

In 1981 Barfknecht came up with the idea for what became a bestselling collection of Michigan trivia called *Michillaneous*, resigned as hockey commissioner, and once again became a full-time author and publisher. In 1983 Barfknecht authored *Murder, Michigan*, a book he describes as "the dark side of Michigan history" and plans to publish *Michillaneous II* in September 1985.

Barfknecht currently resides in Davison, Michigan, with his wife Ann, and two daughters Amy, 18, and Heidi, 13.

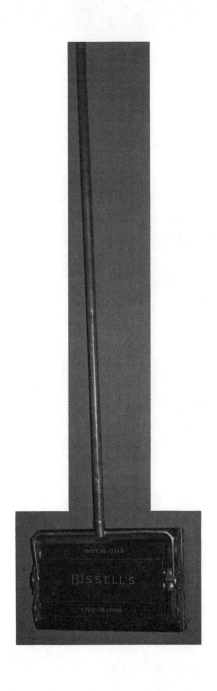

A Michigan man invented the carpet sweeper (see September 19).